DATE DUE

~~NOV 8 79~~		
~~DEC 17~~		

DEMCO 38-296

Roy Head with The Traits
Left to right: Gene Kurtz, Tommy May, Ronnie Barton, John Clark,
Jerry Gibson, Frank Miller
Photo courtesy of G. Kurtz/C. Escott

TATTOOED ON THEIR TONGUES

A JOURNEY THROUGH THE BACKROOMS OF AMERICAN MUSIC

COLIN ESCOTT

SCHIRMER BOOKS
AN IMPRINT OF SIMON & SCHUSTER MACMILLAN NEW YORK

PRENTICE HALL INTERNATIONAL
LONDON MEXICO CITY NEW DELHI SINGAPORE SYDNEY TORONTO

The chapters on Billy Jean Horton, Marty Stuart, Don Everly, and Don Pierce/Starday Records originally appeared in slightly different form in The Journal of Country Music.

Schirmer Books
An Imprint of Simon & Schuster Macmillan
1633 Broadway
New York, NY 10019

Design: Rob Carangelo

Library of Congress Catalogue Card Number: 95-24544

Printed in the United States of America

Printing Number
1 2 3 4 5 6 7 8 9 10

Library of Congress Cataloging-in-Publication Data

Escott, Colin.
    Tattooed on their tongues : a journey through the backrooms of American music/ Colin Escott
        p. cm.
    Includes index.
    ISBN 0-02-870679-X (alk. paper)
    1. Country music—History and criticism. 2. Rock music—History and criticism.
I. Title
    ML3524.E65 1996
    781.642'0973—dc20   95-2544
                                                                  CIP
                                                                  MN

This paper meets the requirements of ANSI/NISO Z39.48-1992 (Permanence of Paper).

" . . . a picture from the past came slowly stealing . . . ";
Billie Jean Williams with Hank in the background
Photo courtesy of C. Escott

Contents

Top left to right: Eddie Hill, Tommy Sosebee, Carl Smith, Ernest Tubb.
Bottom: Carl Shook, Jimmie Osborne, Jimmie Logsdon, Pee Wee King, Louisville, 1954
Photo courtesy of J. Logsdon/C. Escott

Jimmie Osborne and myself worked at the same radio station, WKLO, and became close friends.

He shot himself in 1958, a victim of vodka, depression, and a failed marriage. He was the finest deejay I have ever known—a cross between a Holy Ghost backwoods preacher and a modern-day snake oil salesman.

He was obsessed with death and all things related. He sold millions of records on King Records out of Cincinnati, Ohio.

When we visited his home he would get high, lie down on the floor in his large living room, and tell his wife, "Here is where I want the casket—a blue one."

He would cross his arms & close his eyes and ask me how he looked. I would always say "You sure look natural Jim." This always cracked him up and he would jump up and fix drinks all around.

The day after he killed himself, his wife, Mae, called me and said she had found fifty thousand dollars stuffed into a piece of sewer pipe in the trunk of his Cadillac. She asked me for advice. I said, #1, lock all your doors, and #2, call your attorney!

Jimmie Logsdon, in a note to the author

Introduction

. . . .

So much popular music history is bound up in the memories, often gloriously warped memories, of old men and women. When they go, the history goes, or at least much of its color goes. Chart statistics and discographies are often all that's left.

Popular music is a more difficult area of study than it appears. Even academics, who can be relied upon to document the most arcane areas of human activity, usually louse it up, perhaps because they fail to realize the interplay between art and commerce, or perhaps because they can't quantify dumb luck. The musicians themselves can't be trusted to tell their own tales for the same reason that parents can't be objective about their babies. Why, for instance, did a record fail? Because the record company didn't promote it (a favorite one, that); because it was ahead of its time; because management messed up. Never, never, never because the record sucked.

The real story, which I see as the interaction of art, commerce, and luck— or lack of it—is what makes popular music history so intriguing. The subject itself starts with a contradiction: the very term "music business" is an oxymoron (like "free love" or "British cuisine"). It's the oil-and-water nature of it that I find so compelling. There's another wrinkle, too: You're often trying to deal dispassionately with a record that someone played three times a day for a year. That record is more than mere music now. It can evoke time and place as exactly as a family snapshot.

I truly never fantasized about being a performer. The business always intrigued me, especially for the way that it tried to make commercial judgments about art. "Good" could mean different things on different days. I worked for several record companies after getting out of school, and every now and again I would try to get them to share my passion for what was sitting in their back catalogs. The first record I put together was called *Sun Rockabillys*. The curious plural form of "Rockabilly" probably stemmed from the designer's miscalculation of the number of characters he could get across the top of a twelve-inch record jacket. I, of course, never thought to ask for a proof. The record was compiled with a school friend, Martin Hawkins. The year was 1971 or 1972.

I would never dream of reprinting those first halting attempts at writing, although most of what's here first made its way into print on the back of album jackets or in CD booklets. In the years since *Sun Rockabillys*, I must have worked on hundreds of records that covered the spectrum from an anthology of Texas psychedelia to a Perry Como boxed set. Sometimes the research would consume me to the point that I phoned all over the country, or scoured company, state, or municipal archives in search of a sliver of information that truly mattered to no one but me by that point. I think it was Rudyard Kipling who said that everyone is more or less mad on one point. I've been more or less mad on many.

Celebrity interviews don't interest me greatly, so you won't find them here. The idea of sitting in an anteroom for two hours waiting for a ten-minute audience with someone like Madonna is my private hell. You become a supplicant, and your only revenge is to take a few cheap shots in a piece that she won't even read. Worse yet, the record company publicist *will* read it and won't let you near Los Lobos when they come to town. There's another problem interviewing stars. Their answers usually take the form of set pieces that are as well rehearsed as their set list. These set pieces are trotted out, often with a freshness that can fool you into thinking you're the first person ever to hear them. In most cases, though, the neatly tailored stories have replaced actual memory cells.

For me, it's the supporting cast—the session musicians, the engineers, the record company personnel, and the guys who never made it—who are the real story. They don't always filter everything through an ego as big as all outdoors, and because they don't get asked the same questions every day or every week, the original data is still there. Often, it's warped by time and personal perspective, but memory is—by definition—selective and interpretative. It's the writer's job to give it context.

Of the record labels I've worked for, Bear Family Records in Germany deserves special mention for the way that the owner, Richard Weize, will commit to a historically significant project knowing that he will lose money on it. In fact, he takes a perverse pride in his dogged reversal of the usual music business equation. The first time I became aware of his attitude was when we were in Nashville and he okayed a four-hundred-mile drive into the Ozarks to interview Melvin Endsley, the crippled composer of "Singing the Blues," who was at one time a surprisingly good singer. No other record company would have even considered a Melvin Endsley record, much less bankrolled an in-person visit. Several of the pieces in this collection first appeared in different forms on Bear Family records, and I remain hugely indebted to Richard for letting me learn so much on his dime.

I wanted this collection to be more than just some things I whipped up earlier, so I've tried to rework every one, go back to the original interviews, and add bits and pieces that didn't belong on the record jacket. There are also a few record reviews here. One of the perks of being in the music business is free, or at least cheap, music. Too much music, really. Living with a record for days on end, as I did when I was fourteen, is a luxury I literally can't afford anymore.

Going back through the old pieces sometimes induced the sort of retrospective nausea that is said to afflict people who are drowning. The mistakes appear to be printed in bold face twice the size of regular type, and the clunky phrases make you want to check to see if your old day job is still open. Still, many of these pieces didn't get much exposure the first time around, so there's a chance that the revised and polished versions can now pass for history.

Whatever that is.

COLIN ESCOTT
Toronto, January 1995

I Loved It.
I Took Advantage of It.
I Blew It.

Roy Head

· ·

I BIT ELVIS ON THE LEG

Roy Head was seated in the sightless gaze of a 260-pound deer he had shot and stuffed. He'd cried after he had shot it, he assured me. "Man, I've worked some rough places," he said when the subject finally turned to music. "This one joint, I remember feeling something against my shoe. I looked down and a biker was pissing on my feet, man!" Roy illustrates the story with the appropriate gestures. "Even I knew better than to pick a fight with *that* hairy bastard. The owner of the joint said, 'That's okay, Roy. That means he likes you.' I said, 'What does the son of a bitch do if he *doesn't* like you?'"

I didn't think I'd get to see Roy Head at all. I called from New York and told him I'd be in Houston on Saturday night. He said he had to work a barbecue cook-off during the day, but any time after six o'clock would be fine. I flew to Houston, drove up to Humble (a strangely inappropriate place for Roy Head to live), checked into a motel, and called Roy. No answer. There was no answer at seven, eight, nine, or ten o'clock either. Then, around eleven o'clock, there was a knock on the motel door. I opened it, and someone stood there in the dark leveling a gun at me. A voice said, "Frisk him, Sundance," and a kid stepped out from around the corner and frisked me. Then there was a laugh. It was Roy Head. He didn't appear to care that I didn't think it was so damn funny.

Roy Kent Head is frighteningly intense and perpetually wired. He's been known to pick fights with strangers for looking at him the wrong way, and his nose—broken in five places—attests to the fact that he doesn't always know who to pick on. He had his crack at the brass ring in the fall of 1965 when "Treat Her Right" broke out of the R&B market to become a surprise left-field pop hit in an era dominated by pimply British groups. Television appearances revealed that he was not black, as many had thought, but that—like fellow Texans Delbert McClinton, Doug Sahm, and Bruce Channel—his natural style just owed a lot to black music.

More than anything else, Roy is a performer. After strutting in front of ten thousand people at the barbecue cook-off, he took me out to a honky-tonk near Humble. If just one ol' boy who once got lucky when "Treat Her Right"

Roy Head
Photo courtesy of G. Kurtz/C. Escott

was on the car radio lets out a whoop at the mention of his name, Roy will head toward the stage like a heat-seeking missile and give it everything he's got. He'll do the back flips, splits, microphone humps, and turkey trots that once rivaled James Brown for pure onstage energy.

There have been several Roy Head birthdates quoted through the years, but Roy swears he was born on September 1, 1941, in Three Rivers, Texas, midway between San Antonio and the Gulf of Mexico. His father, George, was from Chicago and his mother, Ellen, was a full-blood Indian from Oklahoma. The family moved to Crystal City, almost within sight of the Mexican border, when Roy was small. His father was an itinerant worker. His mother worked at a spinach factory. "Crystal City is the spinach capital of the world," says Roy. "Honest to God, they got a statue of Popeye in the city square. Where we lived, all my friends were black, and that's when I started listening to R&B. I loved Elmore James, Bobby Bland, B. B. King, Junior Parker. Those were the guys that were layin' it down. My parents loved country music. My mother was the world's biggest Ernest Tubb fan. The 'Louisiana Hayride' was the big thing in our house."

Roy formed his first band after the family moved to San Marcos. He was trying for the blind, butt-shaking energy of early rock 'n' roll. "Guys like Little Richard, Little Willie John, Dee Clark, and so on, they had *something*," says Roy. "You couldn't go out on stage in those days and set your equipment on fire and cover up with loud amplifiers. That was real music back then.

"I used to sing on the school bus, and everyone said I should form a band. A guy named Bill Pennington was a year younger than me. His folks owned a funeral home. They was rich folks and his mother, Edra Pennington, bought us a bunch of spangled shirts—and there was twenty-four of us in the original band. We had *Traits* sewed on the back of our shirts. We looked like heavyweights."

The name "Traits" apparently came from the fact that everyone in the band had different personality traits—as if that was some kind of fresh discovery. Tommy Bolton played guitar, Jerry Gibson (who later played with Sly and the Family Stone) was the drummer, and Bill Pennington played bass. Dan Buie played piano and kept Roy company on his teenage drinking binges. "Every weekend we was in jail. Edra kept it from my mother, God bless her! Now Dan's president of Alcoholics Anonymous."After letting a few guys go and bringing the group down to a manageable size, the Traits started playing the low-life bars around San Marcos. According to Roy, "They had chicken wire to protect us in a lot of those places. I swear to God, that's not just a Willie Nelson story. It wasn't that the audience hated the band, it's just that they didn't give a shit about the band. They had been working all week and they wanted a good time."

The Traits were discovered by Ricky Ware at KTSA in San Antonio, who recorded them performing a song called "Cathy Lou." Ware took the demo to T-N-T Records (Tanner 'n' Texas), which was primarily a polka label then, although Tanner had scored a surprise country hit with Bill Anderson's "City Lights," and had recorded Johnny Cash's brother-in-law, Ray Liberto, singing rock 'n' roll. Roy and the Traits were signed to T-N-T and cut six singles for the label, most of which are on a fabulously rare album released in 1958. There were more singles on little labels like Renner and Suave that did little or no business.

Roy began a hitch in the army reserves in mid-1963, and the Traits continued without him for a few months until he got out. Then a promoter from Houston, Charlie Booth, took the band under his wing and brought them into the studio with Huey Meaux, who promised free studio time. "Every time we'd rehearse something, Huey'd shout 'It's a take!'" said Roy. After the success of "Treat Her Right," Meaux leased some of those early demo tapes to Scepter Records for an album called *Treat Me Right*.

According to Roy, "Treat Her Right" was originally a double-entendre blues called "Talking 'bout a Cow." ("If you don't treat her right/You'll get no milk and cream tonight." You get the idea.) The verses didn't rhyme and didn't scan, but the song was a big hit at dances because it was played to a goosed-up "Mashed Potato" riff. Gene Kurtz, who had taken over on bass while Roy was in the army, cleaned up the lyrics the night before a session that Charlie Booth had arranged at Gold Star Studios in Houston. "I took it upon myself to make the lyrics rhyme and have some continuity," he says. He also inserted a horn riff at the end that he had adapted from a television commercial. And that was "Treat Her Right." A borrowed dance riff, lyrics that had somehow evolved from "Milk Cow Blues," and a horn lick from a television jingle. What mattered was that the Traits had played it so often on show dates that they had that cohesive *thing* that all the great R&B bands have. Roy sang with all the confidence in the world.

Kurtz insists that Huey Meaux did not produce the session, but Meaux was probably the one who placed the master with Don Robey's Backbeat Records. Backbeat was the junior member of Robey's Duke-Peacock label empire, which was run from his headquarters on Erastus Street in Houston.

"Robey was a big, beautiful black guy," said Roy with considerably more affection than many of Robey's former artists. "He impressed me. That man could spit into a spitoon and hit it from six yards away. He gave me a damn Cadillac, and I drove home in style." Robey had reason to be grateful; "Treat Her Right" went on to place higher on the pop charts than any record Robey had ever released—or would ever release. It got all the way to number two, with "Yesterday" keeping it from number one. Exact sales figures from the Duke-Peacock empire are hard to come by, but Roy always quotes two and a half million copies.

Just after "Treat Her Right" went on sale, Robey scheduled an appearance for Roy at a black deejays convention. Roy was scheduled to front Bobby Bland's band, led by Joe Scott. "It was scary, man. This was the time of Watts and the riots and so on. Robey changed his mind and said I shouldn't go on, but Charlie Booth pushed me on stage. With that band behind me I did

Don Robey in his pressing plant
Photo courtesy of Showtime Archive, Toronto

things that they thought was impossible: back and forward flips, splits, you know. I worked my butt off and they went wild. That's how we broke 'Treat Her Right.' Those deejays went back and spinned my record. The record broke big time. Changed my life. Up to that time I was just working in the furniture factory in San Marcos. The biggest event in my life was when I screwed the town whore and the whole football team got clap from her.

"'Treat Her Right' was a whole different trip. One night we were driving our '58 Chevy wagon near Prairie Hill, Texas. There was a big blue cross on the horizon. We had the radio tuned to 'Ernie's Record Mart' show on WLAC, Nashville, and just as we were getting near that cross they played 'Treat Her Right.' The guy who was driving drove off into the damned ditch. We were jumpin' on each other, clapping, goin' nuts. It just mushroomed. Bigger crowds. Limousines. I loved it. I took advantage of it. I blew it!"

Success brought its problems, the first of which was a lawsuit that brought Head into conflict with the other members of the Traits. "Jerry Gibson came to me," said Roy, "and he said, 'Roy, we need you to sign this little piece of paper as a pact to hold everything together.' I signed it. I was big-hearted and ignorant. Then the stupid sons of bitches didn't want to travel. We were fully booked for months—and they wanted to sell fuckin' insurance. These days I don't sign nothing till I've talked to a lawyer—and I don't even trust them. But that's what busted us up back then. It got so we couldn't work but on weekends. They took me to the cleaners. They got me by the nuts and run with 'em." The Traits sued for six-sevenths of all the money Roy had made without them, and they won. "Sure, that lawsuit impeded his career, but it was just one of many things that impeded Roy's career," said the Traits' bass player, Gene Kurtz.

In the meantime, Don Robey's publishing company was being sued over "Treat Her Right." The publisher of "Do the Mashed Potato" saw a similarity between the "Treat Her Right" riff and the "Mashed Potato" riff, and, inasmuch as a riff can be copyrighted, he had a case. "Do the Mashed Potato" was done to a shuffle, and "Treat Her Right" was done as eight-to-the-bar rock 'n' roll; otherwise there wasn't much difference. Roy and his band were hidden away in a hotel room to avoid having papers served on them, but it was a lawsuit with wheels within wheels. "Do the Mashed Potato" was a James Brown record issued under a pseudonym, "Nat Kendrick & the Swans," on Dade Records.

Huey Meaux was subpoenaed to testify as an expert witness at the case when it came to trial.

"Now, Robey had never paid us a dime except front money on 'Treat

Her Right.' I called him one night just before we were due to go to court. You didn't just go down on Erastus Street, where he had his offices, because he had his henchmen. So I called him up and told him to keep his henchmen away because we were going to have a little business talk.

"I got there about seven o'clock. It was drizzlin' rain and the sun had just gone down. I went into his room and he had a deer rifle on his desk. He was polishing it with his handkerchief. I had brought my .38 and I got it out and started polishing it. He'd take his handkerchief every once in a while and polish his bald head with it. He'd say, 'How's it going, Huey?' I said, 'Oh, everything's fine, Chief. I come to talk to you about "Treat Her Right." When I go to court tomorrow I'm either on your side or them other people's side.' He said, 'What you talkin' about, Hue?' I said, 'You know what I'm talkin' about. I want my fuckin' Roy Head money. Forty thousand dollars. I want it in a briefcase, in cash, when I go on that witness stand. Otherwise, being an expert witness, I'm gonna be for the other side.'

"He got fuckin' nervous. He said, 'Oh, Hue, you know that thing didn't make no money.' I said, 'Shit it didn't! It ain't my first hit record and I didn't ride into town on no mule.' I told him I wanted my money and that's just the way it was. He said he'd talk to his lawyer.

"He called me later and said we had a deal. Said I should meet him the next morning at his lawyer's office on San Jacinto. I got over there and Robey says, 'Give Hue a check for forty thousand dollars from the trustee account or something.' Then we got into his limo to go to court.

"I said, 'Let's just drop by the bank and pick up the money.' He said, 'Oh, Hue, we don't have to do that. You can trust me.' I said, 'Look, Chief, I said I wanted the forty thousand in this fuckin' briefcase.' He got pissed off, but he said, 'OK, drive him by the bank.' I went in, cashed the check, put the money in my briefcase, and went to the courthouse.

"When I was sittin' on the witness stand I had that briefcase right beside me. Afterwards I got up to take a leak. I had Eddie Kilroy working for me at that time. I said, 'Eddie, I'm goin' to take a leak in a few minutes. You meet me out in the hall by the pisser. I'm gonna hand you a briefcase and you take it back to the office.' I wasn't taking no chances. Could very well the briefcase *and me* disappear."

The copyright remained in Robey's hands, but Roy's share didn't remain in his hands. As part of a divorce settlement, he signed it away to his ex-wife, Nancy, and after she died in 1988, his oldest daughter, with whom he is not on good terms, got his share of the song.

After the disagreement with the Traits, Roy put together a trio with Gene

Kurtz and Jerry Gibson, but he couldn't recapture the success that had come and gone so quickly. He signed with Mercury in 1967, but by then he was drinking heavily and soon needed an operation to scrape nodes off his vocal cords from screaming James Brown screams too many nights. He was also out of step with much of what was happening in rock music. "When they started blowing up guitars, playing with their dicks on stage, and so on, I knew I didn't belong," he said. "You couldn't even hear your own self for the guitars. I was from the old school. I was lost for several years there. I beat up club owners, choked disc jockeys, and did a lot of things I wish I hadn't done. I just screwed up."

Roy's last fling at rock 'n' roll came with the TMI label in Memphis, co-owned by Jerry Williams at Trans-Maximus studio and Stax studio veteran Steve Cropper. By the end of his stint at TMI, Roy was doing fifties revival music and was in bad shape. When someone suggested a move to country music, Roy thought he had no option.

"Art Chancey, who was a deejay here in Houston, suggested that I learn a few country songs. I sang 'em at some gig he was presenting and he said, 'Boy, you might have something here.' [Club owner] Lee Savaggio bought my contract off Huey Meaux and said, 'Hell, I'll give you a shot.'" Savaggio, interviewed in *Rambler* magazine, remembered Roy coming in one afternoon in March 1974, unshaven, surly, and three-quarters drunk. "He had nothing going," said Savaggio. "He couldn't find a job, not even [here] in his hometown."

"Lee had a little old club," said Roy, "and I played fifties music there. People packed the sidewalks; you couldn't get in. Lee got me a deal with Mega to cut 'Baby's Not Home' and then fixed up a meeting with Jim Reeves's widow, Mary, who had a little label called Shannon. We cut 'The Most Wanted Woman in Town,' and it caught on."

The Shannon contract was picked up by ABC Records in January 1976, and Roy had a run of middling country hits on ABC's Dot label, like "A Bridge for Crawling Back," "Now You See 'Em, Now You Don't," a country version of Rod Stewart's "Tonight's the Night," and half a dozen others.

"Country was real good to me," said Roy, "but I think I was a little too flashy for 'em. You don't see too many country artists standing up there wearing lots of jewelry and stuff. Hell! That's the black in me. I want to look good." Head was thrown off ABC after he phoned the president, Jay Lasker, one night, drunk out of his mind, demanding to know why his records weren't racked in Cut and Shoot, Texas. When he asked for his release, Lasker was happy to mail it to him. Then there was a brief fling with Elektra Records, which was trying one of its occasional stillborn efforts to start a country division, this one with Jimmy Bowen at the helm. Two albums and four fleeting hits later, Elektra Country was history and Roy was adrift again. Since then he has recorded for more labels than he can remember. The last time he showed up in the country charts was in 1985 on the Texas Crude label. "Break Out the Good Stuff" got up to number ninety-three and stalled out.

Roy and his second wife, Carolyn, don't seem to be doing so badly. They have a place out in the country and two children. Watching his son, Sundance, grow up fills Roy with mixed emotions about his own mistakes, but there doesn't seem to be much in the way of regret. "Hell, I've screwed up. I've got thrown off tours because I was having a little more fun than some of the other acts. I bit Elvis Presley on the leg when I was drunk one night and his bodyguards leaped on me, man. I had to go to the chiropractor for three weeks to get straightened out. I'm still not through. If there's one son of a bitch in the room that's paid to hear me, I'll work my butt off for him."

The consensus among those who worked with Roy is that he had self-destruct buttons implanted all over him. "You should have seen the Traits back around 1963," says Gene Kurtz. "If the right person had got a hold of them, Roy could have been as big as Elvis. What he was doing was that unusual for a white performer." Roy doesn't even seem to be able to tap into the lucrative European market. Another golden opportunity came and went when "Treat Her Right" was used in the soundtrack for the film *The Commitments*. He has also missed out on the royalties that came when Len Barry, Otis Redding, Mae West, Roy Buchanan, Barbara Mandrell, the Leroi Brothers, George Thorogood, Lee Atwater, and Jerry Lee Lewis cut the song. It's on a Dylan bootleg, too, according to Kurtz. Treat Her Right is even the name of a better-than-average band from Boston. Roy, though, seems pretty much mired in East Texas. Still, even if no one remembers who he is when he steps up to the microphone, the band only has to break into the "Treat Her Right" riff and suddenly anyone who was listening to the radio in 1965 knows exactly who Roy Head is. ⑥

FOR YOUR LISTENING PLEASURE

Varèse Sarabande has issued a CD of Roy Head's Backbeat recordings, *Treat Her Right*, (VSD 5618). Bear Family issued an LP of Roy's Huey Meaux recordings, *Treat Her Right* (BFX 15307), which includes the original version of "Treat Her Right" and a recreated version of "Talkin' 'bout a Cow." Treat Her Right's self-titled first album, a dark, underregarded classic that admittedly has almost nothing to do with Roy Head, was first issued by Demon Records in England (FIEND 97) in 1987, and subsequently picked up by RCA in the States, which lost what little momentum the band had.

Bobby Charles

. . . .

SEE YOU LATER, ALLIGATOR

It's Bobby Charles's personal preference to maintain a low profile. He has famous friends who get twitchy when they're out of the limelight for so much as a day. They call every now and again and stop by when they're in Louisiana. The mailman brings Bobby checks for his songs. It can be a marginal existence sometimes, but that's the way he wants it. He has written a few of the hardy perennials of rock music ("See You Later, Alligator," "Walkin' to New Orleans," "But I Do," "The Jealous Kind," and "Before I Grow Too Old"), but he's not out there performing them or even trying to persuade other people to cut them.

Surprisingly for someone so shy of the limelight, Bobby has a recording career that spans forty years. It's true the momentum has tailed off since the fifties, but he has a smoky swamp-pop voice that has weathered the years well and still has the power to charm. His chops are intact—engagingly so, in fact. There's something about the white singers from Bobby's part of the country. They have found what the Joe Cockers of this world have searched for throughout their lives: a white R&B voice. Not a voice strangled and crammed with Ray Charles's leavin's, but one with smoky depths and contours, and the knowledge that laying back and holding something in reserve conveys more than all the gargling, gurgling, and screaming.

Bobby is from Abbeville, Louisiana. He was born Robert Charles Guidry on February 21, 1938. "My parents spoke mostly French around the house," he says, "but when I started school the teachers would spank you for speaking French. That stopped a lot of people from being bilingual. In fact, we should have spoken Spanish, French, and English." As a teenager, he and a couple of friends snuck into the juke joints to hear Fats Domino (who was a star on the R&B circuit for five years before the pop market cottoned on to him), Guitar Slim, Lloyd Price, and Joe Turner. That was as much of a musical education as anyone needs, and when Bobby formed his band, the Cardinals, they were playing the R&B hits of the hour. Then Bobby wrote his own hit, a silly little song called "See You Later, Alligator," that he based on a phrase he'd heard when he was leaving a club one night. Right then Bobby

Bobby and the fan club
Photo courtesy of Jeff Hannusch/Showtime Archive

experienced his first songwriter's rush: something was out there in the ether waiting to be received. All he had to do was raise his antennae and get it down before it disappeared.

The Cardinals played "See You Later, Alligator" at their dances and sometimes had to reprise it ten or fifteen times a night. Ace Records, from Jackson, Mississippi, was sniffing around, but Bobby had been warned off them. Then, after playing a dance in Crowley one night, Bobby met Charles Relich, owner of Dago's Record Shop. Leonard Chess of Chess Records had been through Crowley a few years earlier and told Relich that if he ever heard anything he thought would sell, he should call collect. Bobby sang his song over the phone to Leonard, and Leonard told Bobby to go to New Orleans, see Paul Gayten, and arrange a session at Cosimo's studio, the legendary hole in the wall where Fats Domino, Smiley Lewis, and all the others recorded.

Gayten was a bandleader who doubled as Chess's man in New Orleans. Leonard Chess, usually so on top of things, was an hour late and a dollar short when it came to raiding talent out of New Orleans. Between them, Imperial, Specialty, and Ace had scooped up almost everyone worth having. But Chess had Bobby Charles, and one night in the fall of 1955 Bobby and the Cardinals wrapped up their last set in Abbeville and drove to New Orleans. They met Gayten at Cosimo's. Bobby thinks he cut four or five songs, but only two made their way to Chess: "See You Later, Alligator" and the lovely swamp-pop ballad "On Bended Knee."

Chess, of course, was a rhythm 'n' blues label, and, from what he'd heard over the phone, Leonard Chess thought he was getting an R&B singer. Soon after the record came out, Chess brought Bobby to Chicago. "Phil Chess, Leonard's brother, had driven to the airport with a pretty little blonde girl from Tennessee," says Bobby. "He was looking for a black guy, and I was eyeballing the girl, looking at baldheaded Phil wondering what she was doing with him. After everyone had picked up their bags, he came up to me, and he said, 'You can't be Bobby Charles, can you?' I said, 'Yeah, I am.' He said, 'Leonard's gonna have a stroke.' He dropped me off at some hotel with the girl and a hundred-dollar bill. He said, 'You have a good time and come in the office on Monday morning. Leonard will be in.' I knew then I was gonna enjoy working for Chess. When Leonard first saw me, the first word that came out of his mouth was 'Motherfucker!' It was the first time I heard that expression. I said, 'What?' He said, 'You're not black.' I said, 'I know.' The record had already been released then, and it was too late. The toothpaste was out of the tube, and you can't put it back."

Chess issued "See You Later, Alligator" as "Later Alligator," which infuriated Bobby. Leonard thought he was being hip. Bobby called him and set him right. How the song became the lead cut on a Bill Haley recording session on December 12, 1955, is unclear. Perhaps Haley heard it; perhaps Benny Goodman's brothers, who administered Chess's music publishing, got the song to him. Haley knew it was a hit in waiting because he'd seen what had happened with another dumb expression, "Crazy, Man, Crazy." He was so hot you could hardly touch him during that winter before Elvis broke, and his version of "See You Later, Alligator" got up to Number Six, but it would be poor Bill's last Top Ten hit.

Bobby's record of "See You Later, Alligator" might just have clicked if Bill Haley hadn't scooped him. "Haley had more money behind him," said Bobby, "and it was following up a pretty big record. He got more airplay than I did because I was on an all-black label, and it was hard to get airplay on the white stations. That record was never a hit with the blacks. No one black ever did that song." Nothing else that Bobby recorded on Chess did much business, a situation not helped by his distaste even then for going on the road and promoting his records. Around 1958 he started writing for Fats Domino, beginning with "Before I Grow Too Old."

"Fats was playing in Lafayette," said Bobby, "and I went to see him after I'd sent him the song, and he said, 'I wish I'd known you were gonna be here. I'd have brought you a copy of your song.' He said he wanted me to hear it. He said, 'Why don't you come to New Orleans and listen to it?' I said I didn't have a car, didn't have any way to get there. He said, 'Well, find some kind of way to get there.' I said, 'About the only way would be if I walked.' As soon as I said that, I told the fellas I was riding with, I said, 'Let's go, fellas, get me a pencil and a paper quick.' I wrote 'Walkin' to New Orleans' on the way home. Right away I knew it was for Fats." Fats and his producer, Dave Bartholomew, cut themselves in for two thirds of the song, reversing the usual paradigm in which the black guy lost two thirds of his royalties to the white guys.

"It Keeps Raining" was every bit as compelling and hypnotic as "Walkin' to New Orleans," although it did nowhere near as much business. "That was called 'Little Rascal,'" says Bobby. "I put the voice down on the track, but when they sent the record to Fats the voice was left off the damn track. Fats wrote the words 'It keeps rainin' and rainin'' 'cause it was raining the day he got it. He liked the track so much he put the words to it. They tried to get that from me without giving me a piece of it. I said, 'Wait a minute, man, those are my changes on there and everything, you know.'"

"Later Alligator."
Bobby objected to this title and got it changed.

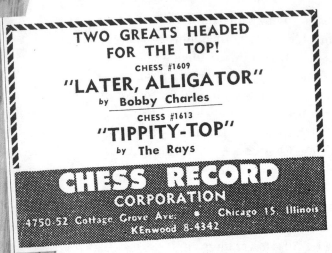

Bobby got his release from Chess, and Dave Bartholomew signed him to Fats's label, Imperial Records, but the deal soon fell apart. Several other deals followed. They fell apart, too.

By 1971 the law was on Bobby's tail for a drug infraction, and he decided to exit the South for a while. He and a friend settled anonymously in a little town in upstate New York. "It was five miles from where they had the Woodstock Festival," he says, "but I hadn't heard of the festival. I was hiding out. At my daddy's funeral, they had some guys looking for me for jumping bail. They were waiting at his funeral with .45s, looking to put me in the same hole. I didn't even know he had died until two weeks after he was buried. Me and this friend were in a house in upstate New York, and I didn't like it. I started looking at the map, and I saw this little town called Woodstock. My buddy said, 'That's where they had the big festival.' I said, 'Let's go take a ride over there, I might see somebody I know from the business.'"

Bobby saw a house he liked. He went inside and saw guitars and records lined up against the wall. It looked like home.

"There were some guys there. I said, 'What do you all do?' One of them said they were musicians, and we got to talking, and he said he had a friend of his coming in from Nashville the next week. I said, 'Who?' He said, 'Ben Keith.' I said, 'I'll be damned.' When I got in trouble, Ben was living right across the street from me in Nashville. I said, 'Just tell him Bobby Charles will be in to see him.' When I said that, the bass player, Jim Colegrove, said, 'Are *you* Bobby Charles?' I said, 'Yeah, but don't say anything.' We got to talking. They asked me if I'd been writing. I said I had, but I hadn't done anything with the songs because I'd been trying to stay one step ahead of the law most of the time."

Everyone told Bobby he should meet Albert Grossman, manager of Bob Dylan, Peter Paul & Mary, Janis Joplin, and The Band. Grossman was a fixer. He might be able to shake the bad guys off Bobby's back and land him a deal. They met at Grossman's restaurant. The Band was there that night. Later, up at Grossman's estate, Bobby sang some songs, including "Tennessee Blues." Grossman was sold, and he promised a deal with his own Bearsville Records. Recording started around November or December 1971.

16

Rick Danko of The Band and John Simon, who had produced the first two Band albums, coproduced with Bobby. As production started, The Band was preparing for its New Orleans-flavored "Rock of Ages" concerts in New York, scheduled to run over the New Year's holiday. The Band offered to include one of Bobby's songs, "But I Do," on the album, but he was in dispute with the music publisher and passed—a little moment of pique that has cost him dearly over the years. Bobby's album was wrapped up just as *Rock of Ages* was being mixed.

His self-titled album, *Bobby Charles,* is a little-known classic from the seventies, a decade not much given to classics. Despite the big-name guests (The Band minus Robbie, Dr. John, David Sanborn, and so on), it's Bobby's record: very Southern, almost an elegy to the life he thought he'd left behind. Garth Hudson's voicings add as much to Bobby's little creations as they did to Robbie Robertson's. Levon Helm's drumming is wonderfully spare and muddy. Amos Garrett's guitar work on "Tennessee Blues" in particular is some of his best. He weaves in and out of Garth Hudson's countermelodies on the accordion, making you pray for another half dozen choruses. "Small Town Talk," like The Band's "The Rumor," takes a swipe at the Woodstock gossip mill. Several people have cut it since, but no one has been able to make a hit out of it. A new version of "Before I Grow Too Old" was the album's only link to Bobby's past life.

If nothing else, *Bobby Charles* served one purpose. It drew the line once and for always between "laid back" and "slow." Everyone was trying for "laid back" around this time; mostly, they were only slow, and often unconscionably boring. "Laid back" is a frame of mind that applies to any tempo.

Bobby hung around The Band's camp during their last good season. Robbie Robertson, he says, was already distancing himself from the others. Bobby was there for The Band's last hurrah in 1976, too. He flew in from Louisiana for "The Last Waltz." Robbie asked him to perform "See You Later, Alligator," but Bobby declined, so Robbie taught him what he could remember of "Down South in New Orleans" and asked Bobby to go write some additional lyrics. It was one of Bobby's last onstage appearances; one of Robbie's too.

Bobby Charles and Albert Grossman had fallen out just after the album was released. Warner Bros., which distributed Grossman's Bearsville label, didn't do much work on behalf of an artist who was off the roster, and who wouldn't go out on the road anyway. Bobby returned to Louisiana. "Maybe big things could have happened," he said. "Maybe not."

The latest album, *Wish You Were Here Right Now,* released on the Canadian

Stony Plain label in 1995, is a mixed bag. The best is very good. It's Bobby and a few of his famous friends. "Willie Nelson was playing in New Orleans," he says, "and he had never heard the Neville Brothers, and the Neville Brothers wanted to meet Willie. I knew the Neville Brothers real good, so I called them and said I'd meet them at the Willie Nelson concert. We didn't tell Willie. We just agreed that we'd wait till he was onstage doing his gospel number and we'd just appear there, backing him up. Aaron looked at me and said, 'Do you think that will be all right?' I said, 'Sure. He's real loose about that kind of stuff.' When we walked up onstage, Willie was singing 'Amazing Grace.' The crowd recognized the Neville Brothers, and there was a little 'Wooo.' Willie turned around. He thought it was for him, I guess. Then we started singing behind him, and he did a double take because he saw Aaron and Art and me up there. I pointed to Willie and said Aaron should sing a verse, and Willie just flipped out. Everybody in the auditorium did.

"After the show, we got on the bus and started talking. Willie wanted to play something with me, and said I should come to his studio. I said, 'Why don't we all do it? Me, the Nevilles, everyone?' He said that sounded great, so he called his manager. They had one date open, April fifteenth—income tax day. A Sunday that year. Willie said it was the only day he had off in six or seven months, but he'd be happy to go in with us. I said, 'I'll be there.'

"The Nevilles backed out, and Willie's manager called me up and said everyone was backing out so we might as well call it off. I said, 'I'm not backing out. Hell, no. I'm gonna be there.' I had Neil Young, who wanted to be there, and some other people that wanted to be there. I drove out to Austin with Rufus Thibodeaux, the fiddle player. We went in the studio and there was two young engineers. They weren't ready for a session at all. They didn't think it was gonna happen. They said, 'Who are you?' They called Willie, and Willie said to set up his guitar. Then Neil Young walked in with Ben Keith and different other people. The engineers' eyes was poppin' out. Neil had bought this guitar that Hank Williams owned, a 1928 Martin. I was with him when he bought it in Nashville. He used it only to write songs and record. I said, 'Just bring that Hank Williams guitar.' Neil had never met Willie, and that night they started putting together Farm Aid."

There are two other things about Bobby Charles. First, he makes the music come together without being able to play any instrument or even call off chords. Once, at the Chess studio in Chicago, Chuck Berry tried to teach him the guitar to no avail, but he seems able to draw what he wants out of people anyway. "Willie was hitting a wrong chord on one song," he says. "Maybe not *wrong*, but it didn't sound right to me. I mentioned it to him. He said, 'Well, which is the right one?' I said, 'I don't know. You'll have to play me the ones you know and I'll tell you when you hit it.' He started going through chords, and he and Neil Young were looking at each other laughing. He hits one, and I said, 'That's it!' Neil said, 'He's right.'"

Then there's "The Jealous Kind," still a classic in waiting. It was Shakespeare who wrote the first great lines about jealousy: "O! beware, my lord, of jealousy/It is the green ey'd monster which doth mock/The meat it feeds on." In a series of three or four everyday images, Bobby tells the story of a man who can't get over what his woman did and who she did it with before he met her:

> If you only knew how much it hurts to hear you say
> How you can't forget that before we met, those were the good old days.

Otis Redding should have lived long enough to cut it. Delbert McClinton and Joe Cocker have done it. The cartoonish Clarence "Frogman" Henry had the first version.

There should be a place for someone like Bobby Charles, who could still make delightful records but doesn't want to bust his ass on the road. All the "shoulds" and "oughts" will probably never put checks in his mailbox, although one day a Bobby Charles song might end up in a movie and the mailbox will be fuller. It has passed into legend now that Nick Lowe got a cool million for getting a few seconds of "(What's So Funny about) Peace, Love, and Understanding" into *The Bodyguard*. If it doesn't happen, Bobby will just stay put in Louisiana. If he's gonna starve out, he swears he'll starve out somewhere warm. ☺

19

FOR YOUR LISTENING PLEASURE

The Bearsville record has been reissued on CD by Stony Plain Records in Canada (SPCD 1202). *Wish You Were Here Right Now* is also on Stony Plain (SPCD 1203); write for details to Box 861, Edmonton, Alberta, Canada T5J 2L8. Two of the Chess recordings, including "See You Later, Alligator" are on the Chess *Rhythm & Roll* boxed set (CHD4-9352). Six of Bobby's Chess recordings are on *Chess New Orleans* (MCA CHD-9355).

Ersel Hickey

. . . .

BLUEBIRDS OVER THE MOUNTAIN

The reason that anyone remembers Ersel Hickey is because of *that* photo. It was taken by Gene Laverne, a photographer in Buffalo, New York, who specialized in what were then called exotic dancers. After the photo session, Laverne stood in his darkroom, pulled the negative out of the tray, held it up to the light, and said, "Wow!" It was a sculpture every bit as much as a photo, the first rock 'n' roll sculpture, perfect in its filigree, its contour, and its symmetry. It told how and why rock 'n' roll was a thing apart.

Laverne gave the negative to Ersel Hickey, who held it up to the darkroom light and said, "Ugh!" He sent the negatives to Epic Records and told them that he wanted the standard head-and-shoulders shot from the same session for his first publicity photo.

Twenty years later, the photo archivist Michael Ochs was trawling through the Columbia Records archives when he found the photo, and it was Ochs who made it into perhaps the most famous pose in rock 'n' roll. *Rolling Stone* used it on a cover, and Ochs put it on the front of his book *Rock Archives*. Since then it's been on T-shirts, postcards, and Christ knows what else. Ersel himself has never been able to unravel the paradox that more people know his silhouette than knew his music.

From the name and the photo you would guess that Ersel Hickey had come from a little town on the Tennessee-Mississippi line and had shared a Coke with Elvis after he'd played the high school gym there early in 1955. Not so. Hickey was born in Brighton, just outside Rochester, in upstate New York, on June 27, 1934, one of a family of eight. His mother was from Kingston, Ontario—just across the lake; his father had been a dancer in vaudeville and had settled in Rochester before Ersel was born. His mother and father had once danced together back in the twenties, but Ersel's dad was working for the WPA when he died. Ersel was four years old then. His sister became an exotic dancer. She was killed in a car wreck when Ersel was fifteen. Her photographer was Gene Laverne.

Ersel won a talent contest in Middletown, New York, in 1950 singing in the petulant style of Johnnie Ray. He didn't have a high school band and didn't

21

***That* photo.**
Photo courtesy of Ersel Hickey

Ersel with Johnny Cash
Photo courtesy of C. Escott

play much locally, but his brother Bill bankrolled a private recording that appeared on a tiny Rochester label, Fine Records, around 1955.

Ersel's sweet, defining moment as a singer and songwriter came one night in 1957 when he wrote "Bluebirds over the Mountain." He called Bill at two-thirty in the morning and sang it for him over the phone. Bill flipped. Everyone who heard it flipped, but how was Ersel to get his song out of upstate New York to where someone with power and influence might hear it? Shuttling between relatives, Ersel got off the bus in Buffalo on his way to his aunt's house. He looked across the street and saw Gene Laverne's Studio of the Stars. He remembered that Laverne had helped his sister, so he went in to see him.

Laverne put Ersel in touch with Mike Corda, a songwriter and personal manager in New York. Corda had managed Enzio Stuarti and had placed him with Epic Records. As a musician, Corda had played in the original cast of Cole Porter's *Kiss Me Kate*. Even with that kind of background, Corda knew that "Bluebirds" stood a good shot, so he paid for a demo session at the National Studio in New York. He brought in Jimmy Mitchell (later the staff guitarist on *Sesame Street*) to play lead guitar, and Corda played bass himself to keep the costs down. The three of them noodled around with "Bluebirds" for hours, eventually coming up with a strange, offbeat rhythm that predated ska by several years. Corda hawked the demo around, eventually pitching it to Joe Sherman, the A&R director at Epic Records.

Even though it timed out at one minute and thirty seconds, making it barely longer than the commercials that would precede it on the radio, Sherman recognized that the demo held the little bit of magic that he would never be able to recreate, so he leased it in January 1958. It was a tiny, perfect record. Another instrument, another note, another chorus, and its logic would have been destroyed. Some knucklehead shipped the wrong take to Canada, though, and a slowed-down version was issued there.

Ersel was playing at Luigi's in Niagara Falls, New York, when he heard that he was an Epic recording artist. He got some acetates of "Bluebirds" and handed them around to Buffalo deejays. George "Hound Dog" Lorenz played it on his popular late night rhythm 'n' blues show on WKBW (originally a religious station, its call letters stood for Well Known Bible Works), and Lucky Pierre aired it over a fifty-thousand-watt station, WBNY. Together, they started a clamor for the record even before its release. It topped some radio station charts in New York and Los Angeles, but *Billboard* reckoned that it only deserved to get up to seventy-fifth place in the Hot 100. A couple of years earlier, when rockabilly was hot, it might have been a Top Five record.

Corda placed Ersel with the Royaltones, a group from the Detroit suburb of Dearborn remembered by chart fetishists for their hit "Poor Boy." With them, Ersel played some clubs in Wildwood, New Jersey, and elsewhere, but the group soon landed their own contract and split. Ersel played a few package shows, MOA (jukebox operators) conventions, and Epic Records conventions, but he needed a convincing hit to be able to put a band together.

For the second session, Joe Sherman brought Ersel to New York to cut at the old Columbia studio in a converted church on Thirtieth Street. Ersel turned up with another good original song, "Goin' Down That Road." Billy Mure played the fiery lead guitar. Once again, the sound was rockabilly, and once again the problem was that it was now 1958—not 1955.

Ersel Hickey was in the wrong place at the wrong time. He was trapped in the old-time New York music business, walking around with guys who were used to forty pieces on a session, dealing with record companies that had bureaucracies like the Kremlin. He should have been cutting in Nashville or Memphis. The New York music mill tried to accommodate rock 'n' roll as best it knew how, but on some level the results were always unconvincing, and everyone was always waiting for it to go away and for business to resume as usual.

The third record, "You Never Can Tell," was co-written by Al Lewis, who had co-written "Blueberry Hill" back in the forties, and Sylvester Bradford. Together, they had written "Tears on My Pillow," and Lewis had just formed a music publishing partnership with Don Kirshner, later the mastermind behind the Monkees. "You Never Can Tell" was one of the demos that Kirshner and his accountant, Alan Klein, presented to Ersel; the other was "I'm Ready." Both demos were sung by Bobby Darin. Ersel picked "You Never Can Tell"; Fats Domino picked "I'm Ready." Ersel's record charted in a few cities; Fats's reached Number Sixteen nationwide.

It was almost unreturned-phone-call time for Ersel, but as 1959 drew to a close, he was given another shot. In England, Adam Faith was scoring a big hit with "What Do You Want." Faith was a Cockney Buddy Holly imitator, last heard of as a discredited financial columnist during the Thatcher years. As a song, "What Do You Want" had the goods. In Faith's hands it had the plaintiveness that the best Buddy Holly records had, and in a reversal of the usual paradigm, several American cover versions of the British hit were rushed out. Ersel had one; Bobby Vee had another. Vee got the hit.

Ersel's final Epic single, "Stardust Brought Me You," was a song he had written sitting at the piano in the Famous Music office—the same piano that Hoagy Carmichael had used to write "Stardust." Then he was off Epic. There was a brief, abortive fling with Kapp Records, and then Ersel began to concentrate on songwriting. He co-wrote one giant hit, "Don't Let the Rain Come Down," which the Serendipity Singers charted in 1964, and had fifty other songs cut by the likes of LaVern Baker and Jackie Wilson. Then in 1968 the Beach Boys bought the publishing on "Bluebirds over the Mountain" and cut it as a single. It didn't do much better than Ersel's version, but it has appeared on countless compilations, and that makes it what songwriters call an oil well; it just keeps on gushing.

Ersel should have written "Bluebirds" in 1955 and left Rochester the same day. He should have used *that* photo to promote himself back then. Ersel himself probably knows this. He appears to be a querulous, self-doubting person who has almost certainly second-guessed every career move he has ever made. He carefully thinks through every response to every question as if under cross-examination in a murder trial.

When all is said and done, Ersel Hickey is a one-hit wonder. Chart statisticians will tell you that it wasn't even much of a hit, but it was a wonderful little record. Ersel is unique among one-hit wonders, though; his contour has outlived his music.

FOR YOUR LISTENING PLEASURE

Sony Special Products/Backtrack Records in New York issued an Ersel Hickey anthology titled *The Rockin' Bluebird* on LP and cassette (P 18750). Bear Family has reissued all of the Epic recordings together with the Kapp sessions on a CD titled *Bluebirds over the Mountain* (BCD 15676).

Jimmie Logsdon

· ·

A ROCKET IN HIS POCKET

For a year or two, in 1956 and 1957, it looked almost certain that rock 'n' roll would blow country music off the planet. As it turned out, rock 'n' roll was very good news for country boys—or some of them, at least. The older country musicians who couldn't or wouldn't change found doors closing in their faces. The younger ones faced a dilemma: should they flirt with rock 'n' roll and risk alienating the following they had built up, or should they stick with the old ways and pray that rock 'n' roll would blow over? Most decided to go with what was selling; to hell with tradition.

One way of covering both bases was to cut rock 'n' roll records under a pseudonym, the same way black gospel singers sometimes cut secular records. George Jones barely disguised himself as "Thumper" Jones, Webb Pierce tried it on as as "Shady Walls," and Buck Owens was "Corky Jones" for a record or two. It was a ploy that never really worked in the commercial sense—the sense in which it was meant to work—so no one had to figure out what they would do if they actually had a hit under the assumed name. The best of the pseudonymous rockabillies was Jimmie Logsdon, who was utterly convincing as a rock 'n' roller recording under the name of "Jimmie Lloyd."

Jimmie hadn't been a best-selling country artist in the way that George Jones or Webb Pierce had been, but he knew that he stood a good chance of alienating what country following he had if he suddenly switched to rock 'n' roll. That was the climate that prevailed in 1957. Rock 'n' roll wasn't some new tune Jimmie was being force-fed, though. He knew and loved rhythm 'n' blues, and he had the natural, spiky energy that rock 'n' roll demanded.

Jimmie Logsdon is a voluble source for his life story, which is just as well, because not much has been written about him. He fell into the void reserved for those who got just so far, but no further. Nick Tosches wrote a wonderful fantasia upon what little was known, and that pissed off Jimmie no end; so, for posterity, the basic biographical entry goes like this: Jimmie Lloyd Logsdon was the son of a preacher man. He was born on April 1, 1922, in Panther, Kentucky. His father, a self-taught man who made it through Methodist seminary, was a circuit rider in Kentucky during his early years as a preacher, and was

Jimmie with Raymond Burr at the Derby Inn, Louisville, early 1950s
Photo courtesy of C. Escott/Jimmie Logsdon

posted to several towns, such as Bowling Green, Corbin, and Olive Hill, while Jimmie was growing up.

Music, for the first fifteen years of Jimmie's life, was gospel music. He and his sister sang in the choir, put on shows, and entered amateur contests. Then, when the family lived in southeastern Kentucky, Jimmie heard blues singers and secular country music at ice cream socials and wienie roasts. Later he latched onto rhythm 'n' blues, and he especially remembers Erskine Hawkins's "After Hours" as a record that made a deep impression on him. Glenn Miller, George Gershwin, and the popular music of the day also had an impact, but not like that of blues and country. "My record collection," says Jimmie, "ranges from Mahalia Jackson to Jimmy Reed to Sonny Terry and Brownie McGhee to Frank Sinatra to whatever. I listen to all kinds of music depending what mood I'm in and what time trip I want to take."

In 1940 he graduated from high school in Ludlow, Kentucky, just south of Cincinnati, and in the fall of that year married his first wife. He started working for Schuster and Schuster in Cincinnati installing public-address systems,

Jimmie Osborne, Jimmie Skinner, and Jimmie Logsdon at the Derby Inn, Louisville, Kentucky, 1953
Photo courtesy of J. Logsdon/C. Escott

Jimmie Logsdon, Ernest Tubb, and Jimmie Osborne at the Louisville Armory, 1955
Photo courtesy of J. Logsdon/C. Escott

Jimmie interviews Goldie Hill on air, WKLO, 1953
Photo courtesy of J. Logsdon/C. Escott

then he sold appliances. In 1944 he went to war in the Air Corps, but got no further than an air base near San Antonio, where he repaired the wiring on B-17s. Down in Texas, Jimmie heard Ernest Tubb and the other Texas honky-tonk singers. Locked up in the stockade for a few days for an offense he won't specify, he remembers singing to a fellow inmate who was facing a term in Leavenworth. "That," says Jimmie, "is where it all began."

Out of the service, Jimmie started a radio shop in La Grange, Kentucky, twenty-five miles northeast of Louisville on the Cincinnati highway. He picked up records to resell and, after two years, decided that he would take a stab at the music business. He had been borrowing other people's guitars for a while, and finally he broke down and bought one from Abe Davis's pawn-shop in Louisville for twelve bucks. He learned all three chords you needed to know, then cut some demos on a recording machine in the back of the radio shop. The demos landed him a nonpaying job on WLOU in Louisville.

After a year on WLOU, Jimmie switched to WINN. He and his band were playing the beer halls around Louisville, and with three hundred dollars from Art Rhoades, a furniture store owner in La Grange, Jimmie cut his first record. It was issued on Harvest Records, a label he started with Rhoades, and one that began and ended with Jimmie's record. Five hundred copies were pressed; most went to deejays.

Jimmie sang one side of his record at the Louisville Memorial Auditorium when the headliner was Hank Williams. "It was a full house," he says, "and I was so nervous waiting to go on, I thought I'd never make it. When I was introduced I ran out and tripped over Don Helms's steel guitar cord and fell flat on my face. My guitar slid across the stage and the house broke up. I looked offstage and I could see Hank laughing.

"After making a fool of myself, Hank come over and put his arm around me. He said, 'Say, son [even though Jimmie was a year and a half older than Hank], I like what you do. Is anybody cuttin' you?' I told him about Harvest Records, and he said he'd talk to someone down in Nashville for me. I did several shows with Hank after that. I'd ask him about getting me on a label in Nashville, and he would say he was working on it."

Hank, of course, had more problems on his plate than landing a contract for a potential rival. Then, in the summer of 1952, Jimmie heard that there was a man in town from Nashville. It was Vic McAlpin, a songwriter and song plugger who had written a song or two with Hank. Jimmie chased him all over town. He told McAlpin about his songs and gave him a copy of the Harvest record. "There were a few months of sweating and writing him back and forth, and finally Vic said he thought he could get me on Coral, which was a subsidiary of Decca. Then a couple of months later, he called me down and I auditioned for Paul Cohen [Decca's country A&R chief] at the Andrew Jackson Hotel. I was sweating bullets. I got about halfway through one song, and Paul said, 'OK.'"

McAlpin became Jimmie Logsdon's agent. "He was a great man," he says. "He could walk up to Carl Smith, and say, 'Carl, you asshole, what're those drums doing on your new record? Ain't you country no more?' And he'd do it in such a way that no one was offended. He knew everybody."

Jimmie's early Coral records were good, late-blooming hillbilly music, firmly in the Hank Williams mold. Then, on January 1, 1953, the news came over the wire that Hank Williams was dead. Jimmie was scheduled to go to Nashville to perform on Ernest Tubb's "Midnight Jamboree" two days later. "I remember being backstage when Red Foley sang 'Beyond the Sunset' at the Opry with everyone crying," he said. "It was a very moving thing. A couple of weeks later, I decided to put my feelings into a song and wrote 'Hank Williams Sings the Blues No More.' I wrote half of it in bed and finished it at Sandy's, the nightclub we played. To me, Hank was the ultimate in country music. He was a blues man, and I love blues."

For a year or two after Hank Williams's death, no one quite knew what to do next. There was a void at the top. A&R men only get creative as a last resort, and for a while they all tried to replace Hank Williams with guys who sounded more or less like him. Jimmie Logsdon was one of Paul Cohen's stabs at filling the void. Cohen even got the nucleus of Hank's Drifting Cowboys to back him on one session. MGM Pictures apparently contacted Jimmie early in its search for someone to play the lead in what would turn out to be the Hank Williams bio-pic, *Your Cheatin' Heart*.

By the time Jimmie was preparing for what would be his last Decca session, he was having what he euphemistically refers to as personal problems. He was hitting the pills: Seconals and Nembutals. Paul Cohen tried to warn him by way of example. He took him to a Red Foley session. "Red was cutting 'Plantation Boogie,' or trying to," says Jimmie. "We stood in the foyer of the studio. He said, 'Do you know how many takes that is?' I said, 'No.' He said, 'Sixteen.' Red had been suckin' on them Seconals and couldn't get his deal up."

The last Decca session didn't produce the breakthrough single, and Cohen, who was as unsentimental as any other A&R man with a sheaf of sales statistics in front of him, dropped Jimmie when his contract was up. It sent Jimmie into a tailspin. He took pills, drank, lost jobs, and alienated friends and lovers. The next time he entered a recording studio, a year and a half later, it was for

Dot Records, a label that had a diminishing commitment to country music and an increasing commitment to Pat Boone.

Jimmie's next single came out on Starday; it was cut in his fiddle player's bedroom. They moved the kids to another part of the house, then sat on the bed, using a broom for a microphone stand. They wanted a Latin beat, like the Opry stars Johnnie and Jack had used, so one of the pickers filled up a baby bottle warmer with beans and shook it. At a deejay convention, Logsdon met Pappy Daily, one of the owners of Starday Records, and Daily agreed to put it out. The group's payment was five hundred copies of the record.

By 1957 Jimmie had straightened himself out and told Vic McAlpin he was ready for another stab at the business. McAlpin got Jimmie a deal with Roulette Records, the New York label eventually controlled by the notorious mob-connected Morris Levy. "I was really hung up on rock 'n' roll like the kid in the street," says Jimmie. "I idolized Elvis. I had him on a remote in late 1955, just after he'd signed with Victor. I told him I'd been playing 'Good Rockin' Tonight' on the radio, at home, all over. I said to him, 'One day you're gonna be as big as Hank Williams.'"

Jimmie's first single for Roulette was "Where the Rio de Rosa Flows." He had got the idea for the song when he was down in San Antonio during the war. "There was a little river down in San Antonio that ran under Houston Avenue," he says. "It was very picturesque, little bridges and so on. Lovers would walk there. I went down there every three-day pass I got. Drink beer, watch girls. I'd go over to the Mexican quarter and sing. I wrote the song in 1951 with Moon Mullican in mind." The lyrics run down all the things to love about San Antonio to a boogie woogie beat. Jimmie gave a half share of the song to Vic McAlpin in exchange for landing the Roulette deal and helping on the arrangement.

"Where the Rio de Rosa Flows" was a hit in several markets, including Memphis, where Carl Perkins obviously heard it, because he covered it on his first Columbia album a few months later. Jimmie was brought down to Memphis to appear on Wink Martindale's television show. "We went in, Vic and me," said Jimmie, "and Wink was on the air. He said, 'We've got the guy in now who's singing "Rio de Rosa" on television with us tonight,' and he looked at me and blanched. He put a record on, shut down the microphone, and he said, 'I thought you were black. I've got you a room at the black hotel here.' Broke me up."

Another promotional foray took Jimmie and Vic McAlpin to the Louisiana Hayride in Shreveport. On the way back, they wrote "I've Got a Rocket in My Pocket." Jimmie insists that it wasn't meant as a dirty song, although "I've got a rocket in my pocket and the fuse is lit" seems fairly unambiguous. "It was just a nonsense thing," says Jimmie. "Vic said, 'Rock 'n' roll is in. We're gonna make a rock 'n' roll song.' I don't know if it's dirty. It's like beauty—it's in the mind of the beholder."

It was a joint decision on the part of Jimmie and Vic McAlpin to issue the Roulette records under the pseudonym Jimmie Lloyd. "Country fans are so loyal," says Jimmie, "and since I was singing so differently, I'd just as soon that the country people didn't know that I'd cut those things." Roulette dropped him after the second single, and Jimmie himself realized that, at thirty-five, he was probably a little old to be rocking or rolling. It took another five years before he went back into the recording studio, and then it was for King Records. In the meantime, he tried to straighten up yet again. He was on the fifty-thousand-watt station WCKY in Cincinnati as a deejay between 1962 and 1964, and after he was dropped, he stayed in radio for another decade, moving as he always had from one station to another.

Jimmie has the radio man's easy patter. He's never at a loss for words and is almost frighteningly honest about how, when, and where he screwed up. "My career in music wasn't as good or as lucrative as I wanted it to be," he says. "But whose is? I blew some opportunities. Who didn't?" Most entertainers who never lived up to what they considered to be their potential will blame everyone but themselves. Jimmie doesn't. Insofar as he blames anybody, he blames only himself.◉

FOR YOUR LISTENING PLEASURE
Bear Family has issued all of Jimmie's Harvest, Decca, Dot, Starday, and Roulette records on *I Got a Rocket in My Pocket* (BCD 15650).

Dale Hawkins

· ·

OH, SUZIE Q

Dale Hawkins is "Suzie Q"; "Suzie Q" is Dale Hawkins. For every artist there is a defining moment. For Dale Hawkins, it came upon a midnight hour in Shreveport when he cut "Suzie Q." The record captured rockabilly's go-for-broke looniness. No white person had never been this crazed on record before. The rockabillies were after the flame of rhythm 'n' blues, and, like most white singers who came after them, they tried too hard to catch it. In the act of overreaching, they created rockabilly.

To chart statisticians, Dale Hawkins came and went quickly. "Suzie Q" cracked the charts in June 1957, followed by another Top Forty entry and two other fleeting hits, and then the story ends. Hawkins, though, ought to get an entry in the *Guinness Book of World Records* for the guitarists he hired. At one time or another his bands included James Burton, Roy Buchanan, Fred Carter, Kenny Paulsen, and Scotty Moore. Even two members of the Newbeats (remember "Bread and Butter"?) came out of his band. Like his cousin, Ronnie Hawkins, Dale was able to attract the best even if he wasn't able to keep them. He and Ronnie had an aura that conveyed in some wordless way that, hits or no hits, they headed an elite corps.

Dale himself was born Delmar Allen Hawkins on August 22, 1938, in the tiny farming community of Goldmine, Louisiana, some thirty miles from Jerry Lee Lewis's birthplace in Ferriday. After his parents divorced, Dale was shunted around to various relatives, ending up in Bossier City, across the Red River from Shreveport. Inevitably, he grew up listening to the "Louisiana Hayride," the country music radio jamboree broadcast on KWKH Shreveport, but the blues figured more prominently in his value system.

Dale enlisted in the navy in 1953 and came back to Shreveport in August 1954 determined to try for a career in music. He started at the ground level, working in Stan's Record Shop. Stan was Stan Lewis, who was also the local Chess distributor and later the founder of Jewel Records and Paula Records. At night, Dale led his own band on the Bossier strip. One of his first guitarists was sixteen-year-old James Burton. His first bass player was Joe Osborn who— like Burton—later played with Rick Nelson and played on almost every record

Dale Hawkins
Photo courtesy of Showtime Archives (Toronto)/C. Escott

made on the West Coast for years. Dale's first drummer was D. J. Fontana.

Shortly after D. J. quit to play with Elvis, Dale cut a demo of "See You Soon, Baboon," which he conceived as a sequel to Bobby Charles's "See You Later, Alligator," at the KWKH studio. Stan Lewis heard the demos on the radio and pitched them to Chess Records, which issued them and gave the go-ahead for another session.

Now the confusion starts. Dale insists that the group that cut "Suzie Q" included James Burton on guitar, Joe Osborn on bass, and one of Stan Lewis's relatives, Ron, on drums, but a session report filed with the American Federation of Musicians for February 14, 1957, lists Burton, Lewis, and three other musicians. On some level, it's all academic, because to all intents and purposes the record is the work of Hawkins, Burton, and Lewis. Burton claims that he and Hawkins wrote "Suzie Q"—something that Hawkins freely acknowledges—but when it appeared it was credited to Hawkins, Eleanor Broadwater, and Stan Lewis. Eleanor Broadwater was the wife of a WLAC deejay, Gene Nobles, who was handed one third of the song in care of his wife as a token of Chess's gratitude for playing their records. In much the same way, Alan Freed was given a piece of Chuck Berry's first record, "Maybellene," and shares of other copyrights.

Contract for Dale Hawkins' "Suzie Q" session.
Courtesy of C. Escott

And what of Suzie Q herself? The title came from a dance craze in the mid-1930s. "Doin' the Suzi Q" was in the "Cotton Club Revue" of 1936, and by 1940 it had even reached Trinidad—"The Lion," calypso artist Raphael de Leon, recorded "Suzi Qu" in Port of Spain that year. Roy Buchanan told Bill Millar that Hawkins had once told him that he had seen Howlin' Wolf in Shreveport down on his knees screaming Suzie something-or-other. Perhaps that's where the title came from. The melody of the song came from a 1954 Clovers record, "I've Got My Eyes on You." But none of this explains the magic of "Suzie Q." It's the bravura, the numbing simplicity, and James Burton's hot lick that make it great. James's kick-off is repeated through the verses, apparently confirming his assertion that "Suzie Q" was originally an instrumental. On the breaks he slashes away wildly; his tone would never be this dirty again. Hawkins takes credit for this, saying that he weaned Burton off hillbilly music and pressured him into listening to singers like Howlin' Wolf.

Leonard Chess sat on "Suzie Q" for several months before Dale decided to force the issue by sending a copy to Atlantic Records. When Jerry Wexler at Atlantic expressed an interest and told Chess, Chess had the record on the streets inside two weeks. Burton, already resentful over losing his share of the song, quit soon afterward when Chess sent Hawkins out on a promotional tour and left the band back in Shreveport without its lead singer. When Hawkins came back to town he recruited Carl Adams and Fred Carter, both stellar guitarists, to fill Burton's spot.

Carl Adams took the lead when Hawkins went back into the studio to cut "Tornado" and "Mrs. Merguitory's Daughter." Adams died young—and almost died even younger. Dale remembers that two fingers of his left hand had been blown off when he stuck them down the barrels of a double-barreled shotgun and pulled the trigger.

Hawkins appeared to be heading nowhere, so Carl Adams went off to join Tommy Blake, and Dale recruited Roy Buchanan, a teenager he had met on the set of "Oklahoma Bandstand." Talking to Bill Millar, Roy said that playing package shows with Dale was a drag, but when they were playing in the clubs they would work up extended blues jams—music without boundaries and certainly without time limits, very similar in fact to the music with which Buchanan would later make his mark. Buchanan can be heard on Hawkins's recording of "My Babe," which was cut in New York. Hawkins and Buchanan were in St. Paul, Minnesota, and apparently drove clear across half the country for the session and then drove back. "Roy was an offshoot of my own way of thinking," Dale told Billy Miller, acknowledging that working with Roy could be a disorienting experience. "There were some times with Roy, you couldn't write 'em down."

Dale Hawkins's solitary Checker album was issued in October 1958. The cover was one of the classic rockabilly poses—down to the acne-pocked face. The shot holds mixed memories for Hawkins himself. He was sick with the measles when it was taken, he says, and Chess had him holed up in a mob hotel on Chicago's South Side. By 1958 Hawkins was on local television in the north and was scoring a few minor and best forgotten hits like "La-Do-Dada," "A House, a Car, and a Wedding Ring," and "Class Cutter."

After leaving Chess, Dale recorded for labels like Tilt and Zonk, as well as more familiar labels including Atlantic and ABC, but he never saw another hit as a singer. By the mid-sixties he had drifted into record production and scored a Top Five hit with his work on the Five Americans' "Western Union" in 1967. He cut another album in 1969, but it was disappointing. He's cagey about the missing years between then and now, and about what he's doing at present. His brother's a millionaire in New Orleans, he says. He wants to get back into recording, he says. Don't they all.◉

FOR YOUR LISTENING PLEASURE

MCA in Europe has reissued Dale's *Suzie Q* album with eight bonus tracks (MCD 30693). "Suzie Q" is available on several anthologies, including Chess *Rhythm & Roll* (Chess/MCA CHD4-9352).

Jimmy Murphy

. . . .

EEE-LEC-TRICITY

At 2:30 P.M. on January 29, 1951, Jimmy Murphy stepped into RCA's makeshift studio in Nashville. There were just two musicians: Murphy himself and Mother Maybelle Carter's daughter Anita, who had been called in to play stand-up bass. Behind the glass sat Steve Sholes, RCA's corpulent boss of specialty singles, who had flown down from New York for several days of sessions. Hank Snow had recorded there a couple of daysearlier, and Chet Atkins was scheduled for the following day. Others, like Murphy, were sandwiched in between. That's the way country recording was done in field locations like Nashville circa 1951.

The Number One spot on the country charts that day was held by Tennessee Ernie Ford's "Shotgun Boogie." Ford was no pioneer, but this record pointed into the future. It was half R&B and half country, with a thunderous backbeat by the standard of the time. Murphy was heading in the opposite direction. His guitar was in an "open E" tuning, which allowed him to play rhythm and melody at the same time. He sang, played ferocious rhythm guitar, and hit his little licks between lines like a man desperately trying to hold down three jobs at once. There were three takes on the first song, "Electricity." By the third, Murphy had nailed it. The song drew an analogy between electricity, still a thing of wonder in many rural communities, and salvation. You can't see electricity; you can't see God. You don't doubt electricity; don't doubt God. Skeptics would be unconvinced by the argument, but Murphy was preaching to the converted.

The four-song session continued with "Mother, Where Is Your Daughter Tonight?" one of many hillbilly morality fables about a daughter who has slipped off the rails. The problem, Murphy decided, was lack of discipline:

> Remember the night she started to stray
> You failed to whip her and make her obey.

Steve Sholes must have known that Jimmy Murphy would have stood a better shot in 1931 than 1951, but there was something strangely compelling about him and about that "Electricity" song, so Sholes released it as a single.

Jimmy Murphy (center) flanked by Carl Story (right) and his Mountaineers
Photo courtesy of Bear Family archives

The entire session had, after all, cost only $120 for the musicians and had used up only two reels of tape. Strangely, the single must have done pretty well, because Sholes called Murphy back in October for another session, this time with a full band. Two more singles were released, neither of them anywhere near as bizarre as "Electricity." Neither sold, and Jimmy Murphy was dropped.

Murphy was an off-breed, a man apart. He was born on October 11, 1925, in the tiny mining community of Republic, Alabama, near Birmingham. According to Richard Spottswood, who annotated Murphy's comeback album on Sugar Hill, Murphy's father liked blues and bought records by Blind Boy Fuller and Leadbelly, which would account for Jimmy's open E tuning and much else besides. The Murphys also listened to the Grand Ole Opry in its infancy: Murphy recalled hearing Asher Sizemore, DeFord Bailey, the McGees, Uncle Dave Macon, and his personal favorite, Roy Acuff.

At the age of five, Murphy took up the harmonica, and for his ninth birthday his parents bought him a guitar. A friend, Bee Coleman, showed him how to tune in open E. Coleman was the son of Dutch Coleman, who had recorded in a secular vein for Vocalion in 1929 and again as a holiness preacher for Victor in 1952. Murphy apparently met the Colemans in 1940, and at some point during the following year he made his radio debut on Happy Hal Burns's show on WRBC in Birmingham, Alabama.

During the war years, Murphy worked with his father, who had quit the mines and had started a construction company. He later worked on his own as an independent contractor, continuing to play when the opportunity presented itself. In 1949 Murphy went to Knoxville, Tennessee, to audition for Archie Campbell's "Dinner Bell Show" on WROL. It was Campbell who introduced Murphy to Chet Atkins, who had been a fixture of the Knoxville scene for several years. Atkins was not the mover and shaker that he became at RCA—he was just a contracted artist—but it was probably his influence that secured Murphy his shot on the label.

RCA's termination notice didn't make much difference to Murphy's routine. He continued his live radio gig on WROL, switching to "Mid-Day Merry-Go-Round" on WNOX at some point in the early fifties. His next shot at recording came in 1955 with Columbia. By now Murphy was only ten years out of date, not twenty. Columbia's A&R man, Don Law, who, like Steve Sholes, commuted in from New York, paired Murphy with a harmonica player, Onie Wheeler. Together, they sounded like Wayne Raney and the Delmore Brothers. One single resulted from the first Columbia session, "I'm Looking for a Mustard Patch," a belated sequel to "Too Old to Cut the Mustard," a huge hit for another Knoxville radio act, the Carlisles.

The arrival of Elvis Presley presented a challenge to Murphy, much as it did to all country musicians. Murphy, who had more of a blues background than almost anyone cutting in Nashville, probably thought he was up to it. The two cuts remaining from his first Columbia session were left in the can, and Murphy came back to Nashville with his idea of a rock 'n' roll song. It was a rockabilly rewrite of Merle Travis's "Sixteen Tons," titled "Sixteen Tons Rock 'n' Roll" ("Go cat, dig that coal"). Thinking himself as up to date as the morning newspaper, Murphy was still locked in a time warp, playing acoustic guitar in open tunings with Onie Wheeler huffing and puffing in the background.

Sales are hard to determine, but the fact that Columbia released another single from the session suggests that they got a little action. The second Columbia record, Murphy's last for a major label, coupled "Baboon Boogie" with "Grandpaw's a Cat." The latter worked the same geriatric rock 'n' roller territory as Carson Robison's "Rockin' & Rollin' with Grandmaw," recorded a month earlier.

Like Steve Sholes, Don Law did not pick up the option on Murphy's one-year term. Murphy stayed around Knoxville, playing music and working in construction. He didn't see another record issued until 1962, when he recorded for Cincinnati-based Ark Records one of the best Hank Williams tribute songs, Jimmie Logsdon's "I Long to Hear Hank Sing the Blues." Like almost everything else in Murphy's career, it came out about ten years too late.

Murphy continued to work out of Knoxville, although the labels that recorded him were scattered far and wide. He was on the lilliputian Midnite Records in Grand Rapids, Michigan, and reportedly cut a session for Starday. He also recorded for Wayne Raney's custom label, Rimrock Records, and Walter Bailes's Loyal Records in 1969.

The story would probably have fizzled out at that point had it not been for the folklorist Richard Spottswood, who became enamored of the original recording of "Electricity" when he was compiling the Folk Music in America LP series for the Library of Congress. Spottswood located Murphy through the music publisher Acuff-Rose and placed him with Barry Poss's Sugar Hill Records in 1978. Poss recorded him with a group led by Ricky Skaggs, then a member of Emmylou Harris's Hot Band. It was an artistically successful album (although God knows how few it sold), which demonstrated that Murphy's powers had diminished little by his fifty-third year. He wouldn't allow himself to be photographed for the cover; instead there was something like an artist's courtroom sketch of a middle-aged man wearing glasses and a toupee.

An overseas tour was discussed, as was a second Sugar Hill album, but they were preempted by Murphy's death on June 1, 1981. Apparently, he had run away from home with a girl half his age just before his death. So, with any luck, he died with a smile on his face and perhaps a song ten or twenty years out of date in his heart. ◉

FOR YOUR LISTENING PLEASURE

Bear Family has collated all of Murphy's RCA and Columbia recordings on *Sixteen Tons Rock 'n' Roll* (BCD 15451). The Sugar Hill album, *E-Lectricity* (SH 3702), can still be found in used record stores.

Tommy Tucker

· ·

SHACKLES AND CHAINS

Tommy Tucker could just possibly have been big, but like so many of the Memphis crowd, he lacked the crucial bit of DNA that would have told him what to do in critical situations. So much talent; so little self-control. His name really was Tommy Tucker: Tommy Ray Tucker—not to be confused with the forties big-band leader or the stubby black guy whose real name was Robert Higginbotham and who cut "Hi-Heel Sneakers." Tommy Ray Tucker was born in Memphis in 1941 and first made waves in 1959, the year he was signed to Hi Records and cut two terrific singles. The first was a Charlie Feathers song, the lilting and melancholic "Man in Love." Tucker sang with all the confidence in the world. Next he recorded the first version of Jack Clement's nonsense murder ballad "Miller's Cave." Cowboy Jack, just recently divorced from Sun, produced both singles. His trademarks are everywhere: the bright, clean production with ringing acoustic guitars and the chorus working hand in glove with the vocalist. Tucker's voice was a lighter take on the Johnny Cash sound, but it had the same gravitas, the same burdened soul.

Trouble seemed to dog Tucker from the very beginning. He was working at Danny's Club and the Cotton Club across the river in West Memphis, Arkansas, when both clubs were padlocked by the police following the murder of a young woman close by. Then, in March 1960, he was playing Hernando's Hideaway when he was busted by the Labor Department for working under the age of twenty-one in a joint where liquor was sold. "I don't think it's fair," said his mother at the time. "He's got a car note coming up, union dues coming up. He can't get no other job. Nobody will take him because he's draft age. He's a nice boy. He doesn't mix and mingle with the people at the clubs and he doesn't drink." Three months later, Hank Snow covered "Miller's Cave" and had a Top Ten country hit with it.

Jack Clement gave up on Memphis and moved to Nashville to work with Chet Atkins at RCA. He brought Tucker down to record a belated sequel to "Ballad of a Teenage Queen," a song Clement had written for Johnny Cash. The sequel was called "Return of the Teenage Queen." Tucker was spirited out to Hollywood to pose awkwardly with Jayne Mansfield. He just barely managed a

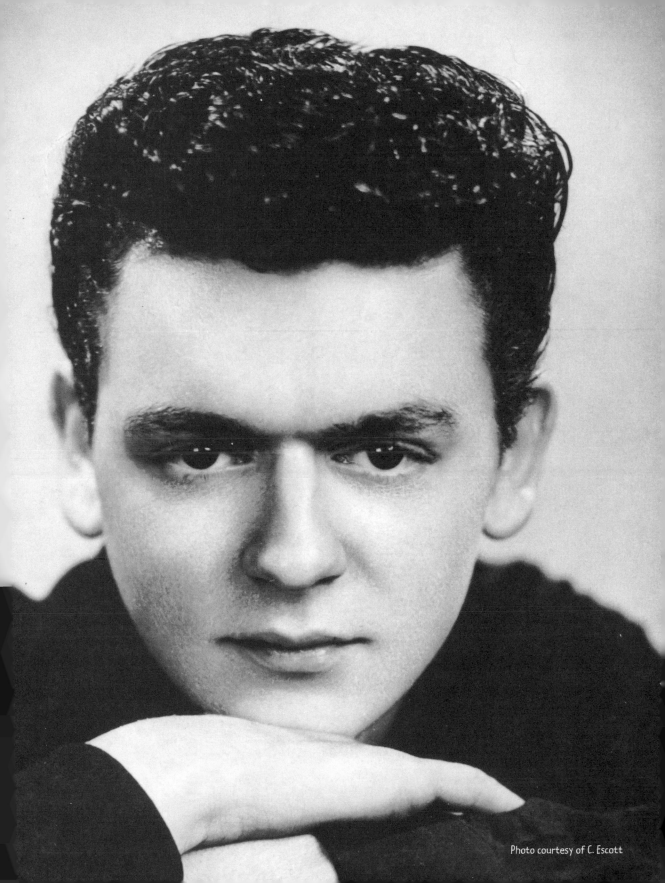

Tommy gives Eddie Bond a copy of his first Hi record
Photo courtesy of C. Escott

smile. A little later, he got a Wednesday-through-Saturday job at the Little Black Book club on Highway 61 in the south end of Memphis.

On the night of October 28, 1961, Tucker finished work around midnight and got in his 1957 Oldsmobile. He'd had a few drinks just to be sociable with the patrons, he said. He was driving very fast up Highway 61 toward Memphis when his car rear-ended another car driven by Leland Payton. Payton's gas tank exploded, killing him and another occupant, then his car spun into the path of a third car, killing the two occupants. It was the worst wreck in Shelby County since 1945, police said. Eight children were orphaned.

Tucker sped from the scene, weaving from one side of the road to the other, running on the wheel rims, spitting sparks from the highway. Witnesses said his car looked like a rocket ship. He was followed by several other drivers until he eventually came to a stop and started to walk away, yelling for everyone to leave him alone. Several people say he got into a Cadillac driven by a woman, although Tucker insisted he went to a friend's house nearby, and then on to his girlfriend's apartment. From there he phoned his manager, Eddie Bond. Bond, who owned the Little Black Book, had driven home later, seen the wreck, and told Tucker that four people had been burned to a crisp. Tucker told Bond that he shouldn't worry, because the runaway car wasn't his. "Well, they think it's you," Bond told him. "You'd better think what you're going to do." Tucker tried to find a lawyer at that late hour, and he was on the phone when the police showed up and arrested him shortly before 3:00 A.M. He was released on bail, which was set at five thousand dollars. Interviewed the following day, he said nothing. His mother said she was praying for the victims.

Tucker's case came to trial on May 21, 1962. He was accused of second-degree murder, along with driving while intoxicated and a variety of lesser charges. A young woman who co-owned another club, and who clearly carried a torch for him, appeared on his behalf. She insisted that Tucker had left the Little Black Book too early to have been involved in the crash. Tucker admitted that he been involved in an accident—but not that one. He said that the driver of the other car had said he could go on home because the damage wasn't that serious. The jury wasn't buying any of this, and Tucker was sentenced to eleven months and twenty-nine days in the penal farm for involuntary manslaughter, fined $250, and handed another six-month sentence for driving while intoxicated.

As he left the courtroom, Tucker said that he was going home to catch up on his prayers and to decide if he was going to appeal. Later, the DWI sentence was dropped, but he was sentenced to another six months for leaving the scene of an accident. "I guess it's either this or the army," Tucker said resignedly on his way to jail. "I received my draft notice last month." RCA Records dropped him, but his mother remained upbeat. "I think we came out pretty good," she said. Tucker went inside on June 27, 1962. He was eligible for parole in nine months.

The memory of that night exacted a penalty that the courts did not. Tucker recorded again. Stan Kesler's X-L Records issued a cover version of "You Don't Love Me" by "Tommy Raye." The pseudonym was probably to avoid conflict with the Tommy Tucker who had cut "Hi-Heel Sneakers" as much as it was to sidestep the scandal. Later in the sixties, Tucker recorded a slow blues for Hi that remained in the can, as well as a doomy, Cash-like version of the strangely appropriate "Shackles and Chains," which also remained

Tucker is booked on four counts of manslaughter
Photo courtesy of C. Escott

unissued. Tucker went to Hi a third time in the early seventies. His voice was gruffer now, but the rough edges suited his new songs. Some were starkly autobiographical. "You Hitched Your Wagon to a Loser" was one that painted a picture of a desperately unhappy man.

Hi released a single in its stillborn Hi Country series from these sessions, but it did no business. That was probably the last Tommy Tucker record to hit the streets. He continued to work on the fringes of the music business, writing songs, playing clubs. Eddie Bond still hired him, and he had fairly steady work at the Western Steak House and Lounge. Several studios used him for backup vocals.

Early in March 1985 Tommy Tucker went around the various studios in town handing out demo tapes. Then, on the evening of March 17, he went to sleep around 1:00 A.M. in his East Memphis apartment with a lighted cigarette in his hand. The apartment caught fire. Tucker woke up, crawled into the second bedroom, but began choking and became disoriented. He fell on the floor and died of smoke inhalation.🌀

FOR YOUR LISTENING PLEASURE
Zu-Zazz Records in England issued a long-deleted LP of Tucker's work called *Memphis Bad Boy*. Several cuts are on *Hi Records: The Early Years* (Demon/Hi, England HIUKCD 127) and *Hi Records: The Early Years, Vol. 2* (Demon/Hi, England HIUKCD 128).

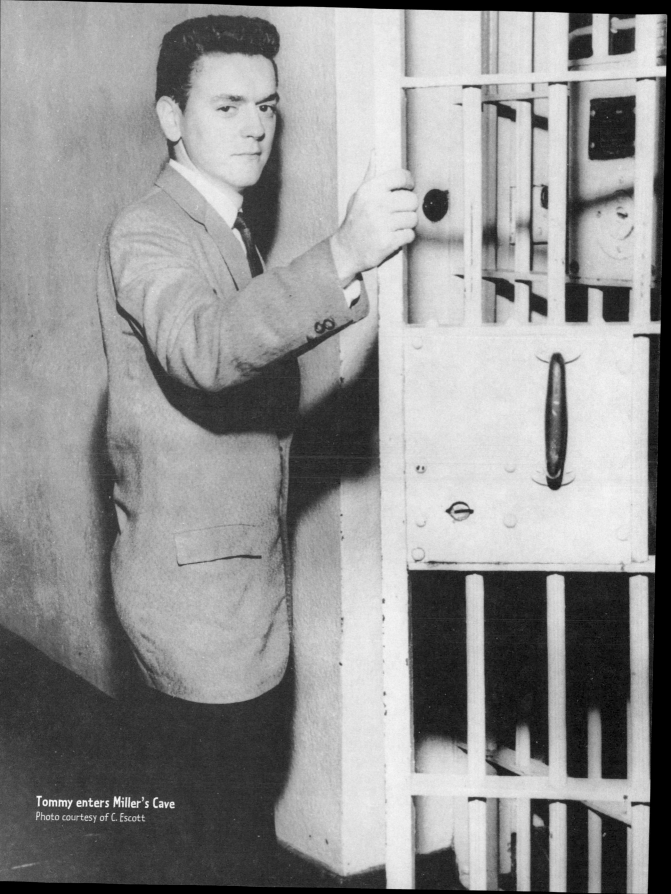

Tommy enters Miller's Cave
Photo courtesy of C. Escott

Republic Records Star, 1953
Photo courtesy of C. Escott/Vanderbilt Archive

Pat Boone

· ·

BORN TO BE MILD

Pat Boone insists he has got a bum rap. "For years," he said over the phone from California, "Elvis and I were nip and tuck, chasing each other up and down the charts. People don't realize this, but we appealed to different instincts in the same people—like yin and yang. A lot of the same people were buying his records and my records. There was this difference in lifestyle: I was playing by the rules and winning; he was breaking the rules and winning."

Pat is almost unnervingly insistent upon this. There's an element of revisionism in what he says, of course, and his statement that kids were buying his records with one week's pocket money and Elvis's with the next is one of those great unprovable assumptions. He might very well be right, though.

There's another thing that galls Pat Boone. Whenever stories are written about the fifties, Elvis is always front and center, and Pat Boone, who sold almost as many records, often barely rates a mention. "In fact," says Pat, "in 1957 I eclipsed Elvis as Male Singer of the Year, and I still hold the record for the highest number of consecutive weeks on the charts—from 1955 until sometime in 1959. You couldn't listen to pop radio without hearing me. At the time, I didn't feel as though I belonged in it. Now I feel as though I *did* belong in it, but everyone's trying to pretend I never existed."

Can this be true? In which poll did Pat eclipse Elvis as Male Singer of the Year? Pat can't remember, but again, it could very well have happened. And what about the statistic for highest number of consecutive weeks on the charts? That's possible too, but as a statistic it's as useful as those baseball statistics like Most Times Butt Scratched During One At-Bat. Still it's true that Pat was unavoidable on radio in the fifties. And it takes uncommon honesty to admit that you didn't think you belonged, but now you want to—and no one wants to acknowledge that you ever existed. Or, worse yet, treats your existence as a joke.

That's Pat Boone. An interviewer's dream. He's there when you phone. He's not surly, offhand, or given to churlishness, and he recognizes the impersonality of the telephone interview and does his best to sidestep it by

At home with Shirley and Debbie in New Jersey
Photo courtesy of C. Escott

being engaging and warm. He has a terrific memory, and the anecdotes are well-rehearsed, perfect little sound bites. You want to like the guy.

Could it, you wonder, be time to listen to those records again? Were they better than you remember? Perhaps they were, especially if you place them in the context of where he was coming from, and not where you're coming from. Still, any serious attempt to rehabilitate Pat Boone is always undermined by those covers of rhythm 'n' blues songs. They're every bit as bad as you thought. The arrangements sound exactly like what they were: note-for-note transcriptions of the original arrangements played by sightreading musicians, proving once and for all that some elements of music just aren't susceptible to notation. The brass parts rattle around the studio like loose change. Echo never sounded so empty. A singer never sounded so tragically white. Pat is trying his damnedest, but he could have been singing Yemenite wedding songs for all he felt or understood R&B.

Pat usually holds out a comparison to Perry Como. Pat recorded "Tutti Frutti," which—if you concentrate on the lyrics—is a pretty dumb song, and Perry recorded "Hot Diggity" and a lot of other pretty dumb songs. But Perry's dumb songs weren't trivializations of songs that, by virtue of their passion

Pat gets a taste of the South; eating barbecue in Memphis
Photo courtesy of C. Escott

if nothing else, had merit in the original versions. Perry's dumb songs were written to be dumb songs. Perry himself brought an insouciant, self-effacing humor to them, as if he were saying, "Sure they're rubbish, but hey, a guy's gotta live." Pat sounds almost desperately serious when he sings his dumb songs. And then, on top of that, he had to go and change the lyrics. Little Richard's deathless couplet "Long tall Sally she built for speed/She's got everything Uncle John needs" became "Long tall Sally's got a lot on the ball/Nobody cares if she's long and tall."

Pat Boone may see himself as part of the rock 'n' roll revolution, but at the time, he was really more an antidote to it. If you didn't want to listen to what your folks listened to, but you didn't really like this rock 'n' roll nonsense either, then Pat Boone was just the ticket. By his own admission, Pat had real problems getting himself hip to rock 'n' roll. "When [Dot Records president] Randy Wood called me to Chicago, I hardly knew what rhythm 'n' blues was," he said a few years ago. "So I took the Charms' original of 'Two Hearts' to Chicago, and for a day and a half I just listened to the two sides over and over. I tried to sing along with the original to get the feeling." Jive: Getting Hip to the, 101.

Pat 'n' Dick
Photo courtesy of C. Escott

Pat's blanket lack of understanding of the blues and country music that underpinned rock 'n' roll would be just about believable if he'd had a sheltered home life in Minot, North Dakota, but he came from Nashville—and, in the one wild-ass move of his life, he had eloped with the daughter of the country superstar Red Foley. How could Boone remain so totally unaffected by it all?

Nashville, of course, was different then. Country music was marginalized to one or two pockets in the city. It had a low profile, but not low enough for the city elders. There were, after all, only four references in the Nashville papers to Hank Williams before he died. WSM, the "Grand Ole Opry" station, devoted a large chunk of its broadcast day to pop music. When Pat went on the radio in Nashville, he was singing pop music. A snippet of him on radio circa 1953, when he was starring in a show on WSIX called "Youth on Parade," is in the Sun Records vault (of all places). Sun had a black vocal group, the Prisonaires, who were confined to the state penitentiary in Nashville but were allowed out to perform on WSIX. One night, in a wonderful cross-cultural collision, they recorded some demos over a tape of Pat's show. Pat comes through between cuts.

Then, on October 20, 1955, Elvis and Pat Boone shared the bill in Cleveland. The reason we know this is that the event was filmed by a local deejay, Bill Randle, for Universal Pictures, although the film itself has never surfaced. By October 1955 Elvis was starting to attract some serious attention in the South, and record companies were ready to mortgage the farm to acquire him. The history books tell us that he was on the verge of next-big-thingdom, but you'd never know it from talking to Pat Boone. "Bill Randle told me, 'I got a guy who's gonna be the biggest thing in the country: Elvis Presley,'" he remembered. "I said, 'Oh yeah?' I had lived in Texas and seen a couple of his tunes on country jukeboxes, and I wondered how in the world a hillbilly could be the next biggest thing, especially with a name like Elvis Presley."

The gulf between the insider playing by the rules and the outsider was never more obvious than on that afternoon when Pat and Elvis met. "He was wearing some odd-looking clothes," said Pat. "He looked like he had just got off a motorcycle. He just slouched around and didn't say much. I said, 'Hello Elvis, I'm Pat Boone.' He just said, 'Mrrrbleee, mrrrbleee.'"

For about two years after that, Pat made a good living reinterpreting rhythm 'n' blues songs for people who didn't like rhythm 'n' blues. "Then," he said, "pretty quickly, the Top Forty stations began to play the original versions, and that little avenue to hitdom vanished."

What saved Pat Boone's career was that someone in his organization, probably his music director, Billy Vaughn, had a terrific ear for a song. Vaughn had been a member of the Hilltoppers, a top-selling vocal group in the early and mid-1950s. Later he scored a slew of hits with his own orchestra. Among the songs he found for Pat Boone was "Don't Forbid Me," probably the best thing Boone ever did. An interesting little story resides there. "I almost didn't record it," says Pat. "We always did at least three songs on a session, and we'd done three and only had maybe twenty-five minutes left. Randy Wood was very pleased, and he said 'Guys, we're gonna let you go early.' I went over to Billy Vaughn at the piano, and I asked him what the other song was, and he said, 'Oh, Pat, you'd have loved recording this one.' He played it for me with that lovely low note, and I went running into the control room. I said, 'Randy, this song could pay for the whole session.' The guys were on the point of going, and we were down to maybe fifteen or seventeen minutes left now, and we might have gone into half an hour overtime, but that was what the excitement of the record business was all about then."

"Don't Forbid Me" was by the rhythm 'n' blues songwriter Charlie Singleton, which in itself showed the strides that black writers and musicians were making to accommodate the wider market. Singleton had sent the song to Elvis, but, as Elvis himself said during the chatter on the Million Dollar Quartet session, it sat around at his house so long that he simply blew the chance of cutting it. "Don't Forbid Me" set Pat Boone on a new course. His records from this point were at least true to the tradition he knew: pop vocals, straight as an arrow. He was still doing well until the Beatles blew him out of the water.

There have been some bad years for Pat since then. Not bad in the sense of having the repo man around, but bad in the sense of knowing that you're not yet thirty-five and your best years are behind you, and bad in the sense that rock journalism is now an industry and it treats you as a joke. That makes Pat Boone anxious to curry favor with critics. He followed up on our conversation by sending me a Christmas card that year. It was personally signed, as far as I can tell.◉

II

Selling Grand Pianos in the Desert

How to Start a Record Company, 1

· ·

DECCA RECORDS, NEW YORK, 1934

Decca Records was launched in the United States in August 1934, when business confidence was mired below zero. If Decca had collapsed, as it almost did, the launch would have been hailed as foolhardy, and everybody would have said, "I told you so"; instead it was a success, and that made it an act of derring-do.

The record business had been in wretched shape since the onset of the Great Depression; it had risen with blind confidence during the jazz age, then stood by helpless as Americans turned to radio for entertainment. Record sales fell by 40 percent in 1932 alone. The Decca story, though, began in England in sunnier times. In 1928 Barnett Samuel and Sons, Ltd., a British company that made musical instruments, copyrighted the name "Decca" to use on a line of record players. The meaning of "Decca," if there ever was one, has been lost to time. One theory is that D-E-C-C-A corresponds to a series of musical notes from a composition by Beethoven. In the summer of 1928 Barnett Samuel and Sons was floated on the London Stock Exchange, and the share issue was handled by a young stockbroker named Edward Robert Lewis. Then, while the shares were on offer, Lewis heard about the imminent collapse of Duophone Records, which owned a pressing plant. He thought he could make the Barnett Samuel share offer more attractive if the company had a line of records to sell alongside its phonographs, so in January 1929 he formed a syndicate to buy first the factory and then the Decca division of Barnett Samuel.

Decca, now separate from Barnett Samuel, was offered to the stock market. The issue was oversubscribed but, because of the market collapse in October, the original investors weren't able to sell at a profit until 1945. The first Decca records were issued in England in June 1929. A bust of Beethoven presided over the middle "C," lending credence to the Beethoven theory of the label name's origin. Predictably enough, the first record was "God Save the King." By September 1930 the company was in serious trouble, and Lewis took over the reins. In November he scored his first coup when he persuaded Jack Hylton, the leader of one of the most popular British dance bands, to join the label.

In April 1932 Lewis was approached by Warner Bros., in the United States. Warners had acquired Brunswick Records in April 1930 but, after record sales plummeted, had sold off the American pressing rights in December 1931 to the American Record Corporation (ARC). Now Warners were trying to off-load British Brunswick as well.

The recording manager at Brunswick in the United States was Jack Kapp. Kapp's father, Meyer, had been a salesman for Columbia Records, and Jack had driven with his father on the rounds, helping to set up a portable phonograph and play samples for the dealers. At age fourteen Kapp had gone to work for Columbia as a shipping clerk, subsequently graduating to salesman. While there, he astonished everyone by remembering the artist, title, and catalog number of all four thousand records in the Columbia catalog. In 1926 he went to work for Brunswick Records. At first he was handed the Vocalion subsidiary, which was the blues imprint. His pop music savvy became evident when he insisted that Brunswick release Al Jolson singing "Sonny Boy," which sold two million copies in 1928. Shortly after Warner Bros. took over Brunswick, Kapp was brought to New York. Among the many acts he signed was Bing Crosby.

E. R. Lewis bought the British Brunswick franchise and represented the label for two and a half years. During that time, he began forging a working relationship with Kapp and the Brunswick treasurer, Milton Rackmil. Lewis's first opportunity to get into the American record business came when Columbia Records was offered to him for seventy-five thousand dollars. He immediately boarded a ship for New York and tried to finalize the deal, but was beaten to the post by ARC, the same label that had bought the American pressing rights to Brunswick.

Kapp and Lewis had first met when Kapp went to England on Brunswick's behalf in 1931. Kapp went again in December 1933, and they talked about forming an American company. Kapp mulled it over for a few months, then told Brunswick that he would quit if he was not made president. In July 1934 Lewis was at Kapp's house in New York. He had just seen his deal to buy Columbia go down, and Kapp had not been offered the presidency of Brunswick. Together, they planned the launch of American Decca. Rackmil and a Columbia Records employee, E. F. Stevens, wanted in on the deal. Lewis held out the promise of the one thing the American partners lacked: capital.

Kapp was fairly certain he could get Bing Crosby and Guy Lombardo to come over, because there was a "key man" clause in their Brunswick contracts stating that their contracts would be void if Kapp left. Kapp also knew that Warner Bros. had a record plant at 619 West Fifty-fourth Street in New York, as well as studios and offices at 799 Seventh Avenue. Warners had hung on to the Brunswick Radio Corporation, which manufactured transcription discs for radio, but the plant wasn't getting much use, and Decca acquired it in exchange for stock. For his part, Lewis would supply the trademark and the capital.

"The question then arose as to the price or prices at which the new Decca records would be marketed," Lewis later wrote. "Jack Kapp wanted to follow the existing pattern with 75, 35, and 25 cent records. I could see no hope of success for this policy. The total sales of records in America then was no greater than ten million, and for us to succeed we had not only to capture some of those sales, but also to increase the total volume. I insisted that only on the basis of a one-price 35-cent record could we agree to go ahead, and as we were to supply the trademark and the finance, [Decca U.S.] could never have been formed without us. I argued that at 35 cents not only would we take business away from competitors, but we would almost inevitably increase overall turnover of the industry at the very moment when it was touching the bottom." Kapp later took credit for the pricing, insisting that his father, who by then was running Kapp's Imperial Talking Machine Shop on Madison Street in Chicago, suggested the lower price because higher-price sales had tailed off so badly.

Lewis was virtually alone in seeing the Depression as an opportunity. He would have none of retrenchment, and he aggressively bought labels in the United States and England, believing that business would turn around and that he would be well positioned when it did. He finalized the purchase of the Warner Bros. offices and plant in New York in exchange for 5,000 of the 25,000 shares in American Decca and sixty thousand dollars in promissory notes. The plant gave him the opportunity to start production immediately. Jack Kapp got 1,250 shares in the new corporation, and English Decca had 18,000 shares.

"Meantime, I was having heavy weather with Jack Kapp, who wanted to be president," wrote Lewis. "For various reasons I felt it would be inadvisable, [but] when Kapp got something into his head he was difficult to move. Late one night, after my only visit to the Empire State Building, I agreed to a compromise. Kapp's main argument for having the title was that he needed the prestige if he was to swing over Crosby and other leading artists. Accordingly, I took the chairmanship, with Kapp as president, and Rackmil as treasurer."

Lewis and his partners set up branches in all major cities, and the company was incorporated as Decca Records, Inc., on August 4, 1934. Kapp was as good as his word, bringing over Crosby, as well as recruiting Chick Webb with Ella Fitzgerald, the Mills Brothers, the Dorsey Brothers, and the Boswell Sisters. Guy Lombardo came over for a short term, then left for RCA Victor, then returned in 1938 after he'd decided that Decca was a sure bet. In terms of artists at least, Decca went from nothing to a major label almost overnight.

Rackmil figured that they could get Decca rolling with $270,000, but the company was in the hole to the tune of $800,000 before the first record was issued. Lewis bought himself a few weeks' breathing space by sending all checks by rail, but every time he went to a New York bank he was told politely that radio had killed off the record business, and that Decca was a bad risk. In the end, he had to find the additional capital in England, where there was an almost blanket lack of knowledge about the American record business, but where he was able to call in enough favors to get the label afloat.

The first 200,000 Decca records went out in October 1934 and promptly came back. They had been sold to jukebox operators, who insisted that the records be nine and fifteen-sixteenth inches in diameter. The first pressings were exactly ten inches and were all returned.

There was never much harmony between Kapp and Lewis. "Jack Kapp had done a fine job with the artists," wrote Lewis begrudgingly, "yet when one of the worst crises occurred and there was no money for the payroll, I remember asking where Jack was and was told that he had gone to a ball game in Philadelphia. On being chided, he said he had nothing to do with finance. Perhaps he was right, for he was president in name only." The profit margin on a thirty-five-cent record was measured in fractions of a cent, and the label teetered on the edge of insolvency for the first two years. The company had a nicely appointed anteroom on Seventh Avenue where creditors would sit and wait while Rackmil would avoid them by scooting down a freight elevator.

American Decca lost $397,000 in its first operating year and $80,000 in its second. Virtually all of this money had to be found in England and cabled across in time to stop foreclosure. One constant problem that Decca faced was a result of the thirty-five-cent retail price: because retailers made only fourteen cents on Decca records, compared with thirty cents on other labels, they wouldn't feature the company's product. In a 1935 lawsuit, Decca alleged collusion between Victor, ARC, and Brunswick to keep its product out of the stores.

According to Lewis, Kapp angled to increase the price to fifty cents, but Lewis was desperately opposed to it. "I was told that everyone in New York was in favor of increasing the price," he wrote later, "and then one day I walked into the Decca office in London and saw John Hammond, [who] was a record critic at that time. I asked him what he thought of the suggested increase, and he told me it would be disastrous. Next day we stopped the projected price change." Decca eventually managed to beat the chain stores' resistance by issuing "albums," several 78s packaged together. Decca took credit for this innovation in 1937, although it's likelier that the company simply brought the concept, long common in classical music, into the pop field. The following year, it launched its own line of phonographs and accessories.

In the end it was Kapp's A&R savvy as much as Lewis's ability to scrounge up money that saved Decca. The label got a boost when another Brunswick staffer, Tommy Rockwell, started a booking agency, General Artists Corporation, in partnership with Cork O'Keefe. GAC began with the Mills Brothers, and through the years Rockwell would direct his clients toward Kapp. Crosby was the label's consistently big seller, but the biggest individual record was a novelty, "The Music Goes Round and Round," cut by the Riley-Farley Orchestra at the end of a Dixieland jazz session. It became Decca's first 100,000 seller. For Kapp, the success was even sweeter because he had bought the song for $125. The Andrews Sisters' "Bei Mir Bist Du Schoen" broke in 1936, and by August 1937 Decca, Inc., was trading at a profit. By 1939 total record sales in the United States were around fifty million; Decca accounted for eighteen million of those, and Crosby accounted for two million of Decca's sales.

From the beginning, Kapp had started jazz/blues and country divisions so that Decca would be a full-line record company. He had also acquired the old Gennett label in 1935 to give Decca some instant catalog. Only classics, a field of music he neither liked nor understood, was unrepresented. In a speech to the Radio Executives Club in February 1949, Kapp spoke of his passionate belief in American as opposed to European culture. Thousands of recordings of European opera and instrumental music were available in the thirties, he said, but there was a very slim amount of American vernacular music. He made it a policy to reverse that imbalance. He was also in favor of recording ethnic material, whether it was hillbilly, Irish, or Jewish, with mainstream American artists, like Crosby. He believed that sons and daughters of immigrants wanted the old songs, but wanted to hear them in a way that made sense to them.

The country division and field blues recordings were handled by Kapp's brother, Dave, who had been working as an artists' manager in Chicago when his brother hired him in July 1934. In October 1935 Dave Kapp moved to Decca's head office in New York, and until 1942 he scheduled two or three mammoth recording trips a year through the South and Southwest, traveling with portable recording equipment loaded into twenty trunks. He hit a grand slam almost immediately with Jimmie Davis's "Nobody's Darlin' but Mine" and, with what was probably a mixture of luck and judgment, built an impressive catalog of hillbilly, blues, Cajun, and jazz artists that ran the gamut from Ernest Tubb to Count Basie.

In 1945 Dave Kapp was promoted to vice president in charge of recording, and the country division was taken over by Paul Cohen, who had been one of Decca's first salesmen in Chicago and had then become the Cincinnati branch manager. From November 1941 the R&B and jazz divisions were handled by Milt Gabler, who had previously run the Commodore record label and store. The Kapps, Cohen, and Gabler laid the foundation of what became an astonishingly rich country, jazz, and blues catalog.

Country, jazz, and blues recordings all worked on the principle that they were cheap to make and would break even quickly. When Dave Kapp started, he paid twenty dollars a man for a three-hour session and would expect six songs and free overtime for his money. Success was measured in the aggregate of modest profits. "I will never forget the first time the [hillbilly] records started to break," Dave Kapp said in a 1951 interview. "I sent Jack a note very exultingly, and I said, 'I just got the figures, and we shipped 50,000 hillbilly records this month.' . . . Jack, on my note, said, 'Tell me about it when it gets to a hundred.'" Every so often, there would be an unexpected windfall, such as Chick Webb's "A-Tisket, A-Tasket," or Jimmie Davis's "You Are My Sunshine," or Ernest Tubb's "Walkin' the Floor over You."

Jack Kapp inspired something akin to love and devotion in most of his artists—none more so than Bing Crosby. "Jack formulated my recording plans," Crosby wrote in his autobiography. "He was wise enough to have me work with a variety of bands and sing duets with different artists so as to give the listeners a change of pace. Jack's progressive plans for me were due to the fact that he had a much higher opinion of me than I had of myself. He selected things a cut above the ordinary popular songs, and [he] saw to it that I achieved a musical variety very few other recording artists—with my limitations—were able to. Jack wouldn't let me get typed. In addition to his desire to make money for Decca, he took a personal interest in me. It was no sacrifice to be loyal to Jack when other recording outfits tried to lure me away."

Lewis had begun to off-load his American Decca stock as soon as the label started achieving profitability in 1937. War was declared in Europe in 1939, and by then Lewis had almost completely sold out, although he held some stock until 1943 and apparently remained chairman in absentia until 1945. Unlike the Kapps, Lewis had no attachment to the record business and saw a huge opportunity elsewhere. Just after the outbreak of war in Europe, scientists at Decca's radio division in London began developing a new navigational tool, RADAR—an acronym for *RAdio Detection And Ranging*. The U.S. Navy passed on the idea, and the British air ministry thought it was too complicated, but Lewis sent a team over to the States to work out the bugs. When the Decca

59

scientists came back to England in 1941, the government showed more interest, and in September 1942 the first full-scale navigational trials were held. Very soon afterward, Radar went into production. "When 'D' Day arrived," wrote Lewis proudly, "the Decca Navigator was there, guiding the leaders of the minesweeping flotillas and then guiding the first landing craft."

Control of American Decca was assumed by Jack Kapp, who bought out not only British Decca's share but Warner Bros.' remaining shares as well. In December 1941, just after Decca had released what would turn out to be its biggest seller, Bing Crosby's "White Christmas," the company was listed on the New York Stock Exchange. After the wartime restrictions ended in 1945, Decca broke ground on two new plants in Los Angeles and Chicago that could produce seven million records a month. In 1946 Decca sales topped $32 million, helped no end by the revival of Al Jolson's career. Two Jolson albums sold an unprecedented one million copies each that year.

With Jolson back on top, Jack Kapp had gone full circle in the record business when he died of a stroke on March 25, 1949, at the age of forty-seven. Kapp was a driven, obsessed man. He would lay awake for hours at night, mulling over new combinations of artists and songs and dreaming up new marketing strategies. He was an unabashed populist whose most famous quote was "Where's the melody?" (although, ironically, that quote originated with Dave Kapp). He was after showmanship on record. His theory, said Dave Kapp, was to "pile as much entertainment into the confines of a three-minute record as it was possible to confine in there, and make it so great that people would have to listen to it, and to make it such that they couldn't get it any place else."

After Jack Kapp's death, Milton Rackmil became president. After gradually chipping away at Dave Kapp's responsibilities, Rackmil ousted him in June 1951. Kapp moved to RCA before starting Kapp Records in 1954. Rackmil jealously eyed the spin-off benefits enjoyed by RCA, Columbia, and MGM Records from their radio, television, and motion picture affiliates, and in September 1951 he went into debt to the tune of two million dollars to buy a controlling interest in Universal Pictures. Then, in June 1962, the Music Corporation of America (MCA), a talent booking organization, acquired 81 percent of Decca's public stock, and Decca and Universal became separate divisions of MCA. Decca was swallowed entirely on January 1, 1966, when it ceased to exist as a separate entity.

When MCA had started acquiring Decca stock, the then-attorney general, Robert Kennedy, had launched an antitrust suit against MCA, which led to MCA's divesting itself of its talent agency. MCA dropped the Decca logo on March 1, 1973, probably because it had the rights to the name only in North and South America; elsewhere, it was still owned by Lewis's Decca companies.

E. R. Lewis reentered the American record business in 1947, when he started London Records in New York. At first he kept the rights to American Decca for the world outside North America and couldn't sign American acts to London, but a deal between the two Deccas that was concluded in June 1949 gave the labels more autonomy. Lewis hung on to British rights to American Decca until 1974, although he lost the rights elsewhere, and he was able to sign American acts to London. His American A&R men made a few local signings, like Teresa Brewer, but London's bread and butter was the distribution division. Lewis, though, always saw London Records as a vehicle for making British Decca product available in North America. This left it well positioned in the mid-sixties when everyone wanted British records, but by 1980 both London Records and British Decca were in sorry shape. Lewis, by then Sir Edward Lewis, was still at the helm, but shortly before his death he arranged to sell off his ramshackle empire to Racal, a British marine technology company. Racal only wanted the navigational equipment division and sold British Decca and London Records to Polygram Records in 1980.

American Decca's fiftieth anniversary passed without fanfare, but by the sixtieth, MCA had revitalized the Decca logo in North America for pop and jazz reissues and was using it as an overflow label in Nashville.

The Decca/MCA Records catalog is now merely an adjunct to the MCA/Universal empire, which produces movies and television shows, operates theme parks, and owns Putnam Books. In 1990 MCA was bought for $6.1 billion by Matsushita, the Japanese electrical conglomerate that owns Technics and Panasonic. Then, in April 1995, 80 percent of the MCA complex was bought for $5.7 billion by Seagram's, originally a Canadian distilling company that had made a fortune during Prohibition selling liquor that may or may not have ended up in the hands of organized crime in the United States.

As you ride the elevators from floor to floor at the MCA Records building in the Universal City complex in Los Angeles, it's hard to believe that this was a company that started at the depth of the Depression on a few promissory notes from England and a prayer that Bing Crosby would come over. E. R. Lewis was not a music man and never pretended to be. He was a businessman with enough of an aristocratic bearing to get people to lend him money. He had the sense to ally himself with someone who was in many respects his complete opposite, the coarse but musically astute Jack Kapp. By the time Lewis sold his shares in American Decca, the label had risen quickly to become one of the three major players in the American record business, and building on Kapp's groundwork, it has one of the richest catalogs in the industry.⊚

61

Sir Edward Lewis with Mantovani
Photo courtesy of Polygram Records, London

How to Start a Record Company, 2

KING RECORDS, CINCINNATI, 1943

"You may disagree with me one hundred percent," said the president of King Records, Syd Nathan, "but somebody has to be the chief, and I am elected. I am spending my money—not yours, so it will have to be as I say." And there in a nutshell was King Records. It was the creation of Sydney Nathan of Cincinnati. He was indisputably the king—self-proclaimed rather than elected, as kings should be. "When the sergeant says, 'Charge,'" he said in another of his favorite aphorisms, "you don't decide if you're gonna charge or not. If you go backward, you're gonna get shot in the ass. The big chief is the one who tells you what to do."

Even before the first King record appeared, Nathan seemed to have a clear vision of what he wanted. Driving up to Dayton in September 1943 with Merle Travis and Grandpa Jones to cut his first session, he announced that his label was to be called King. "King of them all," he added emphatically.

Sydney Nathan was born in Cincinnati on April 27, 1904. By the time he started King, he was nearly blind, nearly forty, and plagued by asthma, which he aggravated by smoking cigars and by maintaining his weight at nearly double what it should have been. He spoke in an almost cartoonishly gruff and wheezy voice and peppered his conversation with profanities. He had tried his hand at many things before he started King. He had been a drummer, a pawnshop owner, a jewelry store owner, a park concessionaire, and a wrestling promoter. He had lived in Arizona for a while to alleviate his asthma, then tried Florida, where his brother David was a doctor. In Florida he operated a photo finishing business, but when he came back to Cincinnati, he opened a record store on Central Avenue, continuing to do photo finishing on the side.

"I sold records in a location that nobody could sell a record in," said Nathan. "It was like trying to sell grand pianos out in the desert. But we done business because we knew how to do business."

King started in November 1943 with two records by Merle Travis and Grandpa Jones, both working under pseudonyms. They were pressed in minimal quantities, and the launch barely qualified as a launch at all. King was relaunched a year later with twenty-five thousand dollars raised from family members. The 1943 records, which had been pressed at the American Printing House for the Blind in Louisville, sounded so bad that they could have been made at a home for the deaf. With no other plant around, Nathan started his own. In August 1944 he took out a five-year lease on a nine-thousand-square-foot factory site at 1540 Brewster Avenue.

To a greater or lesser extent, all independent labels were plagued by the same problems: getting records pressed, getting them distributed, and then getting paid for them. Nathan boldly tried to lick these problems by establishing not only his own studio, his own plant, and his own printing press, but also his own distribution system that, at one point, extended to thirty-two wholly owned branches that sold only King records. Later he had his own design studio for LP jackets, and even a line of record players. In other words, he controlled as much of the process as he could, from recording the song to playing it at home. Only the paper inner sleeves for LPs were brought in from outside. He gave up the branches in 1965, but for twenty years King was a self-sufficient organization. A system of that depth and complexity placed an onus on Nathan to produce something that the public wanted, because that was the one factor he couldn't control.

At first, King was a country label. Nathan had WLW's "Boone County Jamboree" on his doorstep and hundreds of thousands of rural Kentuckians and Tennesseans working in local munitions plants. This gave him a pool of talent and a ready-made market. King stayed exclusively in the hillbilly music business for two years and scored some big country hits, like Cowboy Copas's classic of interracial passion, "Filipino Baby," and a slew of hits from the Delmore Brothers, who were one of the few prewar acts to do well in the postwar era. At a time when Nashville had not yet established its preeminence as a recording center, King could have become a player in the country music business, but Nathan found the pickin's were better elsewhere.

The R&B record business was the major growth area after the Second World War, so it was almost inevitable that a label setting out to be "king of them all" would enter the field. "We saw a need," said Nathan. "Why should we go into all these towns and only sell to hillbilly accounts? Why can't we sell a few more while we're there? You don't make any money while your car is rolling. So we got into the race business." It was probably that simple to him. Who needed studies, consultants, or market testing?

Nathan didn't know much about R&B, but neither did the Chesses, the Mesners at Aladdin Records, the Biharis at Modern/RPM, or most of the others when they started. You could afford to learn by trial and error when you could cut two singles in an afternoon for less than a hundred bucks and you

Syd Nathan
Photo courtesy of C. Escott

owned your own pressing plant. Still, as Nathan was fond of saying, there's only one guaranteed sale: the guy's mother. The R&B market was changeable, much more so than the pop and country markets. This meant that if King was to succeed, then Nathan—a Jewish guy now in his late forties headquartered in Cincinnati—had to stay on top of what young urban blacks were buying on the coasts.

King's R&B subsidiary, Queen, started in August 1945 with Bull Moose Jackson's hasty cover version of Joe Liggins's "The Honeydripper," and the label functioned for two years before Nathan folded it into King, starting an R&B series on an appropriately blue label. The last Queen record was by Earl

Bostic, an artist who would help to assure the future of King's R&B series as well as its uptown image. Very little in the way of cotton-patch blues made its way onto King; the success of Bull Moose Jackson and Earl Bostic convinced Nathan that sophistication was the key. Many of the first generation of King R&B artists were big band veterans.

From 1948 until 1951 King was literally King of Them All in Rhythm 'n' Blues, and it remained a major player in the R&B scene for the next twenty years. Nathan always spoke wistfully of revitalizing his country division, but he probably realized that the major labels had airplay sewn up as much then as they do now. In what must have been a sentimental move, he re-signed one of the first King artists, Hawkshaw Hawkins, in 1962. The gesture was rewarded with a giant hit, "Lonesome 7-7203," but it was a posthumous hit, because Hawkins had perished in the plane crash that took Patsy Cline's life.

In February 1949, when Nathan hired Guy Lombardo's arranger Dewey Bergman, and again in September 1951, when he hired the industry vet Eli Oberstein, he made a pitch for the pop market. He signed the checks for the costly sessions, with their armies of arrangers and copyists, and sold almost no records. The pop market, accounting for 50 percent of overall sales, loomed like a mirage just outside Nathan's myopic field of vision, tantalizing him but never letting him get close. The arrival of rock 'n' roll a few years later gave him another crack at the mass market, this time with product he knew and understood. Almost overnight, the Top Forty format took over radio, and a record that would have been called an R&B or hillbilly record a year or two earlier now stood a chance if the production values were right. Nathan was well positioned to take advantage of this development, but he never found an artist like Fats Domino, much less one like Elvis, who could cross categories and sell literally millions of records to kids. His biggest rock 'n' roll record was Bill Doggett's "Honky Tonk."

By the late fifties King was shipping around 200,000 or 300,000 records a month. It was a decent enough amount, but not enough to justify the huge infrastructure that Nathan had built. King was losing money. "Give me six million records a year [500,000 a month] and you'll see the happiest little fat guy you ever saw in your life," Nathan told his A&R men during one of his perorations. He had gone as far as he could, and the realization was sinking in that he would never be King of Them All.

King began limping badly in the early sixties, and by the time Nathan closed out his distribution system in 1965, his company was almost entirely dependent on James Brown, an artist whose music he detested with all his heart. He had been opposed to signing him and was on the point of dropping him in

1959 when Brown reestablished himself with "Try Me." Freddy King sold respectably well in the early sixties, Hank Ballard still generated good sales, and the huge LP catalog drawn from Nathan's well-stocked vault ticked over, but it was James Brown who kept King afloat.

Nathan, never especially healthy to begin with, showed signs of the onset of heart disease in the early sixties. When he wrote to Little Willie John in jail in August 1965, he said, "I have a very serious illness. It could take me in twenty seconds, twenty minutes, twenty days, twenty months, or twenty years. I sit on a keg of dynamite all the time." Talking to the King staff on the occasion of the label's twenty-fifth anniversary bash (which was unaccountably held in 1967 rather than 1968), he addressed the same theme with his usual gruff humor. "The day will come when I pass on," he said, "and maybe King will be better for it. But I'm gonna wait around, because I don't have a contract with God."

He didn't wait around long. Nathan died in Miami of heart disease complicated by pneumonia on March 5, 1968. He was a month and a half shy of official retirement age, and six months shy of the twenty-fifth anniversary of the first King record. In October that year, King was sold to Starday Records, with the understanding that Starday itself was about to be sold to Lin Broadcasting of Nashville. In July 1971, just before Lin sold King-Starday, it sold off James Brown's contract and catalog to Polydor Records. Immediately afterward, Lin sold King-Starday to Tennessee Recording and Publishing, a company formed by the songwriters Jerry Leiber and Mike Stoller, the former King vice president Hal Neely, and the music publisher Freddy Bienstock. In 1975 Tennessee Recording and Publishing sold the King-Starday masters, but not the music publishing, to its current owner, GML, Inc., of Nashville, owned by Moe Lytle.

How many King records Nathan personally recorded or even liked we'll never know. Perhaps his greatest gift was knowing when to bow out and let his A&R men take over, as well as knowing when to step in to make a decisive signing or call a halt to costs spiraling out of control. "I'm not a genius," he said toward the end of his life, "and I don't have any geniuses working for me. We work at it as if it was the coffin business, the machinery business, or any other business. It has to pay for itself. I know a record company [and here he's probably referring to Vee-Jay] who done a minimum of fifteen million dollars worth of business in two years, and they are bankrupt. If I had done fifteen million dollars worth of business in two years, I would have had five million dollars in corporate funds to show for it."

Nathan demystified the music business. He saw nothing transcendant in what was in the grooves. The contradiction of Syd Nathan, though, was that, as much as he was frugal, he had an instinct for quality. He was also insistent that his records had to have something different. He once stood in his sister's record store and heard a customer say that he didn't want a new record by an artist because it sounded too much like an old one, and he took that admonition to heart. There aren't many dogs in the King catalog, and that can't be attributed to one A&R man or another, because it's a recurrent theme through the country recordings, the R&B recordings, and the gospel recordings cut over a twenty-five year period. The only person there all that time was Nathan himself.⑨

"Uh, take it to the bridge, Syd!"
Photo courtesy of C. Escott

How to Start a
Record Company, 3

· ·

STARDAY RECORDS, HOUSTON AND
BEAUMONT, TEXAS, 1953

For all the recording activity in Nashville over the last fifty years, there
has never really been a thriving independent label scene. Odder yet, the
independent labels that flourished there, like Dot, Excello, and Bullet,
weren't primarily country music labels. Starday Records became the most successful country music label based in Nashville, although it started in Beaumont and Houston, Texas, in June 1953 as a partnership between Jack Starnes
("Star-") and Harold "Pappy" Daily ("-day"). Starnes was a booker who had
managed Lefty Frizzell for a while and was running a club in Beaumont. Daily owned a record distributorship in Houston. In September 1953, when Starday was a few months old, Starnes and Daily brought in a third partner, Don
Pierce, who had previously been with 4-Star Records. Pierce stayed in Los Angeles and was the only partner who worked more or less full-time on the label.

Pappy Daily, born in Yoakum, Texas, in 1902, was raised in Houston and
had been a bean counter for the Southern Pacific Railroad before he started
South Coast Amusements around 1932. While selling and servicing jukeboxes and pinball machines, he had drifted into the music business, running a radio jamboree on KNUZ, where the regulars included Webb Pierce and Hank
Locklin. Daily recorded them and placed the masters with 4-Star Records in
Pasadena, California. Don Pierce, born in Ballard, Washington, in 1915, had
worked for 4-Star since he had got out of the navy immediately after World
War II.

"I'd always go to Houston and work with Pappy down there," said Pierce,
"because he had been so fantastic at not only finding talent for us but recording them. He'd send in the tapes and order a thousand copies of the record,
then go out and promote and sell the record. How often do you find a distributor that will do that?

"I left 4-Star in a dispute with the owner, Bill McCall, and I spent that
summer in Los Angeles not knowing what I was going to do. Then one day I
picked up *Billboard* and I saw some reviews of country records on Starday. I'd
never heard of Starday, so I called up *Billboard* in Hollywood and I said, 'Who

Smoke 'em if you got 'em. Pappy Daily and Don Pierce
Photo courtesy of Don Pierce/C. Escott

is Starday?' They said, 'It's out of Houston. Pappy Daily.' So I called Pappy, and I said, 'Pappy, I saw those reviews. I wondered if I might do something with you.' He said he'd had his problems with Bill McCall too, and he said I should get on the next airplane and get my fanny down to Houston. I was introduced to Jack Starnes. They brought me into Starday and made me president of the company, and we put up three hundred and thirty-three dollars apiece. They already had [Arlie Duff's] 'You All Come' out and in the marketplace, and it was starting to make a little noise around Houston."

Two-way partnerships are hard; three-way partnerships are hell, and it didn't take long for the Starday partnership to break up. "To Starnes, a record label was a means of managing and booking artists," said Pierce. "To me, records were a means of selling a commodity and acquiring copyrights. We did not have the same goals at all. Jack would say, 'I need to get a release on this or that artist, and we need to have records by such-and-such a time because we're going to be traveling up to Arkansas.' I said, 'Well, that hasn't got anything to do with the record company.' We had our releases scheduled for the next month, and all of a sudden he would demand that something else be done that had nothing to do with the record company, something to assist him in booking and promoting. One time he had R. D. Hendon, and when he couldn't get a release date from me, he just went to Plastic Products in Memphis, says 'Press up some records,' gave it a release number, and took off. You can't run a record company that way.

"He grew to dislike me a lot because I was interested in making a success out of the record company, but he didn't give a damn about it. He was only interested in what the record company could do for him and his booking work. He was coming from a different direction. We were at odds, and when 'Satisfied Mind' broke open in Springfield and got recorded twice in one week, he offered to sell his share to Pappy Daily. He said he would not sell anything to me. He took six thousand dollars from Pappy Daily for his one-third share. Pappy promptly offered me one half of what he had acquired so that we would still be fifty-fifty and together."

Starnes's final bequest to Starday was the artist who would assure its future: George Jones. Just out of the marines, Jones was hanging around Beaumont, playing Starnes's club when he could, and getting into trouble when he couldn't. Starnes brought Daily in to help produce the first session, which was cut in Starnes's living room with his fourteen-year-old son operating a Magnecord home recorder. On that first session, George tried imitating everybody he knew. A frighteningly convincing impersonation of Lefty Frizzell remains on tape. Finally, in exasperation, Daily asked him if he could sing like George Jones, and George sang one of his own songs, "No Money in This Deal." It was, as George is fond of saying sourly, a little prophecy, but it got him started.

Starday bumbled on through 1954 and 1955. Daily concentrated on his distributorship, and Pierce was on the road selling Starday records and acquiring copyrights. The veteran country record man Ralph Peer, who owned the Peer-Southern publishing company, saw something of himself in Pierce and put him on a retainer in exchange for the foreign publishing rights on anything Pierce acquired. Then, in mid-1955, George Jones broke through with "Why, Baby, Why, " which led to an offer from Mercury Records.

"Art Talmadge from Mercury approached us at the Country Music Festival in Nashville," said Pierce. "He spoke first to Pappy, because Pappy was a Mercury distributor. He said, 'Since Dee Kilpatrick is leaving us to take over the artist bureau at WSM, it leaves us with nobody in charge of our country department. You guys are in the charts all the time. Would you like to make a deal with us?' Pappy said he had a business to run in Texas, and Starday was something he did on the side. He said it hinged on whether I was in the picture. Art said that they needed someone to help them with promotion and distribution as well as the creation of product, and he asked if I would move to Nashville to replace Dee. Pappy told me about it and asked if I would be interested, and I said I darn sure would. I was just crazy about Nashville. I loved to come to the conventions and come to town any time I could get there."

The Mercury-Starday deal became effective January 1, 1957. Pierce moved to Nashville that April and set up an office on Dickerson Pike, far from the emerging Music Row. "Murray Nash, who had worked for Acuff-Rose and

**The Starday Building in Madison.
That's Don's Mercedes out front.**
Photo courtesy of Don Pierce/C. Escott

Mercury and RCA, told me that the place to be was the old Cumberland Lodge Building on Seventh Avenue North, near WSM, but I said, 'Not for me. I want to be away from the business. These people are my competitors.' I didn't want to be seen as another outlet for these people to sell their songs. I told Murray, 'I'm interested in recording *my* songs, not your songs.'"

Mercury-Starday fell apart in July 1958. Mercury was hoping that Starday would deliver crossover artists, like Elvis or Carl Perkins. Instead, the Mercury brass found that Pierce and Daily were as much in the dark about rock 'n' roll as they were. "Then there was some friction over publishing, " said Pierce. "Art Talmadge said that the publisher was always Starrite, our publishing company, and we weren't always using the strongest material available from Nashville—and he was right about that. We were very much interested in building a publishing catalog. We thought our copyrights were competitive, but they weren't selling, and Mercury decided that they didn't want to perpetuate the agreement. I asked Pappy if they could get out. He said that those Chicago lawyers could get in or out of anything they wanted to. He said it was better not to get in a fight with them. He also said that George didn't want to stay with Starday; he wanted to cast his lot with Pappy and Mercury, and that was disappointing to me because he was important to my plans. Pappy and I became estranged over that and some other matters."

The Starday assets were divided in a deal brokered by Savoy Records' Herman Lubinsky in a Chicago hotel room. "Herman said, 'You two guys come up to my room. I'm going to lock the door, and you're not going to leave until you've settled your differences.' " remembered Pierce. "Pappy spread himself out on the bed, and he said, 'OK. Start talking.'" The Starday masters and the copyrights were divided down the middle: Pierce picked one, then Daily picked one. For the year and a half left on George Jones's Starday contract,

Promoting "Giddyup Go " and "Giddyup Go, Answer,"
both on Starday. Left to right: Red Sovine, Tommy Hill,
Minnie Pearl, Minnie's husband Henry Cannon, Don Pierce.
Photo courtesy of Don Pierce/C. Escott

**Pappy Daily with Art Talmadge (left),
Jay Jacobs (right), and George Jones (front)**
Photo courtesy of D. Daily/C. Escott

**Partners in fashion crime.
Left to right: Don Pierce, Sam Phillips,
Shelby Singleton**
Photo courtesy of C. Escott

Pierce and Daily took turns supplying songs and split Starday's 2 percent override from Mercury.

Daily had already started 'D' Records, perhaps in anticipation of the rift, and he continued his affiliation with Mercury. Two months after Mercury-Starday folded, he issued the Big Bopper's "Chantilly Lace" on 'D,' and after it had sold twenty-five thousand copies in Texas, he leased it to Mercury. He placed several other artists with the label until Art Talmadge quit Mercury in 1960 to go with United Artists Records. Daily followed Talmadge to UA, taking George Jones with him. When Talmadge went to Musicor Records in 1964, Daily followed him there, once again hauling George Jones along. New recordings came out on 'D' until 1979. Willie Nelson's first commercial record was on 'D.' George Strait made some early recordings for the label as well, and Daily's grandson still plays with Strait's band. Daily died in December 1987.

Between 1958 and 1968 Starday was Don Pierce's company, and he decided to stand or fall with traditional country music. He didn't dare to be different; he *had* to be different to survive. He knew he couldn't compete with the majors on their own terms, so he set out to build a catalog that was founded on what the majors wouldn't touch: bluegrass, country gospel, old-timey, older artists who had been dropped in major-label cutbacks, and session pickers.

Pierce's trademark was the in-your-face LP, every one emblazoned with the legend "From NASHVILLE, TENNESSEE—The Musical Heart of America." This was at a time when the country market was still singles driven, and LPs were usually cobbled together in a couple of afternoons in the wake of a hit. Starday LPs were different, and even among casual fans there could be no doubt about who ran the company; Pierce wrote the liner notes to almost every one. "Tradition," "America," "authentic," "Nashville." How often those words appeared.

"I started immediately doing bluegrass," said Pierce. "Pappy, out of Houston, had no feeling for bluegrass at all. I was in Nashville, dealing with Carl Story, the Stanley Brothers, and Bill Clifton, and I had a real feel for it. I had recorded them all for Mercury. Starday was *the* place that the old-timers could get on a record. If they were an established act, I wasn't as much interested in putting out singles because I couldn't get them on jukeboxes, but if they'd played twenty years on 'The Grand Ole Opry,' I knew they could sell albums."

There were a few hits on Starday, usually by artists who had been put out to pasture by the majors. Cowboy Copas's career was born anew on Starday shortly before his death; Johnny Bond scored a huge pop and country hit with "Ten Little Bottles"; Red Sovine did well with "Giddy-up Go." In the hardcore country vein, there was Frankie Miller's "Blackland Farmer, " as well as Wayne Raney's gloriously anthemic "We Need a Whole Lot More Jesus, and a Lot Less Rock 'n' Roll."

Pierce worked the market hard. He made Starday a case study in extracting the last bit of mileage from a catalog. He demonstrated the power of mail order by producing LPs and EPs specially for mail-order clients. He opened up the overseas market when the majors saw no future there for country music. If there was a little time left at the end of a session, he would ask the pickers to dash off some instrumentals, then he would send them out to stations to play as filler leading up to the newsbreaks, knowing that he would collect BMI performance money for that.

Then, at the end of 1968, Pierce got out of the business. He judged, correctly as it happened, that the market had peaked for the type of music he was producing, and he saw that the majors now had a hammerlock on radio. "I could tell from my BMI statements," he said. "All of a sudden we had twelve hundred, fifteen hundred stations playing country music, and it was costing a fortune to service all of them, and I would have Charlie Dick [Patsy Cline's widower] on the road for me promoting. We worked the stations hard, but my performance money went steadily down, and I knew I was getting less and less airplay. The majors were issuing eight or ten albums a month instead of one or two. Singles releases were up too, and they were using up all the airtime, and when I couldn't get airplay I wasn't selling the singles, so I took the opportunity to sell."

Pierce had bought his one-third share in Starday fifteen years earlier for $333, and when he sold out it was for over $2 million. The buyer was Lin Broadcasting. Then, just as the deal was being consummated, Syd Nathan of King Records died. Nathan and Pierce had been friends for twenty years, and King handled Starday's LP-pressing business. Pierce approached Nathan's estate and bought King with the understanding from Lin that they would buy both companies for $5.5 million.

Pierce never reentered the record business. He moved into property development. He's still a tireless booster for his adopted city of Nashville, but knows well that the current business climate in the city would have chewed up his little enterprise and left it for dead years ago. The radio in his office is tuned to a country station, but Don Pierce isn't really listening.◉

How to Start a Record Company, 4

· ·

HI RECORDS, MEMPHIS, 1957

Hi Records came within a hair's breadth of being known only to the handful of nutters who collect bad rockabilly on small Memphis record labels from the fifties. It then came within another hair's breadth of being remembered only for a handful of cheesy instrumentals in the early sixties. As it is, it's impossible now to write even a cursory history of soul music without devoting at least a chapter to Hi Records.

Hi was founded late in 1957 with an initial investment of $3.50 from Ray Harris. As a rockabilly singer, Harris had cut two outrageous but spectacularly unsuccessful records for Sun in 1956 and 1957. Everyone had fooled him into thinking that his second record, a gussied-up version of "Greenback Dollar," would be a smash, so he went out and bought a new Mercury on the strength of the promises. Later that year, 1957, he was working in construction to pay for it. On a site somewhere near Memphis, Harris met Jerry Lee Lewis's cousin Carl McVoy. They went to McVoy's house one night, and McVoy started pounding out a rock 'n' roll version of the old Jimmie Davis hit "You Are My Sunshine." Fats Domino had ushered in the craze for rocked-up standards, and Harris thought McVoy could do it as well as anyone; he had, after all, taught Jerry Lee Lewis. So Harris took McVoy to a house on Poplar Avenue where an old lady he knew had a tape deck and a battered upright piano. He paid her $3.50 and came out with a rough demo of "You Are My Sunshine."

Harris had two partners: a country fiddle player, Bill Cantrell, and a guitarist, Quinton Claunch. They had worked on country music production for Sun Records in the pre–Johnny Cash era, but quit in disgust soon after their song "Sure to Fall" was bounced off the flip side of Carl Perkins's "Blue Suede Shoes" in favor of "Honey, Don't." Perkins and Charlie Feathers had been among the acts they produced for Sun. "We said, 'We got the know-how, but who's got the money?'" said Harris.

The man with the deep pockets was Joe Cuoghi (rhymes with "boogie"). He and a school friend, John Novarese, had started the Poplar Tunes record store in Memphis in 1946 and had expanded it to become a distributor to the jukebox trade and a one-stop (a subdistributor that services small stores with all labels). Cuoghi had already passed up the opportunity to invest in another record company, and now the lure of being able to put his own records on his jukeboxes at a fraction of the price of other people's records was too powerful to resist. He recruited his lawyer, Nick Pesce, and three other investors, Sam Esgro, Bill Brown, and Bill Crudgington. They put up five hundred dollars each. Harris, Cantrell, and Claunch put up nothing, but were to work on the creative end. Cantrell was to be president. Two hundred and forty shares were issued in Hi Records; each of the eight partners had thirty shares. Harris, Claunch, and Cantrell took off for Nashville with the money and recut "You Are My Sunshine." Then, shortly before the record's release, Cuoghi bought out the three silent partners, making him the majority shareholder. He replaced Cantrell as president.

Early in 1958 "You Are My Sunshine" started getting good reaction, but Cuoghi found what others who had been in his shoes had found: he couldn't collect fast enough to keep the pressing plants happy. His hit was bankrupting him. In April 1958, just before McVoy was due to go coast to coast on the "Dick Clark Show" (a spinoff of "American Bandstand"), Cuoghi sold his master and McVoy's contract to Sam Phillips at Sun Records for twenty-six hundred dollars, then watched Phillips's Midas touch work in reverse. The record died.

Harris, Cantrell, and Claunch persuaded Cuoghi to invest the proceeds from the McVoy sale into refurbishing an abandoned movie house at 1320 South Lauderdale Avenue into a recording studio. Cantrell, a qualified electrical engineer who worked for the city of Memphis, converted the projection room into a control room with an Ampex single-track recorder and two Altec boards. Then he partitioned off a little studio in what had been the seating area. This was every record person's dream: no more paying for studio time. After McVoy, the releases trickled out. There was a singing dentist from St. Louis who brushed his teeth between takes, and some teenage pap from a kid named Kimball Coburn. One release by a young rockabilly singer, Jay B. Loyd, landed Hi a distribution deal with London Records; another, the original version of "Miller's Cave" by Tommy Tucker, got covered by Hank Snow. Otherwise, all Cuoghi got were bills. By early 1959 he was at the point of pulling the plug on Hi.

Then one Sunday in 1959 Bill Black came to see Ray Harris. Black and Elvis Presley had fallen out the previous year, and the bassist who had once been one third of "Elvis Presley—Scotty and Bill" was watching the repo man walk away with his household appliances. He and Harris had worked together at the Firestone plant in Memphis and had stayed in touch. Harris had some local pickers in mind to work with Black. He wanted Reggie Young, now

Nashville's premier session man, on guitar. Eddy Arnold's nephew, Jerry Arnold, played drums. Marty Willis from Billy Riley's Little Green Men was on saxophone, and a black pianist, Joe Hall, was brought in from Willie Mitchell's band. "Everyone except Reggie was working on an old Hank Thompson song," said Harris. "Then Reggie come down one night and he said, 'We're going nowheres.' So he tuned down his guitar and started beating around with it. Everyone fell in and we came up with 'Smokie.'" At first listen, the instrumental seemed no more than a bass-heavy Bill Doggett sound-alike, but its simplicity was deceptive. The key was cohesion.

Harris couldn't afford to pay session fees for all the hours the musicians had invested, so he worked out a profit-sharing plan. Marty Willis, who had been burned at Sun, was having none of it, and he demanded his fees. Joe Hall agreed to the plan but later needed twenty-seven dollars to settle a light bill, so Harris gave him the money in exchange for his share of the record. He then returned Hall's share to the group.

"Smokie" was a hit. Elvis sent a congratulatory card, which Black's wife, Evelyn, pasted in the family album. Harris quit his job to concentrate on Hi and persuaded Cuoghi to plow back some of the winnings into a three-track recorder. Willis and Hall quit the combo. Willis was replaced by another saxophonist, Ace Cannon, and Hall was replaced by Carl McVoy in the studio and a rotating cast of pianists/organists on show dates. Quinton Claunch was forced out of the Hi partnership soon after for cutting Bill Black soundalikes for another label. He later cofounded Goldwax Records. McVoy bought Claunch's share for seven thousand dollars, which he earned on the next Bill Black record. He hauled a Hammond organ to the studio on the back of his construction truck and persuaded everyone to redo a clunky pop song from 1957 called "White Silver Sands." If "Smokie" had been no more than a riff, then "White Silver Sands" was a riff overlaid with a melody. The sound of McVoy's organ could curdle milk, but—incredibly—this too was a Top Ten hit in 1960.

Within a year, Ace Cannon was itching to cut a solo album with his own combo, featuring the drummer Johnny Bernero. Bernero had been the session drummer at Sun when Elvis was there, and no one in Memphis could play a shuffle more exquisitely. One of the tunes that Bernero and Cannon cut was cloned from Jimmie Davis's "Columbus Stockade Blues." They called their instrumental "Tuff," although Bill Justis had cut it earlier with Cannon taking the lead when it was called "Cattywampus." "Tuff" was a hit, but when the royalty checks were issued, Bernero found that the only shuffle on the record was the one he had lost out on. He sued Cannon, eventually winning a paltry $1,250 settlement. He quit the music business in disgust and went off to sell insurance. Jimmie Davis threatened to sue but backed off. Ray Harris gave four hundred dollars to Hi's Atlanta promo man to place in the tin cup of the street musician who had reportedly written "Columbus Stockade Blues" before Davis bought it.

The course of Hi Records was set. Greasy blues-based instrumentals became the label's trademark, so much so that it was assumed that "Hi" was an acronym for Hit Instrumentals. The jukebox trade, an aspect of the business that Cuoghi understood very well, was integral to Hi's success. "There was over one million jukeboxes in the country then," said Harris, "and every Bill Black and Ace Cannon release got on two hundred and fifty thousand of them. That's good business. A sale's a sale." Bill Black sold so well in the R&B market that Hi didn't place his photo on albums to foster the illusion that he might indeed be black. It didn't take long for Black to discover that not having his photo on the albums had another advantage: no one knew what he looked like. On show dates most people thought that the saxophonist was Bill Black, so Black stopped touring and franchised several "Bill Black Combos." He formed a record company under Hi's aegis and started his own music publishing company to go with it. He came close to having a hit with the original version of Billy Swan's song "Lover Please," but he was scooped by Clyde McPhatter.

After suffering headaches, dizziness, and memory loss, Black was diagnosed as having an inoperable brain tumor. He set his affairs in order and died on October 21, 1965. Elvis sent another card but didn't attend the funeral. It was business as usual for the Bill Black Combo, though. They continued in one form or another under Larry Rogers's leadership into the 1980s.

There are only so many variations on a theme, and Black and Cannon explored them all. Sales inevitably began to tail off, and by the mid-sixties Hi's most consistent seller was Willie Mitchell, who was essentially recording a punchier version of the same thing. It's still unclear how Mitchell came to join the label. Ray Harris said that Mitchell was working for an automobile upholstery company and they started talking music while Mitchell was refurbishing Harris's Cadillac; Mitchell seemed to think that Joe Hall had introduced him. After working as an artist and producer for the Home of the Blues label, Willie started recording at Hi in 1961. Not long after, he became the house arranger, and then his road band became the studio rhythm section.

By the close of the decade, Mitchell had almost quit touring. He'd had a bad accident and now saw his future in the studio. He started bringing in more of his own signings, most notably Al Green. He had met Green in Midland, Texas, and invited him to check out what was happening at Hi. Green had scored a pretty big hit with "Back Up Train," but was all but washed

Bill Black and Joe Cuoghi, 1959
Photo courtesy of C. Escott

The Hi-est of times. Left to right: Al Green, Nick Pesce (president of Hi), Willie Mitchell
Photo courtesy of C. Escott

up when he arrived on Mitchell's doorstep.

It took almost two years, but in 1971 Green broke through with "Tired of Being Alone." By then, the original Hi partnership had been completely recast. Early in 1970 Harris quit, venturing the suggestion that Green would go nowhere "singing in that sissy voice." A few weeks later, in July 1970, Joe Cuoghi died at the Memphis airport. At roughly the same time, Carl McVoy was going through a messy divorce (as one might expect from a cousin of Jerry Lee Lewis) and sold out. Mitchell bought part of Harris's and McVoy's shares and became the executive vice president. Cuoghi's lawyer, Nick Pesce, who had been a silent partner from the beginning, became president—another lawyer in the record business.

After Al Green broke through, Mitchell tried to get other singers to fit into the elegant production mold he had crafted, but he could never find a consistent winner. Syl Johnson, O. V. Wright, Otis Clay, and others made some wonderful records, but no one was selling like the increasingly troubled Al Green. Mitchell's best shot came with Ann Peebles, who had come to Memphis from her family's gospel choir in St. Louis. Barefoot on the tattered carpet in the old studio, she was intermittently brilliant. "I Can't Stand the Rain " and "I'm Gonna Tear Your Playhouse Down" were as good as anything from the era, but she could never firm up a place in the majors.

Shortly before Al Green went into a self-imposed exile, Atlantic Records reportedly offered nine million dollars for Hi Records. Bill Cantrell and Nick Pesce, the two remaining original partners, were in favor of selling, but Mitchell held the view that if Atlantic was offering nine million this year, they would be offering eighteen million next year. That optimism proved unfounded, and when Hi was eventually sold in 1976 it was for considerably less than nine million dollars. The buyer was Al Bennett. Like Sam Walton, Bennett was an Arkansas salesman who made good. He had sold records for Dot and then worked his way up to the presidency of Liberty Records before selling out to Capitol/EMI. After a short hiatus out of the business, he launched Cream Records out of Los Angeles.

Bennett planned to make Hi a continuing force in the marketplace, but his plans were preempted by disco, which was followed by a sharp downturn in the record business in the early eighties. Bennett also found that Al Green's popularity could not survive his return to the church, and that Ann Peebles was simply not going to make it. He sold off the lucrative music publishing catalog to A&M's Almo-Irving subsidiary and pared back his operation to almost nothing. Shortly after he died in 1989, the company was moved to a squalid little cubbyhole in a Hollywood office block and was put up for lease.

Ray Harris at the Hi three-track, 1960
Photo courtesy of Ray Harris/C. Escott

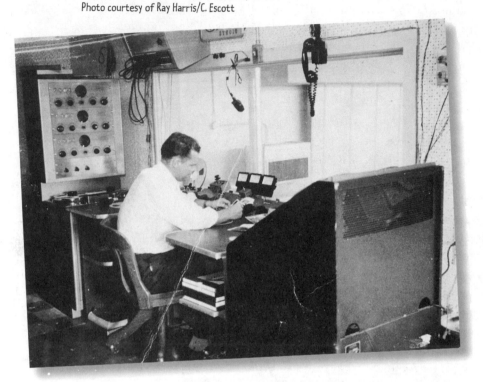

The latest company to take a crack at selling the catalog is Capitol Records.

Hi really was a contender. No label cut better jukebox instrumentals, or made such elegant soul records. No other label knew what to do with Al Green. No one seems to have a lot to show for it, though. Willie Mitchell has his studio, the old Hi studio, and it's ticking over. Guys come in from England and want to stand where Al Green stood. McVoy is dead, and Roy Harris is in retirement in Mississippi. Willie's suing someone or other over something to do with Hi. Bill Cantrell lives modestly in a Memphis suburb. Nick Pesce still has his law practice. The success seems to have left a bad taste in everyone's mouth. The history books are telling these people that they accomplished a lot. So where are the Mercedes? ◎

The Story of a Broken Heart

Marvin Rainwater

· ·

HALF A HALF-BREED

It was something you couldn't get away with today. Back in the mid-fifties, a quarter-Cherokee called Marvin Karlton Rainwater got his career off the ground by trading off his part-Indian pedigree. Today he'd be criticized for reinforcing the media stereotype of First Nations. His fan club journal was called the "Tommahawk [*sic*] Smoke Signal" ("We hope you have heap'um Merry Christmas. We do our best to pleasum you," said the Christmas 1955 issue). Marvin didn't seem entirely comfortable with the image, but he fostered it with a tasseled buckskin jacket and the occasional headband. He knew he needed something to get noticed—and as a gimmick this was as good as any.

The success he found was short-lived, as success tends to be. "Gonna Find Me a Bluebird" broke through in April 1957, but when "Half-Breed" disappeared from the charts a shade over two years later, it was all over. In between, there were two other hits and, odder yet, a Number One hit in England, but it still wasn't much to show for a career that seemed to hold such promise.

Marvin Rainwater's current vantage point for looking back over his life is a house trailer in rural Minnesota, not far from the Canadian border. It gets brutally cold there in winter, but Marvin says he doesn't mind. He owns a sizable tract of land with a lake and the remains of his convenience store, which burned one winter. When Marvin talks about his career, regret percolates to the surface over and over again. Wrong moves, wrong record labels, wrong follow-ups, wrong management advice, wrong investments. Wrong, wrong, wrong. It's not an uncommon litany among performers, but Marvin still has abundant energy and would love to have back the chances that were his in the mid to late fifties.

He was born in Wichita, Kansas, on July 2, 1925, one of five children. His father, Cicero Percy Rainwater, and his mother, Stella, were from Alabama. When Cicero was discharged from the army after the First World War, he listed his occupation as farmer. Cicero and Stella left Alabama in the early twenties to go to Nebraska for the harvest, then came back home before migrating to Kansas. When Cicero settled in Wichita, he drove a bus, and he was still doing that when Marvin was born. He later bought some land in Sunnydale,

fifteen miles from Wichita, and worked as a mechanic and a chauffeur for the Veterans Administration.

Coming from Alabama, Cicero liked "The Grand Ole Opry." He'd haul the battery out of his car on Saturday night and power the radio from it till it ran flat. Then the kids would have to push the car on Monday morning to get it started. Marvin should have grown up idolizing the Opry stars, but he didn't. He started taking piano lessons when he was six years old; his mother took in laundry to finance them. "I was studying classical music, that's why I was so mixed up," he says. "I knew Rimsky-Korsakov, Rachmaninoff, Beethoven, and all them, so when I went into country music, it was just bound to come out funny. I'd heard country music in Kansas, but I didn't like it; all I cared about was my classical piano."

In his teens, Marvin worked part-time at a garage. In a moment of carelessness he lost part of his thumb in an accident. It stopped his classical piano playing cold. "Later," he says, "when I was in the navy I wouldn't even go into a room that had a piano because it broke my heart to see a big beautiful grand and know I couldn't play it properly."

Stella and Cicero separated, and some of the family headed out to the northwest with Cicero; others headed east to Virginia. In 1942 Marvin went to Walla Walla College in Washington State for premed courses before a lack of funds drove him to take a job working with his uncle in the forests near Dallas, Oregon. He was still there when he was inducted into the navy in 1944. He became a pharmacist's mate in the hospital corps.

While he was in the service, Marvin's head was turned around by Roy Acuff. It was "The Precious Jewel" that did it, a song of unbearable loss. After he got out of the navy, Marvin joined his brothers Don and Ray in northeast Virginia, near Washington, D.C. He formed a steady band with Roy Clark and started demoing songs. One of them, "I Gotta Go Get My Baby," was pressed up by 4-Star on a custom label, Rainwater Records, and was then sold to Coral, which promptly covered it with Teresa Brewer. It became a minor pop hit for her in February 1955, and a sizable country hit for Justin Tubb, too.

A couple of months later, Marvin was in New York with his brother Ray and Eddie Crandall. Crandall, later the manager of Marty Robbins and a boyfriend of Hank Williams's widow, Audrey, was a hustler in the D.C. music business. "We were sitting having coffee," said Marvin, "and just on a fluke Ray said, 'Why don't we get Marvin on the Arthur Godfrey Show?' The odds of getting on Godfrey were like nine hundred thousand to one, but Eddie went over there and said 'Marvin's in town.' They said, 'Marvin who?' and Eddie said, 'Marvin Rainwater. He's only filled the Shamrock for seventeen weeks.'

They said, 'How come we didn't know that?' Eddie had neglected to tell them that the Shamrock was not the place in Houston that held twenty-five hundred people, but the one in Georgetown, Virginia, that held about eighteen people. So they said I should come in, and I did all kinds of songs like 'Your Cheatin' Heart' and so on, and the producer said 'We want songs that people know.' So I said, 'What about the Eddy Arnold song "I Really Don't Want To Know"?' He'd never heard of it, so I sung 'I Gotta Go Get My Baby.' This old lady, a spinster, who was one of the senior producers asked me to sing it again, and said she'd put me on the show.

"We got to the afternoon rehearsal and I was just standing there petrified. This gorgeous blonde had just sung 'You Are My Everything' with a forty-four-piece orchestra, and I was strumming my guitar and singing real low, wishing I'd never got into it. That night, I psyched myself up, put on my buckskin jacket and headband, and went out there and won. This girl came over to me and said, 'You didn't sing like that this afternoon.' I said, 'I didn't *feel* like that this afternoon.' From then on I was on every show going. It was like Lady Luck just said, 'I love you.'"

Godfrey ran two shows, the Wednesday night talent show and a regular morning show. Rainwater won the talent show on May 9, 1955, and on July 11 he was called back for a stint on the morning show, variously reported at between one and four weeks. The Godfrey appearances were followed by a call from "The Ozark Jubilee." Back in 1954 Red Foley had quit the Opry, pulled up stakes, and moved to Springfield, Missouri, to host the Jubilee, the first country music show to be broadcast on network television. Marvin relocated to Springfield. "Marvelous days—not much money," is how he remembers it now.

Rainwater also joined the Jubilee touring packages headlined by Foley and starring Porter Wagoner and Ferlin Husky. One night in late 1955 they were in Augusta, Georgia. Backstage, Marvin met one of his father's cousins, who had married a young widow with a precociously talented daughter, Brenda Lee Tarpley. Marvin says that he introduced Brenda Lee to Red Foley and got her on the show. Other accounts don't mention Marvin, but he swears it was his doing.

The Godfrey shows also landed Marvin a recording contract. Ray was talking to Foley's producer, Paul Cohen at Decca Records, when he was approached by Frank Walker, the president of MGM Records. Initially, Walker approached Rainwater to secure the song "Albino Pink Eyed Stallion," which he had heard Marvin sing on Godfrey. Then they talked about Rainwater's becoming an MGM artist. Walker dangled two carrots. The first was that Marvin idolized Hank Williams, and Williams had been on MGM. The second was that the movie division of MGM was planning a Williams bio-pic, and Walker said that he would try to get Marvin considered for the lead. Walker had pushed the right buttons, but the Williams connection was as potent for him as it was for Marvin. Ever since Williams's death, Walker had been trying to find another Hank Williams, because no one had told him that there wasn't going to be another one.

Walker placed Rainwater with Wesley Rose in much the same way that Williams had been produced by Wesley's father, Fred. The first song they cut was "Albino Pink Eyed Stallion." Marvin also cut a tribute to Godfrey called "Tea Bag Romeo," a play on Godfrey's popularity among housewives and the fact that Lipton Tea was his sponsor ("In every living room/There stands an idle broom"). Pretty funny stuff. Marvin Rainwater really was a different kind of country singer.

Just how different Rainwater was became apparent when rockabilly burst onto the scene. Marvin wanted in on it. He cut "Hot and Cold" backed with "Mr. Blues." Roy Clark was all over "Hot and Cold," trading licks with an almost out-of-control steel guitar player named Bill Badgett. "Bill had that fanatical, wild steel sound. Off-the-wall stuff," said Rainwater, adding the bizarre coda that Badgett was killed when a pane of glass fell out of a window and hit him as he was walking down a sidewalk. So many rockabilly records were cut from the same cloth. This was truly different.

Later, Marvin canned Roy Clark for upstaging his country act with rock 'n' roll. "He didn't mean to," he told Bill Millar, "but he upstaged me every night. He was into the Chuck Berry stuff, playing his own lead and wiggling himself back and forth. When I go out singing slow Hank Williams songs, the people would still be hollerin' for Roy."

"Hot and Cold" didn't crack the charts, but Marvin didn't have to wait long. In December 1956 he cut "Gonna Find Me a Bluebird." Wesley Rose was the producer, and in some ways, his production prefigured much of what would later be called the Nashville Sound. A chorus carried the intro that would have been carried by the steel guitar. The fiddle was gone, and Floyd Cramer was on hand with his little trills; Rainwater overdubbed the whistling parts. As he probably knew when he wrapped it up, "Gonna Find Me a Bluebird" was one of those records that's impossible to ignore. Music was bursting out of Marvin Rainwater then. If one style didn't work, he'd try another, but everything was unified by a strange, warped musical intelligence.

The bluebird in his song was an allegory for success—and Marvin found it. In April 1957 the record broke out of the country market, where it crested at Number Three, to reach the pop charts, where it peaked at Number Eighteen. Eddy Arnold, the biggest-selling country artist of the previous decade, tried to cover him, but to no avail. Ray Rainwater claims that even with a record as strong as "Bluebird" on its hands, MGM was asleep at the wheel. He and Marvin went on the road hustling orders from distributors and hyping the record to deejays, he says.

Success was made doubly sweet when Buddy Killen at Tree Music placed Rainwater's composition "I Miss You Already (And You're Not Even Gone)" with Faron Young. It became a Number Five country hit for Young and was a Top Twenty country hit again for Billy Joe Royal in 1988.

The deal with Wesley Rose didn't last long. "We never saw eye to eye," said Rainwater. "He wouldn't go in my direction and that's what caused us to break up. I felt the songs my way, and they didn't want to do it that way. If you give into them, you're not your own artist anymore—you're a horse in their stable doing what they tell you." Frank Walker was on the verge of retirement, and just before he bowed out, he installed Jim Vienneau in the A&R department. Vienneau's qualification for this was that he was Walker's neighbor on Long Island. One of his first moves was to pair Rainwater with an unknown named Connie Francis. The results were dire.

Marvin thought he had hit the big time. He quit "The Ozark Jubilee" and moved to New Jersey. He and Ray started a management office at 48 West Forty-eighth Street in New York. After the follow-up to "Bluebird" sputtered and died, Marvin went back into the studio with a rock 'n' roll song called "Whole Lotta Woman." Cut in Nashville, it was underpinned by Grady Martin's six-string electric bass guitar, which was mixed so up front it could rattle windows two blocks away. The song spent two weeks on the charts, peaking at Number Sixty—a fact that Rainwater attributes to a ban because of imagined obscenity ("She's a whole lotta woman and she's gotta have a whole lotta man"). There was no mention in the trades of any banning, though. Perhaps if it had been banned, it might have done better.

By the middle of April 1958 the record was in retreat in the States, but even before it charted there it was starting to break in England, where it eventually reached Number One. Thirty years later, Marvin can only bemoan the lost opportunity afforded by "Whole Lotta Woman." "It's all trial and error until you find a vein that works for you—then you stick with it. After 'Whole Lotta Woman,' I should've stuck with that and concentrated on it. I didn't realize at the time, it's not your first hit that's important—it's your second and third. I have songs today that I would love to have followed up 'Whole Lotta Woman' with. The first hit just buys you a lot of hard work; it's the second and third hits where you make your money. Back then, I'd have a hit in some field or country and then move on to something else.''

Marvin went to England in April 1958. The tour wasn't a success. With his strange propensity for remembering in minute detail the things that screwed up in his career, Marvin says, "I had a Number One record over there and I thought I'd invented music. Ray and I spent eighteen hundred dollars having arrangements made in the States for the songs I was to do over there, mainly because of the Palladium. We had parts for the second piccolo and so on. I was going to sing songs from *Oklahoma!*, but during rehearsal they said, 'What is this?' so we backed off. I had to start from scratch and ad-lib everything.''

Reviewing a performance at the London Coliseum, *Melody Maker* began by noting, "Many musical comedies have been presented during the 58 years of the London Coliseum. On Sunday yet another was staged.'' Apparently, the first act was a jazz band led by Basil Kirchin, who was followed—after a long break—by an expatriate American, Johnny Duncan. Then came Phil Fernando, an Indian rock 'n' roller, and then came Marvin, who was inaudible for the first few songs and was offstage soon after that.

Marvin's last glimpse of Hot 100 action came with "Half-Breed, " a song specially written for him by John D. Loudermilk. "I wrote the beginning, the narration, and so on and never got any credit, " said Rainwater. But it wasn't the narration that sold "Half-Breed"; it was the pop market's infatuation with pseudo-folk songs in the wake of the Kingston Trio's "Tom Dooley.'' "Half-Breed " fitted into that mold and rose up to Number Sixty-six in the pop charts and Number Sixteen in the country listings.

Marvin eventually dropped the Indian image. "It was my idea to start it,'' he says, "but it wasn't such a good one. I'd go onto Indian reservations and they'd say, 'You're not Indian, you've got blue eyes.' So the Indians didn't like me, and the white people didn't like Indians.'' Before then, Marvin played two more variations on the theme. One was his own "The Valley of the Moon,'' and the other was a Loudermilk composition, "The Pale-Faced Indian.'' In one of those weird twists of fate that the record business delivers up, "The Pale-Faced Indian" was covered ten years later by an English busker, Don Fardon, who cut it as "Indian Reservation" and took it up to Number Three on the British charts. Then it was covered in the United States in 1971 by Paul Revere and the Raiders, who took it to Number One. Marvin has always maintained that he and Marijohn Wilkin wrote part of "Pale-Faced Indian," "but,'' he says resignedly, "you get tired of suing people.''

Marvin and Ray had the idea of using Marvin's money to launch a country music magazine, *Trail*. Initially, Marvin dissented—he wanted to buy up some bowling alleys—but in the end he went along with the idea. Ray knew how many washed-up hillbilly singers there were, and he wanted something that he and Marvin could fall back on when Marvin no longer wanted to perform 250 days a year. The example of Roy Acuff was uppermost in Ray's mind. Acuff had funded his retirement by investing in Acuff-Rose, and Ray saw *Trail* as a comparable venture.

"It took all the money I was making to keep that thing running, but it was a hard row to hoe," says Marvin. "The telephone bill was twelve hundred dollars a month, and the print bill was sixty thousand dollars a month, and the magazine just wasn't moving. We'd get covers back every month by the bale. It was a good idea, but we didn't have quite enough money to see us through that initial period. By the time we could go out and start getting full-page ads, we didn't have any more money left." *Trail* started in February 1958 and continued for seven issues—three full-sized and four digest-sized.

Marvin and Ray parted company soon after that. Ray went into the excavation and waste disposal business in the D.C. area and has made a small fortune at it. Marvin soldiered on, but his problems were mounting.

The new decade dawned with Marvin Rainwater still an MGM artist—just. By now his voice had been scorched by too many one-nighters in smoky clubs, where he would play three sets a night with a pickup band. Calluses were forming on his vocal cords. "After my voice started going, we had a lot of problems," he said. "I'd overdub and rerecord and rerecord, sometimes seventy-five takes. One night Jim Vienneau was walking around the studio holding a twenty-dollar bill that he'd set fire to—seeing if I'd get the message. I started drinking gin, and Jim just walked out."

The low point came with a New York session. "They were making fun of me," he says. "I could see them up in the control room making jokes. My wife was in tears because I was trying to sing, and my voice was just shot. The node on the vocal cords meant that I was hitting a note in two places instead of one—it's like you're singing in harmony with yourself, except you're not in key." MGM's termination notice was mailed soon after. Marvin now had no voice and no money.

There were many more records for many more labels, and even one more hit in Europe. The stuff worth listening to, though, is an eccentric collection of rock and country songs Marvin made for that least eccentric of labels, MGM. "In country music," he says, "you're supposed to find a groove and stick with it. I'd get a good pattern going and then, next record, I'd change it. Each song was like a complete little symphony to me. It'd frustrate everyone who worked with me because they couldn't figure me out. Every time I'd get something good going, I'd head down another road. I was stubborn about it, too.

"Some people have it so easy. They just walk up and everything just opens up. I don't know how hard they worked to do it, but no matter how hard I worked, it always turned around the other way." ◉

FOR YOUR LISTENING PLEASURE
There is absolutely nothing available in North America; "Gonna Find Me a Bluebird " isn't even on a budget CD. In Germany, Bear Family has issued all of Rainwater's recordings on a four-CD set, *Classic Recordings* (BCD 15600), and excerpted the rock 'n' roll sides on a single CD, *Whole Lotta Woman* (BCD 15812).

Jimmy Swan

. . . .

DAMN IF THAT'S SO!

Every now and again, on the twenty-fifth anniversary of something or other, there's a PBS documentary about Mississippi during the civil rights era. Do you ever wonder what happened to those white guys in their white shirts and their broad-brimmed Panama hats, cleaving so unbendingly and unflinchingly to the old ways? Their faces were intransigence itself. Do you ever wonder if they warmed a little to the changes that overtook their society as the years wore on?

If Jimmy Swan is anything to go by, the answer is that they didn't. He hewed as closely to the old ways as anyone, and his South has almost gone—in its visible aspects, at least. Swan was born in Alabama and hoboed to Mississippi in his teens. He shined Jimmie Rodgers's shoes, walked a few hundred miles behind a mule, played the joints, worked with Hank Williams and Elvis Presley when they were on the brink of next-big-thingdom, and twice stood for governor of Mississippi on an avowedly segregationist platform. In retirement, he was careful not to use the inflammatory language he once used. He trod lightly around his controversial political past, preferring instead to talk about his six-year-old great-grandson.

Jimmy Swan, originally Schwann, was of mixed German and Cherokee ancestry. He was born in Cullman County in northern Alabama, an area first settled by a German named Cuhlmann in the nineteenth century. Jimmy's parents farmed the part of Cullman County known as Sand Mountain, which was also home to the Louvin Brothers. His grandfather Sidney Schwann was from Germany by way of North Carolina, and his grandmother was a full-blood Cherokee from Tennessee.

Jimmy was born on November 18, 1912. His father left earlier than Jimmy could remember, and his mother moved the family to Birmingham in 1922. Jimmy grew up there shining shoes and selling newspapers. He remembered buffing Jimmie Rodgers's pointy-toed shoes in a pool hall, and when he started singing he took his cue from the Singing Brakeman, as did so many others. In 1928, calling himself "The Singing Newsboy," he won a talent contest sponsored by WKBC in Birmingham. His mother died not long after that, and times got tougher still. He remembered railroad workers throwing overripe bananas to him down at the yards. Some days, he said, that was all he had to eat.

Swan and a buddy hoboed into Mississippi when he was fifteen. He married at seventeen and worked on farms in Jasper County. In 1944 he settled in Hattiesburg, one hundred miles northeast of New Orleans, so that his kids could get an education. By then, he had already put in a stint in the Mobile shipyards, and it was in Mobile that he put together his first band. He had been classified 4-A for military service because of problems with his right eye, so he worked on Liberty Ships at the Alabama Shipyard during the day and played the joints on weekends. Every Saturday morning he had a thirty-minute show on WALA. His first band included Hank Locklin, who went on to rule the airwaves in 1958 with "Send Me the Pillow You Dream On" and with "Please Help Me, I'm Falling" two years later. Among those who sat in from time to time was Hank Williams, classified 4-F and making a minimal contribution to the war effort in Mobile.

After the war, Swan returned to Hattiesburg, worked live radio on WFOR, and played the local beer halls during the week, and the Hattiesburg Civic Center every Saturday night. Then, as he said, "I got tired of those ol' honky-tonks. I never was a drinker. I ain't saying I'm a saint, but I got values. These were knock-down, drag-out honky-tonks—fightin', killin', all that stuff. One night a whole lot got killed where I was playing, and I told my wife, 'I'm gettin' tired of gettin' on radio and invitin' all them people to come out and kill each other.' I wasn't getting no money for singing live on the radio, just a little sponsorship from a beer company, so I went into disc-jockeying." This was 1948 or 1949, and disc-jockeying was a relatively new phenomenon in country music. After the switch, Jimmy played live only on Saturday nights at the Civic Center. He remained a deejay until 1991 and, at the time he quit, reckoned he was the oldest active deejay in the country.

On April 17, 1952, Jimmy signed with Trumpet Records, based ninety miles north of Hattiesburg in Jackson, Mississippi. With all the music coming out of Mississippi, there should have been record companies dotted all across the delta; as it was, Trumpet was just about the only game in any town between New Orleans and Memphis. The story of Trumpet is almost a made-for-TV plot. The label was started in 1950 by a twenty-eight-year-old white woman, Lillian McMurry. She and her husband, Willard, operated a furniture store and picked up some R&B records in a salvage lot. Lillian thought they would sell better if people could hear them, so she set up a PA system and made a believer of herself. Some Trumpet sessions were cut right in the furniture store, with mattresses acting as baffles. Her most famous discoveries were Sonny Boy Williamson and Elmore James.

Jimmy wasn't the first white artist on Trumpet, as he said, but he was the first to have a hillbilly record that amounted to anything on the label. McMurry was from the Hattiesburg area, and she heard about his band and came down to check him out. The first session was cut in the WFOR studio; Jimmy's first record was "I Had a Dream," a song full of images as dark and haunting as any Hank Williams ever conjured up:

> I cried, I cried,
> I called your name,
> But never one answer you gave,
> And when the storm had passed us by
> Another had stole you away.

Swan insists that he wrote the song and that Lillian McMurry took the composer credit. Certainly McMurry never wrote anything else remotely in that vein; Swan did. "I Had a Dream" was a good seller, although it didn't chart nationally. The country charts had only fifteen positions then, and releases on independent labels in out-of-the-way places usually didn't show up at all, so its failure to chart really means nothing. The fact that it was covered by Ann Clark on Ace, Billy Walker on Columbia, and Jean Chapel on RCA attests to its popularity.

"I Had a Dream" came out in the summer of 1952, and Swan was already promoting a follow-up when he heard over the wire on New Year's Day 1953 that Hank Williams had died. Jimmy and Hank had stayed in touch since the war and had played a date together in Biloxi just a few weeks before Hank's death. Hank hadn't seemed in such bad shape then. His new bride, Billie Jean, was with him, and they were making goo-goo eyes at each other. Jimmy had even gone to their wedding in New Orleans a few weeks before that.

Hank had recorded for MGM, and in the hours after his death, the president of MGM Records, Frank Walker, had sat down and written an open letter to him in care of "Songwriter's Paradise." That sort of gesture lends itself to oily insincerity, and Walker's open letter stands with Jerry Lee Lewis's 1958 public apology as among the oiliest and most patently insincere ever written:

> Do you know, I think HE wanted to have you just a bit closer to HIM.
> Nashville's pretty far away, so HE just sent word this morning Hank, that
> HE wanted you with him. . . . You'll be writing for the greatest singers too,
> the Angels, they're so wonderful—I know they'll want you to join them.

Jimmy saw the letter in *Cashbox* and got the notion to record it as a nar-

99

Mississippi, 1944. Jimmy (second from left) leads the Blue Sky Playboys
with Hank Locklin (second from right)
Photo courtesy of C. Escott

ration. At the same time, Luke McDaniel recorded "A Tribute to Hank Williams, My Buddy" for Trumpet. Apparently, McDaniel's credentials for being Hank's buddy were that Swan had introduced them at the benefit in Biloxi. From his vantage point in heaven, Hank might have reflected that if he'd had as many buddies in life as he appeared to have in death, he might not have died in the wretched circumstances he did.

Lillian McMurry sensed an opportunity. She rushed dubs of both Swan's and McDaniel's records to Frank Walker by Air Express. "The Last Letter" touched the old man's vanity, and he issued it in two couplings; one with Hank Williams's "I Saw the Light" on the flip, and another with Jimmy's own gospel piece "The Little Church." Hank Williams tribute records were now hitting the stores in droves. Some seemed to have been pressed before rigor mortis had set in. Jimmy's wasn't the first, and certainly wasn't the last. Royalties were to go to the Hank Williams Memorial Fund, whatever that was.

Walker, who would spend the last five years of his presidency at MGM signing moderately good country singers believing them to be the next Hank Williams, heard his first potential successor in Jimmy Swan and offered to buy his contract from Trumpet. Swan insists that McMurry wanted so much money for it that Walker and Fred Rose at Acuff-Rose (who had been Hank Williams's producer), decided that they would wait out the contract and sign Jimmy when it was up in 1955.

Unfortunately for Jimmy Swan, Fred Rose expired before the Trumpet contract did. Jimmy still got his deal with MGM, but he believed that Rose could have helped him shape his songwriting, as he had helped Hank shape his. "When I was in Nashville one time waiting for my contract to run out, I mentioned to Fred Rose that I had the same problem Hank had," said Swan. "I could put together good lyrics, but I had problems with the melody. Fred said, 'Well, wait till you get here, and we'll straighten you out.' Fred dying like that was the worst thing ever happened to me."

In truth, the worst thing that happened to Jimmy Swan was that country music changed. His vision of the music was as stern and unbending as his politics. There was a fiddle, a steel guitar, a broken heart, and retribution—if not on earth then for sure in heaven. His fourth MGM record, "The Way That You're Living (Is Breaking My Heart)," is firmly in that mold, and it was a minor hit in 1956. It marked a last sweet flowering of hillbilly music: "My head now is bowed, you've tored me apart/The way that you're livin' is breakin' my heart."

"Time come for the next session," said Jimmy, "and I sent up six songs to Fred's son, Wesley, for consideration, and he picked four. I come up and I

Jimmy's stationery when he was running for governor
Photo courtesy of J. Swan/C. Escott

heard that the fiddle player, Tommy Jackson, was going out on tour on Monday, and the session was set up for Monday. I went to Wesley and I told him we'd better cut the session on Sunday. Wesley said, 'We're not going to use Tommy.' I said, 'Whaddya mean?' He said, 'We're going to use the Anita Kerr Singers.' I said, 'Man, no, no.' I told him we'd worked hard and finally got a hit, so why change? He said, 'Everybody else in the country is changing, we're changing with 'em.' I said, 'Damn if that's so. I'm going home.'"

So while everyone else in country music was gritting their teeth and cutting rockabilly or pop-flavored country, Jimmy Swan stuck to his guns and went back to Hattiesburg. He later alienated Wesley Rose even more when he testified on behalf of Hank Williams's second wife, Billie Jean, at the hearings that preceded the copyright renewals on Williams's songs. A protracted series of court cases eventually saw the Williams estate and Acuff-Rose lose half of the renewal rights to Billie Jean and Hill and Range Music.

Jimmy Swan didn't record again for three years after he and Wesley Rose parted company. In late 1959 he cut a four-song session on his own dime in Biloxi and sold it to the local representative of Decca Records. Decca issued one single, which sold so poorly that the other two cuts were kept in the can. Still, Jimmy carried on recording into the sixties for ever smaller labels, and his records showed that his concept of country music wasn't changing much. Remarkably, a decade or more of spinning current hits on the radio had left his own music more or less untouched.

Shortly after the Decca single was issued, Jimmy bought a stake in WKBH in Hattiesburg, and he used his local profile to run for sheriff, then venture into state politics. He first tossed his hat into the ring in 1966 when he announced that he was trying for the governorship the following year on a platform of state's rights and against what was then called the Great Society. He pointed out the similarities between himself and Jimmie Davis, who had twice moved with apparent ease into the governor's mansion in Louisiana after a career in music.

Speaking at the Jimmie Rodgers Day celebrations in Meridian, Swan said he was running on principles that Mississippians held dear: "God, then states' rights, honest government, and segregation." Federal judges had, according to Swan, "torn our constitution to shreds with the help of the Communist Party." Outsiders trying to meddle in Mississippi would have their "communist pink hides [slammed] in jail. These so-called Federal judges can turn them out, and I'll slam them right back in," he promised. He placed third in the race for the Democratic nomination.

Four years later he tried again, and he reckons he came close to winning the nomination in 1971, when he stood against the black mayor of Fayette, Charles Evers. His platform hadn't moderated much, and on the occasion of his first formal speech in June 1971, he called for segregation and declared that those who wouldn't join the fight were "not worth the powder and shot it would take to blow their brains out."

Later in life he took a slightly more conciliatory view of his position, saying that he was primarily opposed to busing schoolchildren to achieve a racial balance in the classroom. Even so, time didn't mellow Jimmy Swan much. He trod warily around the question of how he saw the state of affairs in Mississippi. "I don't come out and make any statements at all these days," he said. "I don't like it, but I just tolerate it. Don't get me wrong, though, I'm not a hater, and I'm not a racist. I always want to make that clear."

Jimmy Swan just barely tolerated it. The Great Society was always the welfare culture to him. All it had done, he said, was raise four generations of people on handouts. Why couldn't these people work their way out of their problems as he had done? "I hear today," he said, "about poor blacks and poor whites, but shoot, man, ain't none of them ever had the time I've had."

Jimmy Swan's music was hard-bitten music, and his politics were hard-bitten politics. If he was any indication of what those white men in their broad-brimmed panama hats thought about the changing face of Mississippi, it's that they once knew a much happier time and place.

Early in 1994, Jimmy Swan married for a second time. He moved to Jackson, Mississippi, and died there in December that year. ⊚

FOR YOUR LISTENING PLEASURE

The only anthology of Jimmy Swan's music is Bear Family's *Honky Tonkin' in Mississippi,* which includes all of his Trumpet, MGM, and Decca recordings, as well as some that Jimmy made later for small labels in Mississippi.

Photo courtesy of C. Escott

Melvin Endsley

· ·

NEVER FELT MORE LIKE
SINGING THE BLUES

Drasco, Arkansas, is small. A crossroads, a store, and maybe one hundred people. It's in the Ozark foothills, close to the heat, the dust, and the inexorable flatness of east Arkansas, but a world apart from it. There's a large ranch house about a mile out of Drasco. It's the house that "Singing the Blues" built.

Melvin Endsley never moved out of Drasco, although he was tempted to sell and go to Nashville a couple of times. He is a short man, confined to a wheelchair. A wife and kids are in the background, but they're never introduced. Endsley's conversation doesn't give much away in terms of his feelings. The most that he is willing to share is information relating to his career. It's not hard to infer the rest, though.

On some level, the guardedness is understandable. Endsley wants to be viewed as a songwriter and performer, not as a cripple. He doesn't want special consideration or dispensation. He was born on January 30, 1934, and when he was three years old he contracted polio, which withered his right arm and left him without the use of his legs. His parents sent him to the Crippled Children's Hospital in Memphis. "I was there for two years, between 1946 and 1947," he says. "It was lonely; my parents only came down once all the while I was there, but that's when I started playing the guitar. Wayne Raney and the Delmore Brothers were on radio in Memphis at that time. I got interested enough to know what I wanted to do. I wanted to write and sing and get on radio like them."

Endsley went back to Drasco and enrolled at Concord High School. By the time he graduated in May 1954, he had already written one of his best songs, "It Happens Every Time." A couple of people later had minor hits with it. His first stab at performing was on KCON in Conway, Arkansas (the town Harold Jenkins lit upon when he was casting around for a new name—a minute or two before he found Twitty, Texas). At the same time that he was starting to write songs, Endsley was writing himself an insurance policy by enrolling at the state teachers' college.

KWCB in Searcy broadcast a Saturday afternoon jamboree with Wayne

Raney, who was a big noise in that part of Arkansas; he was a local hero who had done well on King Records with novelties like "Why Don't You Haul Off and Love Me " and "Pardon My Whiskers." "Wayne was the host and star of the jamboree," says Endsley, "and he'd bring us all on. I guess there was maybe half a dozen of us local artists trying to get started." It was the Saturday afternoon listeners to KWCB who first heard "Singing the Blues." It got a good response, and Endsley drew encouragement from that.

A little later, he read an article in *Country Song Roundup* that explained the steps that amateur songwriters needed to take in order not to be ripped off. Endsley took the advice to heart and, in July 1954, sent off lead sheets for "Singing the Blues" (then called "I've Never Felt More Like Singing the Blues") and "It Happens Every Time" to the Library of Congress, together with eight dollars to register them for copyright.

From the outset, Endsley had a gift for crafting melodies that seem so familiar you think you've heard them before, even if you haven't. Then the words, which were usually fairly inconsequential, fell into place as if guided by the unseen hand of the melody. All the lessons Endsley ever had came from the radio: Hank Williams, Lefty Frizzell, and Ernest Tubb.

Endsley knew that songs sent on acetates from podunk towns in Arkansas usually had a bleakly predictable future in Nashville, so he decided to go there in person. In July 1955 he traded in the old car he had bought to get to and from school and bought one that he felt might make the long round trip. Then he borrowed thirty dollars from his family and got into the car with his next-door neighbor, Jimmie Douglas Grimes, who had $2.50 left from his wages at a rock-crushing site. They headed for Nashville and arrived one Thursday night. They slept in the car, knowing that their best shot would come on Friday and Saturday nights when the Opry stars came back into town. Endsley hoped to pitch his songs to Webb Pierce.

"I met Marty Robbins before he went on the 'Friday Night Frolics,'" said Endsley. "I asked him if he could find time for us to get together and listen to half a dozen songs. He said, 'Well, I'm signed up with Acuff-Rose, and they don't care if I listen to anyone else's material or not because they want mine.' I said, 'If you don't like something well enough to record it, I'd still like for you to hear it.' He said, 'OK, we'll get together after the show.' After he'd been on, we met back in his room. Jimmie Douglas borrowed Marty's guitar and I sang my songs. 'Singing the Blues' was the last one. The others didn't impress him, but he knew he needed 'Singing the Blues.' He called up Wesley Rose [the president of Acuff-Rose Music] and made me an appointment for the next morning. I stayed across the street from Acuff-Rose, at the York Motel. Marty told Wesley that he should hold 'Singing the Blues' and 'Knee Deep in the Blues' for him. Wesley gave me a contract on all the songs I brought down. They all got cut, too.

"We drove back on Saturday night and the Opry was coming through loud and clear in the car. Marty was on that night. He did 'Long Gone Lonesome Blues.' Jimmie Douglas said, 'If he can make that song sound so good, just imagine what he can do to 'Singing the Blues.'"

It was a blessing in disguise that Endsley hadn't got to Webb Pierce. If he had, his songs might still have appeared, because Pierce was nothing if not a good judge of a song, but they would have had the mysterious addition of Pierce's name to the composer credit, and that would have cost Endsley some hundreds of thousands of dollars over the years. Robbins and Acuff-Rose were almost embarrassingly honest.

Robbins was in no rush to record "Singing the Blues," though. The face of country music was changing, and he was trying to keep abreast of it all by cutting rockabilly records. "Singing the Blues" went on a back burner. It was too country, and Robbins couldn't find an arrangement he liked. He was on the point of pitching the song to Faron Young when his steel guitar player, Jim Farmer, suggested that he inject a little yodel into it, like Hank Williams's yodel on "Lovesick Blues." Robbins tried it and liked it, and the arrangement fell into place. His next session was slated for November 1955, but because "Singing the Blues " sounded too country, it wasn't released until the following August. Country as it was, it damned the smart money by entering the charts, then monopolizing the Number One spot from mid-November until the following February. It was the first hit Robbins had seen in two years.

Robbins might have taken the song into the pop charts as well, but he was thwarted by his own record company, Columbia Records. Guy Mitchell covered "Singing the Blues " on Columbia, so while Robbins sat at Number One in the country charts with the song and sold six hundred thousand copies, Mitchell sat at Number One in the pop charts and sold over two million. Endsley didn't care; he was collecting one cent per copy in songwriter royalties, with cover versions, airplay royalties, and sheet music sales kicking in on top of that. Robbins, though, was furious, more so after exactly the same scenario played itself out with Endsley's "Knee Deep in the Blues."

Between the time that Robbins cut "Singing the Blues" and Columbia released it, the other three songs that Endsley had brought up to Nashville were cut. Don Gibson recorded "It Happens Every Time," Billy Worth cut "Too Many Times," and Bud Deckelman did "I Love You Still." They all appeared on MGM, where Wesley Rose acted as producer. Then, at the beginning of 1957, Janis Martin cut another of Endsley's songs, "Love Me to Pieces," which later became a pop hit for Jill Corey. Almost overnight, Melvin Endsley was the writer most in demand in country music.

With all this attention focused on his songs, Endsley had enough ammunition to get his own recording contract. He convinced Wesley Rose that he deserved a break as a singer, and Rose talked Chet Atkins into signing him to RCA's Nashville division. Looking back, Endsley has mixed feelings about his RCA deal. He saw himself—with good reason—as a singer, but he came to believe that both Rose and Atkins saw him as a song quarry. "I knew they wanted me for my songs," he says. "I think Wesley talked to Chet and said, 'We need to get all the material we can.' There were only one or two who really believed in me as an artist, and three or four who thought I'd better concentrate on my writing"

Endsley saved some prime cuts for his crack at performing; still, they became better known through cover versions than through Endsley's performances. "I Like Your Kind of Love," from the first session, was scooped by Andy Williams for the pop market, and "I'd Just Be Fool Enough" was later covered by Jimmy Newman, Johnny Cash, the Browns, and Faron Young. Other songs, like the haunting and eerie "Bringing the Blues to My Door," somehow missed being covered. The shame of it all was that Endsley was no slouch as a singer. In fact, he was really very good. He got better projection from a wheelchair than most singers get standing up, and he sang with riveting conviction. Transcribed on a page, his words often seemed like rejuggled clichés—some from Hank, some from Lefty—but Endsley made them all desperately real.

Country fanzines gave Endsley some ink, emphasizing the Cinderella aspects of his story, making it seem as though his songwriting career had somehow been visited upon him, ignoring the fact that Endsley had, through pure ambition, stubbornness, and cussedness, made it happen. His misfortune was that he was signed to RCA at the very moment that most RCA salesmen could make their month's quota in a day on Elvis records, then head for the golf course. He still has fond memories of working with Chet Atkins, though. "Chet would turn you loose in the studio," he says, "and let you sing songs the way you felt them. I'd put down the songs on tape for the musicians, and they'd learn from the tape. We'd work out the arrangements right there. I'd want to use little things I'd heard in my head, and Chet would say, 'Let's use Melvin's licks.' A lot of guys wouldn't let you express yourself that way in the studio." Endsley also played the chunky rhythm guitar on some cuts. Naturally left-handed, he was unable to form chords with his withered right hand, so he played in open tunings with the butt end of a silver knife laid across the strings.

After two years with RCA, Wesley Rose signed Endsley to MGM. He got a one-year deal that saw three singles hit the market, but they didn't chart, and Endsley was cast adrift when his term was up. In 1960 and 1961 he recorded for Acuff-Rose's house label, Hickory Records. The label was doing well then, but none of its success rubbed off onto Endsley. He left the label when he quit Acuff-Rose to sign with Marty Robbins's publishing companies.

Few country songwriters are hot for long, and as his success tailed off, Endsley almost gave in to the temptation to move to Nashville. It first crossed his mind in 1957. In 1971 he got as far as buying a piece of land in the Nashville area, but in the end he stayed in Drasco. After the Hickory deal ended, he recorded for his own Mel-Ark label, but has since ceased recording altogether. His last major writing success was his coauthorship of the 1960 Stonewall Jackson smash "Why I'm Walkin.'"

In late 1956 and all through 1957, Melvin Endsley was golden. "Singing the Blues," "Knee Deep in the Blues," "Love Me to Pieces," and "I Like Your Kind of Love" were all riding high, and Endsley's own career looked promising. He was guesting on the "Friday Night Frolics" and touring with "Grand Ole Opry" and "Louisiana Hayride" package shows. Everyone wanted first crack at the next Melvin Endsley song.

If it's hard to warm to Endsley, it's not hard to admire him. He never let his disability become an excuse for inactivity. He wrote one of the half dozen most memorable songs in country music, a distinction that has usually fallen to men with troubled minds rather than troubled bodies. He never achieved the success that he felt was his due as a singer, but his songs are still producing like a bottomless oil well. ◉

FOR YOUR LISTENING PLEASURE

Bear Family has issued all of Endsley's RCA, MGM, and Hickory recordings (*I Like Your Kind of Love*, BCD 15595), and Endsley himself has reissued his Hickory and Mel-Ark recordings (*Getting Used to the Blues*, Mel-Ark NR 19405, available from specialist mail-order outlets or from Endsley at 1289 Greers Ferry Road, Drasco, AR 72530). Marty Robbins's recording of "Singing the Blues" is available on just about every Robbins hit package.

Johnny Horton

. . . .

DEATH OF A HONKY-TONK MAN, 1

The paradox of Johnny Horton is that he is remembered for his music, but unlike most musicians, he had no deep-seated commitment to it. It was just something else he tried; if it hadn't panned out, he would have moved on. Fishing, hunting, even dabbling in spiritualism were more important to him. His voice had a sunny good-naturedness to it, apparently a reflection of his character, but the amiability masked a complex soul, a soul as elusive as all the wraiths he chased.

The Hortons came from Alabama. Johnny's father, John "Lolly" Horton, and his mother, Ella Claudia Robinson, married on December 15, 1912, and settled on a land grant near Tyler, Texas. Their first son, Fred, was born in 1914; their first daughter, Nola Bea, in 1915; their second son, Frank, in 1918; and their second daughter, Marie, in 1922. A little later the family moved to San Diego, California, and subsequently to East Los Angeles. It was there, on April 30, 1925, while Lolly was working with a construction crew building Garfield High School, that the Hortons' last child, John LaGale, was born. When asked, Johnny Horton always said he was born in 1929 in Tyler.

The Horton family moved constantly. Like a tape loop of *The Grapes of Wrath*, they shuttled back and forth between East Texas and southern California. Once their car caught fire on the wooden roads that crossed the desert. "The grass was always greener somewhere else for my dad," said Frank Horton. "He'd say, 'Better get goin'.' " They made the trip between Texas and California as often as four times a year. They picked cotton and fruit along the way.

The older children left home during the thirties. Fred went to California, and Frank followed him, abandoning his day job to be a professional gambler. Johnny graduated from high school in 1944 and briefly attended a Methodist seminary with one eye on the ministry. A few months later he moved on to Kilgore College, then Baylor University in Waco for ten days, and then he too went out to California. By 1947 he was working in the mail room at Selznick studios and living in an apartment with Frank on La Cienega Boulevard. At Selznick

The honky tonk man
Photo courtesy of C. Escott

Horton and Johnny Cash on the streets of Cash's hometown, Dyess, Arkansas, 1959
Photo courtesy of C. Escott

he met Donna Cook, who would later become his first wife. Her mother ran a liquor store in Culver City, a dream come true for most hillbilly singers, but Horton didn't drink then and never would, probably because he had seen his father's alcoholism tear the family apart.

"Frank and Johnny were two of the most handsome men you ever met," said Donna. "Even then Johnny had a certain charisma about him; you couldn't help but like him. He had an easygoing charm that could sell snow to Eskimos. He was trying to overcome his family background. He never had a sense of social inferiority, but he didn't want to be that poor. Ever." Frank and Johnny enrolled at university in Seattle in the fall of 1948 to study geology, but they dropped out a few weeks later. Compulsory French and math had derailed them. They headed off to Florida, then backtracked to California. Johnny stopped off to work in a fruit-packing plant for a while, and Frank went back to Seattle to manage a sporting goods store. Johnny arrived later and decided to go on to Alaska to work on construction sites. In the back of his mind, he had the idea that he would look for gold. He took paid passage to Anchorage for a winter's work, and there, in the endless night, he started writing songs and singing.

Back in Seattle, he joined Frank for the trip to Los Angeles. Frank stayed in Los Angeles, where he married in 1950. Johnny headed on to Texas. His sister Marie encouraged him to enter a talent contest hosted by the then-unknown Jim Reeves at the Reo Palm Isle club in Longview. Horton won, and he came back to Marie's house with the prize: an ashtray on a pedestal. Insubstantial as it was, it gave Horton the impetus to try for a career in music when he went back to California late in 1950.

"I was really amazed when he announced he was going to try for a career in entertainment," said Donna. "I'd never heard him sing, although he could pound out a little boogie-woogie on the piano." Unlike most musicians, Horton had no deep-seated need for applause, but he gave music his best shot. He bought some western clothes and entered more talent contests. At one of them he was noticed by Fabor Robison.

Robison was a transplanted Southerner—the consensus is that he came from Arkansas. By the late forties he was in Los Angeles trying to hustle his way into the movie business. He bore a passing facial resemblance to Robert Young and is rumored, although the rumor could have originated with Fabor himself, to have worked as a stand-in for Young on some movies. Robison was one of the hyperbolic characters who populated the music business before it was run by accountants and lawyers. He had a bottomless fund of stories; some of them might even have been true. He once claimed to have looted a bank in Germany after the war, buried the money, but then forgotten where he had buried it by the time he got back there. If true, it was a metaphor for his life. He would discover, manage, and record a rich variety of artists, lose them all, and have them hate him. When the record business went sour, he would turn to other scams like the cold-weather tanning tube. When everything went sour, he would disappear; Brazil was home for a few years. He became Johnny Horton's manager in late 1950 or early 1951.

One of Fabor's music industry contacts was Les McWain, the "Mac" in the small Cormac label. "I suggested to Johnny that he make a record," said McWain, "but he resisted. He was very shy and didn't think he could sing, but I liked the little yodel he worked in at the end of a line, and I thought he had a very pleasant voice." Robison also got Horton on several Los Angeles–area western dance parties, such as "Hometown Jamboree." Horton even had his own show on KSLA-TV, in Pasadena, for a while. He appeared as the Singing Fisherman; he'd sing a few songs, then do party tricks such as casting a sugar cube into a jar of water at the other end of the soundstage. To make ends meet, he was a professional fly tester for a tackle manufacturer and an assembly line worker for an aircraft manufacturer, but he had what amounted to a phobia of regular day jobs. Fred's wife, Ann, remembers him saying, "I'm not going to work like you do." And he rarely did.

Horton's first Cormac record was released in the spring of 1951. The label folded after his second single. Robison got the masters, then started Abbott Records with the express purpose of recording Horton. Abbott appears to have been a partnership between Robison and the proprietor of an Abbott drugstore in Los Angeles. By November 1951, when he placed an advertisement in *Billboard* on Horton's behalf, Robison had six Johnny Horton records out on Abbott, two of them reissued from Cormac. Most of them were in the western tradition: breezy, amiable, but utterly undistinctive.

At the end of 1951 Horton finally married Donna, over Fabor's objections. Almost immediately they moved to Shreveport so that Johnny could make regular appearances on "The Louisiana Hayride." His parents were living nearby in a small house on their daughter Nola Bea's property.

Early in 1952 Fabor peddled Horton's recording contract to Mercury Records. "He was totally dedicated to Johnny," said Mercury's Dee Kilpatrick. "He made a trip to Nashville, and he had some tapes, and I suggested that he bring Horton in. We talked for two days, and I tried to get on a frequency with Horton, but it was hard to tell where he was coming from. He was so involved with fishing and tackle demonstrations. He was a top man in that field and knew it inside out. Fabor complained that he couldn't get the distribution he wanted, and I guess he figured he could make more off the management if he could sell some more records." The first Mercury record, "The First Train Heading South," was an improvement over any of the Abbott records. It was a homesick Southerner's lament, like Johnny Cash's "Hey! Porter," with a side order of Hank Snow. It didn't do much business, though.

Donna quickly became disenchanted with life in Shreveport. She moved to a small apartment by herself for a short period, hoping that things would work out, but in the end she gave up and went back to Los Angeles. "I'd try to get involved in his career, going around to radio stations and so on, " she said, "but it felt as though Fabor was running our life. It was like Johnny was married to Fabor, and I was an afterthought. Fabor handled all the money, and he had convinced Johnny that he couldn't do anything without him. He was driving a big car and we were putt-putting along."

Horton cut a dashing figure on the Hayride. He was tall, gregarious, good looking, and immaculately outfitted in the western shirts that Nola Bea had hand-tailored for him. The only item of clothing more likely to be seen on him was a hat, and that was because he was losing his hair fast."He was real temperamental about that," said his guitarist, Bob Stegall. "We'd check into the motel after a show, and he'd make us massage stuff into his scalp, trying to make some hair grow. Then he'd read something and lie upside down, and we'd massage something else into his head. He was really tryin' to grow some hair."

Three months after Horton joined the Hayride, Hank Williams returned. Now the biggest name in country music, he was almost unbookable. "The Grand Ole Opry " had canned him for habitual no-shows, and he arrived back in Shreveport in September 1952 to try to regroup. A month later, he married Billie Jean Jones in front of two paying audiences in New Orleans. Horton toured with Hank on several short Hayride tours. On one occasion, Hank had Billie Jean with him. "One of these days," Hank told her in a blinding insight afforded by alcohol, "you're gonna marry him."

Hank Williams's last gig was at the Skyline Club in Austin, Texas—the site of Horton's last gig, almost eight years later. There is an apocryphal story that Horton and his band heard the news of Williams's death while they were driving through Milano, Texas—later the site of Horton's death. Hank became one of Johnny Horton's fixations. The window would rattle; Horton would say, "That's Hank trying to get in touch."

"Hank knew Johnny better than I did," Billie told the journalist John Prime. "Hank was actually a fan. He would stop the car if we were riding along and Johnny came on the radio. I remember the last record Hank heard him sing, 'The Child's Side of Life,' which was a real dog. After it was over, he turned it off and said, 'No son, this one ain't gonna make it.' But he told me that one day Johnny would be one of the biggest stars in the business."

Johnny Horton married Billie Jean on September 26, 1953. At first the living was easy because of the settlement she had received a month earlier from the Williams estate, but Horton was still a long way from making ends meets as an entertainer. He and Fabor soon parted company. Fabor had discovered Jim Reeves, and Reeves had scored his first hit, "Mexican Joe." The singlemindedness that Fabor had once applied to Horton's career was now applied to Reeves's. Then, in November 1954, *Billboard* reported that Horton had quit the Hayride, and it's possible that he got out of music altogether for a short spell. He was back working Hayride packages by the middle of the following year, though. The repo man was a familiar visitor at the Horton house; another out-of-work musician repossessed the Hortons' fridge.

There was no consistent vision behind Horton's Mercury recordings. Horton had no musical vision as such, and Dee Kilpatrick was unable to supply it. On the slower sides he was often incorrigibly wimpy, with an annoying vibrato. "It was difficult to find songs where he could express the emotion he

With Elvis and deejay Paul Kallinger, Shreveport, December 1956
Photo courtesy of C. Escott

had within him," said Kilpatrick. "You could find plenty of songs that he could sing, and he learned songs fast, but it was hard to find songs to bring him out." If his reputation had to stand or fall on the basis of his Mercury and Abbott recordings, Johnny Horton would be no more than a footnote in the history of country music.

During the last months of the Mercury deal, Horton saw a monster unleashing itself from the bottom of the Hayride bill. Elvis Presley became the show's star. Horton saw the change that Elvis was ushering in. His fishing buddy Claude King remembers Johnny introducing him to Elvis. "Johnny said that Elvis was about to have a new record out, and he asked him to sing it.

Elvis sang 'Milkcow Blues.' We left, and Johnny asked me what I thought of him. I said, 'What did he used to do?' and Johnny said, 'He used to drive a truck,' and I said, 'I hope he kept his job.' Johnny laughed and said, 'Ace, I'm gonna tell you something. That young guy will be the biggest singing star who ever lived. Bigger than Sinatra, Crosby, or anyone.' I asked him why he thought that, and he said, 'When he goes out onstage, he does this little bop step, and the teenagers go nuts.' He said it would be that way all over the world."

For his part, Horton never tried to copy Presley's little bop step, although he tried to graft a little rockabilly passion onto his last few Mercury records. Even then, the results were only slightly more dangerous than the uptempo numbers he had done all along. It didn't help that Kilpatrick detested rockabilly with all his heart.

In late 1955 Horton quit Mercury, probably with no great regret on either side, and took on a new manager, Tillman Franks. Born sixty miles north of Shreveport, in Stamps, Arkansas, Tillman had been in Shreveport since he was two years old. After the war he had managed Webb Pierce, Bill Carlisle, and Jimmy and Johnny. When Horton came to see him, Tillman was broke. His on-off relationship with the Hayride was off, and he had split angrily from Jimmy and Johnny. "I hadn't worked in four or five weeks when Johnny Horton come to the door, " said Tillman. "He was broke, too. He and Billie Jean had spent the money they got after Hank died, and she'd told him to get his ass out and make some more. He said, 'If I can get Tillman Franks to manage me, I'll get to Number One.' I told him that I just didn't like the way he sang. He said, 'No problem. I'll sing any way you want me to.' And he was serious!"

Tillman wanted Horton on a label with some kind of commitment to the changes taking place in country music. "I called Webb Pierce," he said. "Webb was a partner with Jim Denny in Cedarwood Music, and Webb told Jim about Johnny Horton, and Denny told Troy Martin, who was running Golden West Melodies for Gene Autry. Troy and Jim Denny talked to Don Law and got a Columbia contract for Johnny." As part of the deal, Golden West Melodies would get the publishing on two songs per session, and Cedarwood would get the other two.

Columbia wasn't mortgaging the farm to acquire Horton. Don Law signed him to a one-year deal calling for a minimal 2 percent royalty, with two options to renew at 3 percent. Before one hour was up on the first Columbia session, though, Johnny Horton had elevated himself to greatness. He had cut "Honky Tonk Man," a song pitched to him by its composer, Howard Hausey. "I played him two or three slow numbers backstage at the Hayride," said Hausey, "and Johnny said he was looking for something uptempo. I just played him the bridge of 'Honky Tonk Man' and he was hollerin' for Tillman." With some prompting, Hausey gave one third of the song to Horton and another third to Tillman Franks.

Elvis was in Nashville for his first RCA session during the week that Horton was there for his first Columbia session. Tillman, wary of his competence as a slap bass player, recruited Bill Black to moonlight for Horton. "We was after bear on that session," he said. "We was hungry, boy!" "Honky Tonk Man" crackled with life; it had all the character and vibrancy that had been lacking on Horton's earlier records. The guitarist Grady Martin played some outrageous single-string leads. Picking the bass strings as close as possible to the bridge, his harsh, pinched lines played nip and tuck with Horton's vocals. If Steve Sholes and Chet Atkins, who had been trying to produce Elvis for RCA, had been in the control room, they'd have thought they'd bought the wrong boy—Horton was that good.

Tillman had the same singlemindedness as Fabor Robison, but he had a musical vision to go with it. Horton himself came to believe that Tillman had the power to visualize a goal, then realize it. "Johnny said I could clairvoyant things," said Tillman. "I believed things so strong, he thought I could make them happen just by believing in them." You can see some of this in the onstage photos. Tillman on bass is goading Horton, much as he would in the studio. "When we was recording, Johnny would keep singing a song until I looked him straight in the eye and said, 'Boy, it's a smash,'" said Tillman. "If I didn't say that, he'd say, 'Let's cut her again.' He knew I'd be thinking hard about it and wouldn't be thinking of nothin' else."

It took some maneuvering to get "Honky Tonk Man" released. Don Law despised the song, but both Franks and Horton believed in it. In the end, Tillman called Jim Denny and asked him to prevail upon Law. "If I hadn't given Tillman one third, he might never have done that, and the song might still be unreleased," said Howard Hausey. Denny came through for them again a few weeks later when Faron Young wanted to cut the song, but Denny persuaded him to hold off.

By May 1956 "Honky Tonk Man" was selling in every major country market, and Johnny Horton had arrived. With his cowboy hat hiding his receding hairline, he more or less looked the part of the unreconstructed rockabilly. The hot streak continued with "I'm a One Woman Man" (a song Franks and Horton had written to the tune of an old two-step, "Schottische in Texas"), "I'm Coming Home," and Tommy Blake's "Honky Tonk Mind." Then things went cold. Between March 1957 and September 1958, nothing hit. They were cutting wonderful late-blooming rockabilly, but its hour had come and gone.

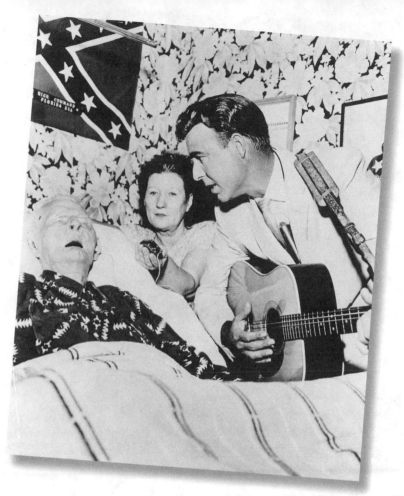

Horton sings "Johnny Reb" to the last surviving Civil War vet, 116-year-old Walter Williams. The old campaigner's daughter, Willie Mae Bowles, holds the hearing aid.
Photo courtesy of C. Escott

Horton fell back on the scams that had supported him in other lean times. "We lived almost next door to each other on Rodney Street in Bossier City," said Merle Kilgore. "I was a deejay and singer on KCIJ then. Johnny was one of the world's greatest pinball players. I had to go to work at eight o'clock A.M., and he called and said, 'Pick me up at seven-thirty and bring a hundred dollars with you.' I said, 'A hundred dollars!' 'cause I was only making one-fifty a week. He said, 'We'll make some money, I promise you.' When he said, 'I promise you,' it always paid off. I dropped him off at this restaurant that had three pinball machines that paid in cash. He said I should pick him up when I got off work at five-thirty. I went by at five-thirty and he had those wrappers that hold quarters up past his ankles. I said, 'How're we doing?' He said, 'Chief, we killed 'em. You got two hundred dollars coming to you.' " Billie Jean and

Newly schooled in rugmanship, Horton returns to Shreveport, 1960
Photo courtesy of J. Barham/C. Escott

her mother owned a little eating joint called Eat 'n' Run. Horton cleaned out the pinball machines so often that the amusement company pulled them out.

Horton hit automobile dealerships too. "He had a brand-new Cadillac," said Kilgore, "and I had an old Buick. Around midnight one night he woke me up and said I should meet him at a truck stop. I didn't ask any questions and went to meet him. He said, 'Have you got money to change these wheels?' I said, 'Yeah,' so he told the man to take the wheels off the Cadillac and put them on my Buick, then put the Buick wheels on the Cadillac. My tires were worn down to nothing, so I asked him what he was doing. He said, 'They're coming to repossess the Cadillac in the morning.'"

The darker side to Horton was his preoccupation with spiritualism. He became a devotee of Edgar Cayce and later built himself a little meditation shed on the back of his property. His preoccupation divided those close to him. His mother saw it as devil worship. Billie Jean had no use for it, and the always practical Tillman Franks saw it as meddling in an area best left alone.

The honky tonk men: Tillman Franks, Horton, Tommy Tomlinson
Photo courtesy of C. Escott

Merle Kilgore and Johnny Cash went with Horton, though, and they were joined by a local psychic, J. Bernard Ricks, who became Horton's spiritual counselor.

Ricks, a short, ruddy-faced man and a lifelong bachelor, had a complex philosophy that mixed predeterminism, transmigration of souls, extraterrestrialism, and white supremacy. A firm believer in reincarnation, he believes that, in previous lives, he was Peter the Great, Sir Thomas More, and George Washington, who, it must be admitted, he faintly resembles.

Ricks first met Horton in 1952 backstage at the Municipal Auditorium in Shreveport where the Hayride was held, but they didn't meet again until 1957. Ricks had attracted some local attention, and Horton got in touch with him. "He phoned at eight o'clock P.M. on March 14, 1957," said Ricks with his usual disconcerting accuracy, "and he told me he'd like to come out to see me that night. He came out and stayed till midnight." It was Merle Kilgore who first experienced dramatic proof of Ricks's powers. "I was watching television with a friend, deejay Ed Hamilton, and Bernard Ricks called and said, 'How are the children?' I said, 'They're fine.' He called back and said, 'Something's wrong, I can't breathe. Go check the children.' My youngest daughter, Kimberly, was six months old. I looked in her crib; the covers were over her head, and she was blue. Bernard Ricks was still on the phone, and he said, 'Spank her,' and I did, but I couldn't make her breathe. My wife had gone to the movies, so Ed stayed with the other children, and I took Kim to the hospital. When I got there, a nurse came by with a stainless steel tray, and something told me to place Kim on that tray. The cold steel shocked her back to breathing."

Johnny Cash shared Horton's faith and curiosity. "One time," said Tillman Franks, "Horton hypnotized Cash and took him back to when he was six years old in the classroom. Cash would tell what color the teacher's dress was, and sing the first song he wrote, when he was twelve years old. Then one time they went into the future, and Cash was screamin' and hollerin' about how it was dark in that room. 'Don't make me go in that room!' he kept shouting."

The spiritual side of Horton tied in with his respect for Native American lore. He frequently played Indian reservations in New Mexico, and, according to the guitarist Jerry Kennedy, "Horton was an honorary chief and all that crap." Horton apparently believed in "all that crap," though, and championed Native rights long before it was chic. He even recorded a demo of a chant called "The Vanishing Race" that Cash later cut on his *Bitter Tears* album. As an outdoorsman, Horton appreciated a value system that placed humans in the broad context of animal and plant life.

By late 1958 Horton was in deep trouble. He was involved in an insurance scam that cost Tillman his home, and he might have gone to jail but for a hit that turned his career around again. "When It's Springtime in Alaska" fit right in with the craze for ersatz folk music that had started with "Tom Dooley." It sounded like it had been written a hundred years earlier, although Tillman and Horton had cooked it up. It became a Number One country hit.

Then Horton cut "The Battle of New Orleans." Based on an old fiddle tune, "The Eighth of January," the song first appeared in 1958 on an album called *Newly Discovered American Folk Songs* by Jimmie Driftwood. It was an album a year ahead of its time, which meant that it sank without a trace. Porter Wagoner and his manager, Don Warden, had got Driftwood his deal with RCA and secured his publishing for their company, Warden Music, and it was Warden who pitched "The Battle of New Orleans" to Horton and Tillman Franks.

Tillman was unimpressed, partly because the song ran over four minutes. Then Ralph Emery played Driftwood's version one night just as Tillman was falling asleep. "I had a dream that Johnny was recording it," said Tillman, "and

I called him up, and he said 'Chief, that's our next record.'" Horton phoned Driftwood and invited him to Shreveport to play a guest spot on the Hayride on January 24, 1959. After the show, they set about shortening the lyrics. Horton was enthused now. He told Driftwood that it would be a monster country record, maybe even a pop hit, too. "You don't want a pop hit, do you?" Driftwood recalls asking. "Johnny said he did, and I asked him why. He took off his hat, and he was bald as a coot. He said he'd like to trade in his old cowboy hat for a new toupee."

Tillman called Don Law and insisted that they book studio time and schedule a release on "The Battle of New Orleans," even though "Springtime in Alaska" was peaking. They cut it on January 27, 1959, three days after Driftwood was in Shreveport. Law was absent that day, and Grady Martin took charge of the session and ran the board; Troy Martin logged the takes. "We cut the thing," said Tillman, "and I walked down the steps in the old Quonset hut down into the studio, and I was crying. It tore me up. Johnny grabbed me by the arm and asked me how I liked it. I looked away, and he said, 'Let's cut her again, boys.' Then I held him, and he looked me right in the eye and said, 'Is it that good?' I said, 'Johnny, it is.'"

"Springtime in Alaska" knocked Johnny Cash's "Don't Take Your Guns to Town" off the top of the country charts on April 6, 1959, and Columbia rush-released "The Battle of New Orleans" a week later. It reached Number One on the country charts on May 18 and stayed there for ten weeks. It was Number One on the pop charts for almost as long. On June 7, 1959, Horton performed the song on "The Ed Sullivan Show." He looked strangely wraithlike in an all-white Davy Crockett outfit, almost static against an all-white backdrop, with dry ice smoke in the background.

Bernard Ricks that insists he had an early intimation that "The Battle of New Orleans" would be a worldwide smash. Horton called him over to the house, sat a little portable record player on the floor, reached under some newspapers, and pulled out a test pressing. "A blue haze appeared," said Ricks, "and in it I saw a dollar sign with two zeros, a comma, and three zeroes. He said, 'What do you think?' I said, 'I don't have to think. In sixty days you will get a check from Columbia for more than ten thousand dollars. It will be an international upheaval.'"

"The Battle of New Orleans" became the best-selling record of 1959, prompting Don Law to renew the Columbia contract before it expired. The follow-ups, Merle Kilgore's "Johnny Reb" and Claude King's "Take Me Like I Am," failed to make anywhere near as much impact, though. "Sink the Bismark" and the awkwardly contrived "Johnny Freedom" did no better. Then

Horton was offered the chance to write the title song for an upcoming John Wayne movie, *North to Alaska*.

The original writer credit on "North to Alaska" was "M. Phillips," a pseudonym for Martin Michel, an executive at 20th Century Fox. If a deposition by Tillman Franks before a U.S. district court is to be believed, he and Horton wrote the song and gave Michel the composer credit in order to secure a movie contract for Horton. Billie Jean, though, said that Michel had been given the composer credit so that Horton could get another five movie title songs. In the same set of hearings, held as the copyright came up for renewal, Claude King claimed that he had written the song with Horton. Billie Jean claimed that Horton had written the song alone at home. The court somehow determined that Horton and Franks had written it.

By the time "North to Alaska" was released, Horton's premonitions of an early and violent death were getting stronger. As early as July 1960 he began visiting those close to him to say good-bye. He saw his sister Marie that month and, she recalls, he said, "'Sis, I gotta talk to you. I want you to pray for Billie and the girls.' He knew he was going to die a tragic death—plane, car, or something like that. He said I was going to have to hold up the family. I didn't want to talk about it, but he insisted. He said he'd quit smoking, and was trying to get his life in order because he'd had these strong premonitions."

This talk infuriated Billie Jean. She had already been through all this with Hank Williams, who was tormented by visions of Jesus coming down the road to get him. "After 'North to Alaska,' " said Billie Jean, "we were laying in bed and he asked me what I'd do after he was gone. He'd raise up in bed and say, 'Bill, I'm fixing to die. It's close. I've got to prepare and so have you.'"

Horton went to see Merle Kilgore, too. "He said the spirits had told him he was gonna die within a week," said Kilgore, "and they wanted him to see all of his old friends. He said, 'I want you to have this old guitar. Don't you ever sell it.' He was adamant. He said a drunk man would kill him. He thought it would be a drunk in a bar at one of the places he was fixing to play in Texas. He accepted it. I asked if he'd heard a voice, and he said that it wasn't like a voice, but a brain message."

Paradoxically, Horton accepted his fate but also tried to avoid it. He backed out of attending the premiere of *North to Alaska* on November 16, 1960, and, according to Kilgore, tried to cancel the gig in Austin, Texas, scheduled for November 4. It has never really been clear why Horton, now one of the top recording stars in the country, was going to play a honky-tonk in Austin. It was probably a quick grab for some ready cash. Horton had some hot checks out and owed taxes on his earnings from "The Battle of New Orleans," and Tillman had some medical bills from a recent hernia operation.

On his last morning at home, Horton tried to phone Johnny Cash to make a pact that he would look after Billie and the kids if he died. Horton then left for Tillman Franks's house. Over Billie Jean's objections, he had taken his $250 velvet jacket and $150 shoes that he was supposed to save for top bookings. Before he left his house, Horton picked up his older daughter, Yanina— or "Neenah," as he called her—and held her tight. "Melody [the younger daughter] is already tough as a boot, " he told Billie Jean, "and you'll make it, but Neenah will need special care."

Tillman was recovering from his operation and was not supposed to go on the road. "My wife said I couldn't go," he said, "but Johnny went to the icebox and got something to eat, and he said 'Hurry up' like he hadn't heard her. I got my stuff, and she said, 'You can't go.' I got in the car, and she was starting to burn up. Johnny opened the car door and made a little motion with his hands, and he said, 'Virginia, hon, do you know what that is?' And she said, 'No. What is it?' He said, 'The world's smallest violin playing "My Heart Cries for You.'"' Then we drove off." They picked up their guitarist, Tommy Tomlinson. Horton talked a lot about God on the drive to Austin.

Before the show, Horton stayed in the dressing room. He'd had a clear premonition of being killed by a drunk, and he thought it might be a drunk in a bar. Warren Starks, owner of the Skyline, found a stand-in bass player to replace Tillman, who couldn't play. Horton did two shows and then started to drive the 220 miles back to Shreveport. Tomlinson had driven down, so Horton drove back; Tillman had never learned to drive. Horton wanted to get home, change, and head down to a lake in southern Louisiana for the start of the duck-hunting season. Claude King was already waiting for him out in the bush. They stopped for a cup of coffee and then got back on the highway. Tillman went to sleep, slumped against Horton. The last words he remembered Horton saying were, "Do you realize how good God has been to us this year" Horton had turned his career around once again. They had needed another hit record and had found it with "North to Alaska."

They passed through Milano, Texas, around 2:00 A.M. "Johnny was driving too fast," said Tomlinson. "All he had on his mind was getting out to the lake. We were crossing a bridge, and the guy who hit us was drunk and was weaving all over the road. He hit the bridge once on each side before he hit us. That pickup truck went down the side of our Cadillac like a can opener."

"I woke up when Johnny was fighting that steering wheel," said Tillman. "At first I was mad from being woke up like that, then that pickup truck come in on us. It was like I was floating on a cloud, like 'Don't worry—you're all right.' When I come to, I was laying right against Johnny, and I asked Tommy what had happened. Tommy was moaning in the back. He said, 'Tillman, we was in a bad wreck. Johnny's in a real bad way,' and I went back out. Tommy's leg had been mashed, but he was conscious through it all."

The irony was that Horton had prepared for a head-on collision: "'You don't have to worry 'bout being in a wreck with ol' John,' " he had told Claude King, "'cause John's gonna take the ditch. Ain't nobody gonna hit me head-on.' He'd trained his mind, probably spent hundreds of hours mentally preparing himself to take to the ditch—and he did it a time or two. Then he got hit on the overpass with nowhere to go."

Horton was still breathing when he was pulled from the wreck, but he died on the way to the hospital in Cameron. There was a report that he had suffered irreparable brain damage when a sun visor rod penetrated his skull. His monogrammed ring flew off with the impact of the collision and was later returned to Billie Jean by a farmer who found it in his field. Tillman received head lacerations. Tomlinson's left leg suffered multiple fractures and had to be amputated the following August.

The funeral was held on the afternoon of November 8, 1960. Tillman Franks's brother, Billy, preached the service; Tillman attended in a wheelchair. Johnny Cash read the twentieth chapter of the Book of John. Bernard Ricks drew pictures of fish and passed them up to Billie Jean during the service. It was meant to be a signal from Horton that he was fishing in heaven and that he was all right.

That afternoon had a deep impact on Frank Horton. "My wife and I were having trouble," he said. "I was drinking and we were fighting. I'd just gone to sleep when someone called and told me that Johnny had been killed. I came unglued. I was numb. Fred and I flew back for the funeral. Everyone was in the front room except me, Johnny Cash, and Billie Jean. We were in the bedroom. Tillman Franks's brother, Billy, saw what misery I was in. He said, 'Frank, would you like to pray about this?' I blinked my eyes, and I said, 'Yes, I believe I would.' I knelt by Johnny's bed, and the load lifted. I accepted Jesus that afternoon. I got back to California and I told my wife, Lorna, that I wasn't going back to working in the gambling joints, and that I'd accepted Jesus. Now, I'd said many times that I was going to quit working the joints, but I hadn't done it. Lorna said, 'Can't the Lord wait thirty days till you find a job?' But I got a job as a salesman. I know how badly Johnny wanted to get me out of the mess I was in, but it took his death to really change my life."

Horton had always promised those close to him that he would try to get in contact from beyond the grave. "I ain't heard nothing yet," said Billie Jean.

Tillman, though, believes he has heard something. He was driving to Nashville with David Houston, then his client, for an Opry gig: "The radio was out and the CB was out, and suddenly on the CB we got the start of 'One Woman Man.' It sounded like a jukebox, real full, much louder than a CB could be. The whole song played, and then the CB cut out again. I just froze; David did too. The song wasn't on an eight-track tape, so someone would've had to tape it onto an eight-track and play it within a two- or three-mile radius. There's just a million-to-one chance of that. I told Merle Kilgore, and he said, 'Johnny's telling you that the song's gonna be a hit all over again.' I said, 'Well, it didn't do too well the first time out.'"

Johnny Horton's message from beyond the grave, if that's what it was, was premature, but as 1988 closed, George Jones's version of "One Woman Man" was in the country Top Ten. ☺

FOR YOUR LISTENING PLEASURE

Greatest Hits (Columbia CK 40665) concentrates on the saga songs; *American Originals* (Columbia CK 45071) is a random sweep through the catalog. Bear Family's *Rockin', Rollin'* (BCD 15543) has twenty uptempo songs in premium sound quality. The complete Cormac, Abbott, and Mercury recordings are on Bear Family's *The Early Years* (BFX 15289; seven LPs), and the complete Columbia recordings are on *1956–1960* (BCD 15470; four CDs).

Billie Jean

· ·

A GIRL NAMED "SUE!"

As she's the first to admit, it's difficult to tell from Billie Jean Horton's language that she is a minister, although sources say that she was ordained in 1978. The way she naturally expresses herself isn't consistent with any religious order that leaps to mind—except perhaps Toronto's Reverend Ken and his Church of the Open Bottle ("Let the spirits enter the body"). It's not that Billie Jean is a heavy drinker, although she has been the centerpiece of a few parties; it's that her conversation is littered with expletives and the occasional threat. She's at least forthright, and never shy of speaking her mind, and there *is* a curious spirituality about her. It becomes apparent once she sets aside her eviscerating manner and places her life, and the lives of those close to her, into a broader sweep that can almost make you misty-eyed in its tenderness and compassion.

"I knew when I was five years old, dragging that cotton sack, that if I ever got off that son of a bitch, I'd never be back," she said during one of our first conversations. The one-time girlfriend of Faron Young and wife of both Hank Williams and Johnny Horton has been true to her credo, and she now guards her assets with the tenacity of a rottweiler.

Billie Jean Jones was born on a farm near Shreveport. Her father became a policeman across the Red River from Shreveport, in Bossier City, soon after the Second World War ended. Beginning in April 1948, Shreveport played host to "The Louisiana Hayride," a Saturday night radio jamboree in front of an audience along the lines of "The Grand Ole Opry." There were hundreds of other Saturday night jamborees, but the Hayride had Hank Williams—then a virtual unknown. His star and the Hayride's rose in tandem. "I went to school with Lycrecia [Hank's wife's daughter by her first marriage]," says Billie Jean. "We rode the bus together. Hank had a radio show, and I'd see him driving toward his house, and he looked so lonesome; he looked like he'd rather go anyplace than home. He lived in the nicer section; we lived up in the colored part of the street. He had black eyes and a cowboy hat, and I told Mama, 'One of these days, I'm gonna marry that guy.' You know how girls dream. He was just my ideal cowboy. He had that haunting look."

Photo courtesy of LSUS

Young Billie and ol' Hank
Photo courtesy of C. Escott

When Billie Jean first married, though, it was to a serviceman, Harrison Eshliman. She was sixteen, and she quickly became pregnant without ever really understanding how. She thought Eshliman had had a heart attack atop her that first night, and didn't realize that he had left his seed. Her first daughter, Jeri Lynn, was born in March 1950. By then—or shortly afterward—Eshliman was history. Soon Billie's mother was baby-sitting and Billie was going to dances in the Municipal Auditorium, where the Hayride was held. She looked stunning: flaming red hair, a natural commanding beauty, a luminosity that attracted stares from the married and unmarried alike.

Hank Williams had left town by then, riding the success of "Lovesick Blues," but the Hayride had an ability to attract and subsequently lose an astonishing roster of talent that at one time or another included Kitty Wells, Slim

Whitman, Webb Pierce, Red Sovine, Elvis Presley, Johnny Cash, Jim Reeves, and Faron Young.

Faron Young and Billie Jean Jones started stepping out together early in 1951, and when Young received the inevitable call to Nashville, Billie Jean rode up with him. "He was wild as a bear cat," she says. "Oh, God! He knew he could sing, and he was about halfway wise, but nothing could ever have worked out between us. I was dating him and about a hundred others, but my dad cosigned a note on a car to get us up there. My daughter stayed with my mother. I was just gonna go up and back."

Billie sat in the visitors' box while Young played his first guest shot on the Opry. By her own admission she looked especially radiant that night, in an off-the-shoulder figure-hugging black dress with white lace trim. She caught the eye of the show's star, Hank Williams, now adrift from his first wife, Miss Audrey. "He came in, sat down beside me. Just sat there and looked at me. I tried to ignore him. Finally he said, 'Girl, who you up here with?' I said, 'Faron Young.' He said, 'Is that the kid that's guesting up here from Shreveport?' I said, 'Yes, sir.' About that time, Minnie Pearl came up to the glass, and he motioned to her, he said, 'Minnie, find Faron Young, tell him ol' Hank wants to see him.' So here comes Faron. Hank said, 'Faron, you gonna marry this girl?' Faron said, 'Hank, I don't think so. She's got too many boyfriends, I can't keep up with her.' Hank said, 'Well, if you ain't gonna marry her, ol' Hank's gonna marry her.' He said, 'Faron, go out there. You see that ol' black-haired girl in the front row with the red dress on? She flew down here from Pennsylvania to see me. After we get through working tonight, let's us go out and party. That gal, she's gonna be your gal, and Billie's gonna be my gal.'"

Sensitive New Age men may recoil, but Billie Jean was won over by Hank's brusque approach to courtship. "He chased me," she says, "but I'm glad he caught me." Faron Young later insisted that Hank dispelled any notion he might have had of another fling with Billie Jean by pulling a gun on him. You never know quite where you stand in relation to the truth with a Faron Young story, but that one could well be near the mark.

Billie Jean got a transfer to the Nashville phone company, and she and Hank quickly agreed to marry in October 1952. They drove to Shreveport to tell her parents; Hank dictated thirteen songs along the way. When they returned to Nashville, though, they found one of Hank's old flames camped in his house. There was a knock-down-drag-out fight. Billie and the driver who had taken them to Shreveport stood incredulous as Hank and his old flame wrestled. Billie told the driver to take her back to the boardinghouse. She packed her trunk and caught a Greyhound bound for Shreveport. It was that move, she claims, that precipitated Hank's longest and worst bender, the one that got him sacked from the Opry in August 1952.

"A couple weeks later—maybe three," says Billie Jean, "he called. He said, 'Baby, this is ol' Hank. I do believe we've got a date October 19,' which was the date we'd planned to marry. I said, 'Well, we *had* one.' He said, 'In a coupla days ol' Hank's gonna be down there. I want you to find me a place.' And a couple of days later, he turned up with two cars. Everything he owned was in there."

The Hayride took Hank Williams back, but it was a very different Hank Williams from the one who had left just three years earlier. This one had nothing left to prove. The civil war with Miss Audrey and three years' hard grind on the road had depleted him. Spina bifida, a condition in which the spinal cord herniates through the discs in the spine, now caused him ceaseless pain and left him with only marginal control over his bladder. It also, according to Billie Jean, left him almost impotent. The alcoholism, precipitated in part by the spinal condition, was growing worse. The fact that Hank was still the biggest star in country music was adding to the pressures that eventually felled him. Not yet out of her teens, Billie wasn't equipped to handle any of this. She and her brothers, Sonny and Alton, chaperoned him, took him to the North Louisiana Sanitorium to dry him out from time to time, but neither the doctors—of whom Hank had a morbid fear—nor anyone close to him could do much to alleviate the conditions that Hank was self-remedying with booze.

The wedding happened more or less on schedule. It was a three-ring circus in New Orleans. There was a "rehearsal" and then the wedding itself as the high point of a hillbilly variety show. Admission was charged. Hank had spitefully invited Audrey, and she threatened to do more than attend; she said she would disrupt it. With the invitation to Audrey looking certain to backfire, Hank, with the help of local bandleader Paul Howard, quickly devised Plan B. He would miss the second Hayride show on Saturday, October 18, and go to Minden, where a justice of the peace would marry him and Billie Jean. Then if Audrey were to disrupt the show weddings, they could produce their marriage certificate.

The wedding photos show that Hank, who had been anorexically thin a few weeks earlier, was now almost chubby. This has been variously attributed to the edema characteristic of some forms of heart disease or to the side effects of the various drugs he was taking. Billie Jean attributes the weight gain to regular meals at her mother's house. She despises the standard photos of him with cheekbones gauntly protruding. The weight gain or puffiness made Hank look younger than he had in years, despite his thinning hair. The photos also cap-

133

Billie and her daughters, Yanina, Melody, and Jeri-Lynn
Photo courtesy of C. Escott

ture a few moments of undeniable tenderness in a stage-managed day. The reward for Hank was furnishings for his new home, but the cost was physical exhaustion. He and Billie were supposed to depart for Cuba immediately after the ceremony, but the demands on his strength and the overavailability of champagne meant that Hank collapsed shortly after his third "I do" in two days.

Hank and Billie Jean were married for a shade over ten weeks. The portrait that has always emerged is that of a hapless drunk living out his last days in a drug- and alcohol-induced haze. Billie is anxious to show the other side of the picture. "After we married he had a reason to live. We had a simple home that we rented. I didn't want carpets—I'd never seen 'em. I was simple, young, and I was a kid. Hank was truly a kid. He was funny, man, I'm telling you. We were a lot alike. You would think Hank had grown up with Southern [blacks]. He had their style of humor. He'd love to sit and pick with them too. He was the complete opposite of what you'd think.

"He just illuminated when he sang. Every pain he had in his back—and it was ungodly—was gone. You couldn't tell he had a pain in the world. I've got some stage shows on cassettes where he's talking, and I like to listen to him 'cause I understand him. I understand how innocent he was. He wasn't educated, yet you listen to songs like 'Be Careful of the Stones That You Throw' or my favorite, 'I'm So Lonesome I Could Cry,' and you wonder how such a simple man with no education could throw that out of his brain. He projected. He lived what he sang. He put everything he had into it. He had like a picture in his mind when he sang. Hank was very sensitive. We had a record player and we'd sit on the floor, and he would listen to some of his sad songs. I remember when Tommy Edwards came out with 'You Win Again' and they sent Hank a copy. We sat on the floor and listened to it and tears was running out of his eyes. He said, 'Just think, a pop artist cuttin' ol' Hank's songs.'

"Money meant nothing to him. It was irrelevant to me. It never crossed my mind or his. The drastic switch from a mansion with chandeliers and stuff to an apartment with bare floors didn't bother him. He was right at home."

Billie understood Hank's need for love, and there's no doubt that she beguiled him with her beauty and gregariousness. The few photos of them together make it clear that, for a while at least, she worshiped the quicksand he walked on. "Hank had never been held," she says. "I knew this. I was wise for my years. I knew I had to be a lover and a mother to him." She didn't understand the complexities of his career or the desperate seriousness of his physical problems, though. Nor did she realize that by this point in his life Hank Williams was beyond help.

It was a measure of Hank's unreliability that he was mostly confined to

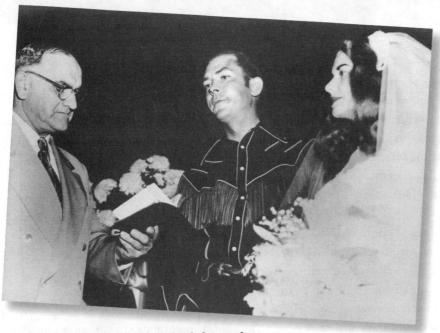

Hank, a welt clearly visible on his left temple, supposedly from a prenuptial encounter with Audrey, marries Billie Jean in New Orleans.
Photo courtesy of C. Escott

short tours in East Texas and Louisiana, and in mid-December 1952 he went out on a short swing through Texas. Two days out, he became so sick that his mother, Lillie Stone, flew in from Montgomery to take care of him, and she finished the tour with him. Billie's heart sank when she saw Lillie, who detested all the women in Hank's life, sitting next to Hank as the limo pulled up. That same day, she packed their bags. Hank took a leave of absence from the Hayride. He was going home to die.

Hank's only outstanding commitment was to play two show dates on New Year's Eve and New Year's Day. Billie maintains that she intended to go on Hank's New Year junket with him, but the weather looked too grim. She was back in Shreveport when the call came on New Year's morning to tell her that Hank had died en route to Ohio. "There's no way to describe how it feels when they tell you," she says. "There was a person-to-person call to my dad at home from Virginia. I thought Hank was in some kind of trouble. My daddy said, 'Oh, Lord,' and asked the driver some questions, then hung up. I was sitting up by that point. He held me and said that Hank was dead, and I was screaming and crying. I said, 'Don't let them touch him. He often pretends he's asleep.' I thought they were going to bury him alive."

The wrestling over the estate began before Hank was in the ground. Lillie Stone and Billie Jean physically fought in the washroom of Lillie's boardinghouse while Hank lay in state in the front room; Billie stood on the toilet seat to get better aim at Hank's mother, who was now built like a logger. Lillie had seized many of Hank's physical possessions, including his automobile and his wedding ring, but the true value of the estate lay in the records and the copyrights, and the haggling over those had hardly begun.

At the funeral, Billie and Audrey sat uncomfortably close in the front row, but Billie was ignored by the Nashville music community, which was busy reclaiming Hank in death. "Money begets money," said Billie. "They thought they were gonna have all the money. When Hank was alive it was a different story. None of them crossed him. Ernest Tubb, who was pretty close to Hank when he was alive, wouldn't speak to me. He looked at me kinda stupid. I stopped to speak to him, and he looked at me like he didn't even know me. I was thinking to myself, 'All right, all you bastards that's mistreating me and hasn't raised a hand to help Hank all these years, hoping that he would go down, so you'd have a shot at being the king, I'm gonna get even with you.'"

In the weeks after Hank's death, Billie Jean said, she didn't know which way to go. "Then hadn't two weeks gone by and Paul Howard said he had this good idea. He asked me if I could sing, and I said I'd been singing all my life, in churches and at the officers club. Paul said, 'G-o-o-d, because I'm fixing to make us a lot of money.' We rented a costume and took a picture of me with a hat on. We were making two thousand or more a night not counting pictures. We could have sold as many pictures as we had. I was sending money home every day—wiring it to my daddy. I started buying houses as an investment because I liked the game Monopoly."

Audrey also wasted no time in putting a band together and hitting the road. Both billed themselves as "Mrs. Hank Williams." "One time up in Missouri," says Billie, "Audrey was playing thirteen miles down the road. We were playing the parks up there, and I said over the loudspeaker, 'If you guys hurry up, you go on down the road you can catch my husband's ex-wife down there.' I used to pull crap like that all the time." It wasn't long before Audrey's lawyers approached Billie Jean with the notion of a buyout. Billie Jean would relinquish her rights in exchange for a one-time payment. The thirty thousand dollars looked like a lot of money at the time, and it avoided a lawsuit in which Billie might have lost everything: her marriage to Hank was technically illegitimate because her divorce from Eshliman hadn't been finalized.

Billie had another reason to settle. She had already met another Hayride star who was pressuring her to give up singing. "Johnny Horton [wanted] to get married," she says, "but I really didn't want to get off the road. I was booked up two years in advance." Horton had joined the Hayride in 1952 and had been recording for two years, with no success at all.

"Johnny loved me, or I'm assuming he did," says Billie cagily. "He needed a family. He wasn't hung up on music like Hank. He'd rather fish and hunt. He certainly wasn't into working all day, either. He would have quit music. He was tired of all that crap out on the road—the pills and so on. He didn't like to be around drunks. He said to me, 'If I quit the business, you'll leave me, won't you?' I said, 'In a heartbeat. You'll go out that door with what you came in with,' which was nothing. I got him out of debt when I married him. He owed the world, and it took everything I had. I'd just bought me my first new car. The finance company had just repossessed Johnny's, so I loaned him mine, and Johnny was somebody you didn't loan your car to, not even to go downtown, because you never saw it in a whole piece again. He finally put that car in the Mississippi River. He drove too fast."

Horton scuffled along for another six years, supporting himself with flim-flam moves and by booking out on Hayride tours. The frustrating thing for everyone involved with his career was that he had the goods; all he lacked was commitment. He went to Nashville only to record and never hung around to schmooze. He preferred to stay in Shreveport, where the fishing and hunting were better.

"To get Johnny to play a gig was like pulling teeth, even after he saw the money he could make," said Billie Jean, "and the more he made the more he threw away. He opened a damn bait factory in Natchitoches, puttin' all our money into it. No money was coming into the household, and that wasn't sitting well with me. Just before he died I made him shut it down. Johnny just wasn't good with money at all—and he was educated, so there was no excuse for him throwing his money away like that. I had to feed the kids, so my mama and I opened a bar, and we had a restaurant just to keep him fishing."

In a bizarre coincidence, Horton's last gig was at the Skyline Club in Austin, the final venue on Hank Williams's last tour. After Horton was in the ground, Billie Jean resumed her performing career. She recorded for 20th Century Fox and scored a fleeting country hit with "Ocean of Tears" before deciding that she preferred management. Meanwhile, Hank Williams was becoming a bigger star in death than he ever had been in life. After years of dickering, Audrey finally agreed to authorize a bio-pic. *Your Cheatin' Heart* had been discussed the year that Hank died. Elvis was up for the lead at some point, but when it finally went into production in 1963 it was with George Hamilton IV as the unlikeliest Hank Williams imaginable. Ten years after the fact, Audrey was finding it harder every day to differentiate between the Hank Williams who had once walked this earth with her, and the Hank Williams who should have walked by her side, taking her admonitions and advice to heart.

Billie and Johnny at Johnny's thirtieth birthday party, April 1955
Photo courtesy of C. Escott

138

Vixen
Photo courtesy of C. Escott

It was the latter who appeared in *Your Cheatin' Heart*, with the Audrey-who-should-have-been walking selflessly at his side until the credits rolled. Billie Jean was cast as little better than a harlot, and she sued.

So began the chain of lawsuits that still continues in one shape or another. Billie Jean has come to enjoy court appearances, and her track record has been enviably good. When Hank Williams's copyrights came up for renewal twenty-eight years after they were first logged, she sued for half of the publishing, contending that she hadn't signed away her right to the renewals because she couldn't sign away what she didn't have. She won, and Audrey got the news that she had lost just days before she died.

Billie married again; husband number four was an insurance executive, Kent Berlin. Billie admits that the lawsuits were consuming more of her time than they should have, and the marriage ended in divorce. It was during her marriage to Berlin that Billie bought the block-long Stutz that sits in her driveway. Until recently, she lived in the house on Shreve Island that she and Johnny Horton had bought with the royalties from "The Battle of New Orleans." She owns other properties in town and has just built herself a house that she promises is the gaudiest property in Shreveport.

For her troubles, Billie Jean has buried two giants of postwar country music, one of them perhaps the most powerfully mythic figure in the music's history. She has also recently buried her father and a brother to whom she was especially close. Her feistiness both in the courtroom and outside cannot occlude the sense of loss that permeates her conversation. There's bravura in her voice when she declares she's making her living off bones, but on closer inspection, one is reminded of Jerry Lee Lewis's aphorism: It's not the years that bring you down, it's the passing of the caskets. ⑥

Tommy Blake

. . . .

DEATH OF A HONKY-TONK MAN, 2

On Christmas Eve 1985 Tommy Blake came home drunk and stoned again. Home was a trailer park in Shreveport, Louisiana. His wife, Samantha, had trimmed the Christmas tree and spread the presents around it, but Blake was in a vile mood. The underlying reason was always the same: too few people knew the name "Tommy Blake" or any of the other pseudonyms under which he worked. He started kicking at the tree, ripping up the presents. Finally, he turned on his wife. They started punching and kicking each other, then suddenly Blake produced a .38 pistol with a hair trigger. He pushed Samantha onto the floor. She got up and lunged at him, the gun went flying, and she reached for it.

"I never meant to pull the trigger," she said later. "I just wanted to get it away from him. He died in my arms. My last words to him were, 'You know I love you.' I'll never forget the gurgling in his throat when he died. I closed his eyes and laid him down on the carpet."

Samantha Carter spent Christmas 1985 in jail but was released and subsequently acquitted. Blake's history of alcoholism, drug abuse, and spousal abuse would have made any other verdict a joke. He was one of the guys who never really made it but got close enough to know what "making it" was all about. Close enough to know that he wanted it badly. Some guys can give it a shot, accept that the public doesn't want to buy what they have to sell, then move on, happy that they at least tried. Not Tommy Blake. He couldn't accept the public's verdict with good grace. After his performing career was over, he tried to experience success vicariously by becoming a songwriter. Once again, he came close, even wrote a few hits, but never quite had Nashville beating down his door.

Thomas LeVan Givens was born illegitimately in Dallas on September 14, 1931. He never knew his father and could never do right in his mother's eyes. He was jailed for rape in his teens and entered the military in 1951. He told people he lost an eye in Korea, but in truth he lost it before he even left boot camp in North Carolina. Discharged, he went to Louisiana, working on KTBS in Shreveport and KRUS in Ruston as a performer and deejay. He played

Photo courtesy of C. Escott

guest spots on the Saturday night jamborees: "The Big D Jamboree" in Dallas, "The Louisiana Hayride" in Shreveport, and "The Grand Prize Jamboree" in Houston.

It was on the Hayride that Blake first became aware of the fresh breeze blowing through the country music scene. Elvis was on the show just about every week starting in October 1954. The audience was at first incredulous, then ecstatic. Watching intently backstage, Blake was among the first to declare himself for rock 'n' roll.

143

Recording at RCA, Nashville, April 15, 1957;
from left: Carl Adams, Selby Coffeen (engineer),
Chet Atkins, Tommy Blake, Eddie Hall
Photo courtesy of C. Escott

Blake's first record was for the Buddy label in Marshall, Texas. Then he signed with RCA in April 1957. He was brought to Nashville, where he recorded four songs with Chet Atkins supervising. The problem was that he had already pitched his best song, "Honky Tonk Mind," to Johnny Horton for a Columbia session a week earlier. RCA was upset, Columbia was upset, and two music publishers were upset. Horton's manager, Tillman Franks, rushed "Honky Tonk Mind" onto the market under another title and credited it to a Cedarwood Music staff writer, Lee Emerson. Blake's version was held back. He sued for composer credit on Horton's record and won, but it was a hollow victory because the song didn't do much business.

Chet Atkins, sensing a troublemaker, issued only one single; the two unissued cuts were finally issued on the Country Music Foundation's rockabilly anthology *Get Hot or Go Home*. Blake sat out his one-year contract with RCA, and when it was up he signed with Sun Records in Memphis. Around the same time he was signed as a regular to "The Louisiana Hayride."

The first Sun single, "Flat Foot Sam," wasn't one of Blake's songs. The measure of Sun president Sam Phillips's faith in it was that Sun didn't even own the copyright. It had been written and recorded by T. V. Slim for Ram Records in Shreveport, then leased to Chess Records in Chicago. It was about a scam artist who can't win for losing:

Flat Foot Sam stole a ten dollar bill
Told the judge he done it for a thrill . . .

Blake could relate. The flip side, "Lordy Hoody," was a rewrite of one of the unissued RCA sides, "All Night Long." "Flat Foot Sam" sold well enough for Sun to keep the faith for one more try. When that failed, Tommy Blake was no longer a Sun artist.

While still at Sun, Blake had pitched a song, a lugubrious ballad called "Story of a Broken Heart," to the departing Johnny Cash. Phillips had put out the call for songs because Cash was holding back his own songs for his pending deal with Columbia. Sun later issued "Story of a Broken Heart" as a single, but by then Sam Phillips had caught Blake in one of his many moments of need and bought the song from him.

Several more recording contracts followed for Blake with Recco, 4-Star, Paula, Aetna, and Chancellor. Nothing came of any of them. Blake's longest relationship was with Bill McCall at 4-Star, who was a magnet for down-on-their-luck hillbillies. He'd keep feeding them small advances in the hope that they'd come up with a song he could use. Then he would cut himself in (as he did on "Release Me" and hundreds of other songs) or buy the copyrights outright. The only winner in a Bill McCall deal was Bill McCall.

In 1954 Blake had married Betty Jones in Carthage, Texas. They had six children. Shortly after one of them was born, Blake went to the store to buy cigarettes, saw Faron Young's tour bus, jumped on board, and disappeared for six weeks. It was the critical choice of his life: success—even experienced tangentially or vicariously—was preferable to absolutely anything else. Yukkin' it up with guys backstage or finishing a song in a pill-induced frenzy beat sitting on the couch watching television with the wife and kids. Betty followed Blake to California, then back to Texas and Louisiana, and on to Nashville. With six kids, she felt she had no other option.

During the late fifties and sixties, Blake—now working as Van Givens—formed a songwriting partnership with Carl Belew. They wrote "Tender Years" and sold it to George Jones's buddy Darrell Edwards for one hundred dollars just before Jones cut it. It was a Number One country hit. Blake also claimed that he had written part of "Lonely Street," a hit for Andy Williams in 1959, and "Am I That Easy to Forget," a hit for Belew and then Debbie Reynolds. Reynolds's version was especially poignant because Eddie Fisher was dumping her at that time for Elizabeth Taylor. Some songs still bear Blake's name. Patsy Cline, Tammy Wynette, George Jones, Ray Price, and Jim Reeves took his songs into the lower reaches of the charts, but whenever he was broke, he would sign away his share of a hit—often more than once.

The seventies found Blake working as a carpenter; Betty was still hanging in. In 1972 he had a heart attack, swore off the pills and booze for a short period, and settled back in Carthage, Texas. Then, in 1976, he left Carthage, heading for Nashville again. Interviewed in the local Carthage newspaper as he was packing, he talked of the sickness that drove him: "I'm looking for the big one, and this time I'm gonna find it. The Big Song. The Big Hit. I've been close to the edge several times. This time, I'll get it in two or three years. Music's a one-way door. Once you go through it, there's no walking back. You're hooked. It's worse than any drug in the world. In this business, you can see a guy out on the street one day without a nickel in his pocket, and maybe by next week he'll be driving a Cadillac. It only takes the right three minutes in a recording studio."

Like a dice player, Blake was looking for the win so high and wild that he would never need to roll again. This time nobody wanted to listen, though, and Blake ended up in Georgia without Betty. There he met Samantha, and they moved to Shreveport. Brutalized as a child, pregnant and then married in her teens, Samantha saw Blake as a conduit to the entertainment world, where her own dreams lay. A photo of Blake and Elvis Presley that sat on the dresser wherever Blake went was proof positive that success had lived there, and would, he assured her, do so again.

Despite the heart attack, Blake soon resumed drinking and popping pills. He cut his demos on a home cassette deck. His vocal range had shrunk to nothing and his voice was now tragically off-key. He left a mountain of tapes, unfinished songs, and a twisted little poem about his songwriting days with Carl Belew:

146

> Victor's the label—Belew was the name
> Nashville the town where they played the game
> Both writer and singer of country type songs
> His partner named Van played both zither and gongs
>
> They'd been in the business since birth some folks say
> Others claim a bad car wreck made their faces look that way
> Now Van had a chin big as half a football
> While Belew was opposite—no chin at all
>
> To write their songs I've heard their friends say
> It took a twenty buck prescription of bennies each day
> They both knew a million seller was their only chance,
> So they existed from advance to advance
>
> One night at the Poodle, as they checked out the new hides
> They conspired to write an album—twelve brand new sides
> Well they did, and Chet dug, then cut with Belew
> And everyone was so excited, their advances grew and grew
>
> Three months later, no album, not a single in sight
> And that's why we're here and this poetry we write
> No bookings, no bennies, we're as low as we can get
> Get up off your asses, use the phone and call Chet

By the time Blake died, the music industry had chewed him up and spat him out. No one made demos in an off-key voice and with an out-of-tune guitar in front of a home cassette deck anymore. Song plugging was no longer a business in which you wandered in to see Chet and said, "Chet, listen here to what

I got." It was a business of lawyers, power brokers, professional song pluggers, more lawyers, and points spreads. Blake was out of the loop. Howard Hausey, one of Blake's cronies from "The Louisiana Hayride" who wrote some of Johnny Horton's biggest hits, summed it up in a song (unpublished, of course), called "Songwriter, Don't Go to Nashville in the Summer (Or You'll Freeze to Death and Won't Know Why)." Tommy Blake never understood why. ⑥

FOR YOUR LISTENING PLEASURE
Two of Blake's RCA recordings are on the Country Music Foundation's five-star anthology of RCA rockabilly, *Get Hot or Go Home* (CMF-014-D); the Sun recordings are scheduled for issue on Bear Family's ongoing *Sun Singles Collection.*

A glimpse into what might have been: Tommy and Elvis, with two members of the Jordanaires, Shreveport, December 1956
Photo courtesy of C. Escott

An Everly Brother in Winter

WALKIN' RIGHT BACK WITH DON EVERLY

When rock 'n' roll arrived, it triggered a three-alarm anxiety attack in Nashville. Many hoped that they would wake up one morning to find that it had all been a terrible dream. It really wasn't until the Everly Brothers broke through in the summer of 1957 that there was a consistently successful rock 'n' roll act based, recorded, managed, and produced in Nashville. The Everlys also confounded the notion that Elvis had opened the door and that everyone marched through with a little different slant on what he was doing. Rather, the Everly Brothers were rooted in country music's tradition of absorbing outside influences, and they insist that Elvis barely figured in their thinking. Their sound was that of the country brother duet in the duck-tail era. Gone were the homilies to God, Mother, and Home; in their place were more pressing concerns: How can I meet her? Should we tell him? When will I be loved?

After fifteen years in Los Angeles, Don Everly returned to Nashville in 1975. He's renowned among his friends as a gourmet cook, and his girth betrays it. He hangs out in Brown's Diner, which has the best graffiti in town ("I think therefore I'm not sure," for one). John Prine plays the games machines; Don Everly holds court at one of the back tables. He's a great raconteur, seemingly oblivious after all these years to what should or should not be said, and what can or cannot be printed.

The Everly Brothers' hillbilly pedigree was come by honestly. Their father, Ike, grew up in Muhlenberg County, Kentucky, and after one too many narrow escapes down the mine, he and his brothers went to Chicago to work as musicians. After they left, Ike returned briefly, when he met and married Margaret Embry. Their first son, Isaac Donald, was born in Brownie, Kentucky, on February 1, 1937. Shortly after, Ike took his family back to Chicago, and Philip was born there on January 19, 1939. The original Everly Brothers band didn't last long, and in 1944 Ike struck out for Iowa to work on live radio and play the schoolhouses and joints.

Phil with future father-in-law Archie Bleyer and Don, Nashville, 1958
Photo courtesy of C. Escott

Ike Everly was much, much more than a journeyman musician with two famous sons. He was a virtuoso country picker—*picker* in the true, original sense of the word. Ike and his buddy Mose Rager based their style on the black guitarists they'd heard back in Kentucky, and the two of them can take much of the credit for bringing the fingerpicking style to country music. Merle Travis heard them, and Chet Atkins heard Merle Travis. That's the genealogy in a nutshell. Ike was an innovator who just never got the breaks.

The entire family worked on radio. Don and Phil grew up in front of a microphone, and life never presented any other serious option. Brother harmony acts, like the Bailes Brothers, the Delmore Brothers, and the Blue Sky Boys, were still very popular, and before they could wonder how they'd done it, Don and Phil had perfected that unerring sibling harmony where one brother intuitively knows where the other is heading. Don, though, claims to have been more influenced by solo singers. "Acuff-Rose would send out sheet music and I'd learn all the Hank Williams stuff from that," he says. "Lefty Frizzell and Hank were my two favorites. I loved the Sons of the Pioneers as well, and much later I cut 'Tumbling Tumbleweeds' on a solo album. Bob Nolan [of the Sons of the Pioneers] called up the radio station and said, 'Take that piece of shit off the air.' I really felt bad. I just wanted to twist it around a little bit. That was one of the big disappointments in my life."

By 1952 Ike's career was winding down as live radio sputtered and died, and the family act finally dissolved in Knoxville the following year. It was there that the brothers met Chet Atkins. Ike had written to Chet in care of the Carter Family in Springfield, Missouri, and the meeting came through a chain-link fence while Chet was playing a fair. His sons were talented performers in their own right, Ike told Chet, and Don wrote songs, too. Chet promised to see what he could do. He wasn't yet the mover and shaker that he would become in Nashville, but he knew his way around. He also had a small music publishing company, Athens Music, and he signed Don to it, pitching one of his songs, "Thou Shalt Not Steal," to Kitty Wells. Miss Kitty cut it on September 1, 1954, and it was a minor hit, spending one week on the charts that December.

Hoping for a break, Ike moved his family to Madison, near Nashville, and Chet introduced the brothers to Troy Martin, who was tight with Don Law, Columbia's chief of country A&R. Law was based in New York and commuted to Nashville and elsewhere for sessions. Martin brought the Everlys to Law's hotel room for an audition. Law's girlfriend thought they were cute, and lo! they were on Columbia. They cut four sides in twenty minutes at the tail end of a Carl Smith session, and their first record, "The Sun Keeps Shining," was released in February 1956. Troy Martin took half of Don's composer credit in exchange for landing the deal, but the record failed to budge. Law didn't exercise his option on the Everlys, and in truth, there was little on that first session to convince him to do so.

The brothers kept hustling. "We stood in the alley out back of the Opry with our songs," says Don. "I got a few cut. I was already a writer when I came to town, and that validated my credentials. The whole family was here for a little while, then Dad went up to get work in Hammond, Indiana. He helped us out for about a year, then all of a sudden we got some work. I had a few bucks coming in from the songs, from a Hill and Range advance, and from the Columbia session, but the Kitty Wells money was the biggest—a couple of thousand dollars."

The brothers had a manager of sorts in Eddie Crandall, once manager of Marvin Rainwater and then the boyfriend of Hank Williams's official widow, Audrey. "Then Audrey ended up advising my first wife on how to divorce me!" says Don. "What a shrew!" Chet Atkins kept trying to open doors for them, and Ernest Tubb's daughter, Elaine, took up their cause. She nursed a crush on Don and placed two of his songs with her brother, Justin. "She was a girl-friend-manager," says Don. "A year or so older—but a little more worldly. I was a very naïve young boy. Mom and Dad had never left us alone before. We'd traveled together, done everything together. Elaine got us on the 'Ernest Tubb

Friends and nemeses; left to right: Phil, Wesley Rose, Boudleaux Bryant, Don

Photo courtesy of C. Escott

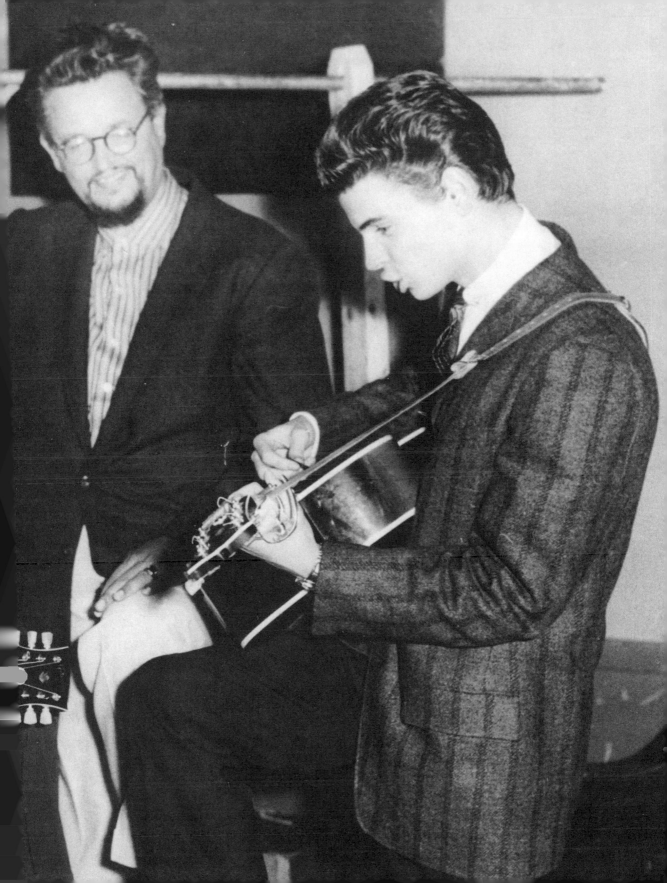

Midnight Jamboree,' and we got up and sang with her and by ourselves."

Elaine also introduced Don to one of her girlfriends, Mary Sue Ingraham. The combination of newfound freedom, youth's recklessness, and limitless access to a bedroom led to an enforced elopement across the state line to Georgia, but soon after the marriage, Sue miscarried. For a while, Don, Phil, and Sue all lived in Madison waiting for a decent break. Don says he never came close to getting a day job—there was always a glimmer of promise from some quarter. Meanwhile, he and Phil were trying to figure out Bo Diddley's music, and in the process, Elvis passed them right by. "Finally, the guitar was cool," says Don, "but Elvis didn't have the kind of voice I liked, nor a sound I liked. I was listening to Ray Charles, Brownie McGhee and Sonny Terry, and Bo Diddley." It was Diddley's open tunings that intrigued him, and the way Diddley made the guitar into a percussion instrument.

Just how far they'd come in a year and a half was obvious when they finally landed another deal. The arbiter was Wesley Rose, the president of the music publisher Acuff-Rose. "Chet had said, 'Watch Wesley!'" says Don, "but Wesley said he would get us a record deal if we signed our publishing with him. The problem was, we were signed with Hill and Range, so I went to Grelun Landon at Hill and Range. Grelun said, 'Nobody gets out of those contracts.' You signed for five hundred dollars for, like, the rest of your life. He got us released, though, bless his heart.

"Our whole idea was to get a record deal. Wesley had Cadence Records coming in. He said if Cadence wouldn't do it, he'd put us on Hickory [the Acuff-Rose house label]." Cadence was a pop label, but its owner, Archie Bleyer, was interested in getting into country music because much of what is now considered first-generation rock 'n' roll, like Elvis, Carl Perkins, and Gene Vincent, was then considered mutant country music. Bleyer, who had been the music director of the Arthur Godfrey show, asked Rose to line up some acts for him to listen to. Up to then, his big acts had been Julius LaRosa, the Chordettes, Bill "Ballad of Davy Crockett" Hayes, Andy Williams, and Bleyer himself. From the acts presented by Rose, Bleyer picked Gordon Terry, Anita Carter, and the Everly Brothers.

One of the songs that Rose offered the Everlys was Boudleaux and Felice Bryant's "Bye, Bye Love," a song that several acts had already turned down. Don and Phil agreed to cut it at their first Cadence session, slated for March 1957. Don doesn't like to hand out many kudos to Bleyer, but he gives him credit for suggesting they lift a riff from one of his publishing demos and graft it onto the intro of "Bye, Bye Love." The arrangement used four guitars: Phil played in regular tuning, Don played a guitar tuned to an open G chord with a capo way up on the neck, and a Nashville session man, Ray Edenton, played in regular tuning, but with the G string tuned up an octave. Chet Atkins was also on hand to play electric guitar fills. The end product had the local pickers sitting up nights. "All the guitar players in Nashville were trying to figure out how to do it," says Don.

One of the first to try and figure it out was Webb Pierce, the best-selling country artist of the mid-fifties. He cut "Bye, Bye Love " six weeks after the Everlys. "Webb was on his way to a session," says Don. "He heard it on the radio, turned around, canceled the session, got the record, and went back to the studio and cut it. He covered everybody. He'd covered Mel Tillis over and over. Mel was with us on a tour, and he said, 'I hate to tell you this, Don, but Webb Pierce has covered "Bye, Bye Love."' I called up Archie Bleyer. I said, 'Archie, we're really in trouble—Webb Pierce has covered "Bye, Bye Love."' He said, 'Who's Webb Pierce?' Then he said, 'Don't worry about it, we're hitting pop.' " Their worlds were so far apart that Bleyer didn't know that a Webb Pierce cover version was usually the kiss of death for the original, and the Everlys had no inkling of what "hitting pop" meant.

When "Bye, Bye Love " broke in May 1957, the Everlys were playing on a traveling tent show in Mississippi as a supporting act for Bill Monroe. Right away, the industry that for two years had been telling them, "Don't call us . . ." was calling. It was the moment of epiphany that every performer lives for. Even Ed Sullivan was leaving messages. Don and Phil bought a new 1957 Oldsmobile and were whisked onto a tour with Johnny Cash.

"The Grand Ole Opry" brought them in from the alley, signing them to the cast on June 1 after a successful guest shot two weeks earlier. This was a fulfillment of Ike Everly's dreams as much as Don and Phil's. With hindsight, the Everlys didn't need the Opry and soon realized as much, but in the early months of 1957 there was still no telling if rock 'n' roll would blow over. The smart money was already on calypso as the next craze. It took a while for the Everlys not to view their career from a country music perspective, a transition made no easier by Wesley Rose, who became their manager.

From the beginning, Bleyer and Rose bickered over whose copyrights were to be used. "They sat in the control room and fought," says Don. "We got it done in spite of them. Chet, Boudleaux, Phil and I, and the band were the ones that produced those records." The Bryants in particular became linked with the Everlys after lucking out with "Bye, Bye Love." They whipped up little two-and-a-half-minute confections for them. Some, like "Wake Up Little Susie" and "Bird Dog," were weak or marginal entries made special by the arrangements, but others shone, like "All I Have to Do Is Dream," introduced by Chet Atkins's single, heavily echoplexed chord.

In August 1958, just as "Bird Dog" was confounding Don's expectations by climbing to Number One, he and Phil went back into the studio to cut a second album, this one a retreat to country music's prehistory. The songs weren't big country hits from the last decade or so—something Rose would have preferred, with his huge back catalog. Instead, some reached back several hundred years, and only one came from the 1950s. It was an adventurous concept; the brothers were accompanied by just their acoustic guitars and Lightnin' Chance on bass. *Songs Our Daddy Taught Us* drew a straight line from the Everlys to groups like the Blue Sky Boys and the Louvins and makes the case for them as consummate country performers.

There was another motive behind the album. "I knew we would be leaving Cadence," said Don, "and I wanted the last album to be something musically that I loved, but I didn't want them to have any possible singles which they would have kept releasing [to] interfere with our career. I suggested *Songs Our Daddy Taught Us*, and everyone went for it. It touched what folk music ought to be—country folk music, songs people would sing sitting on the porch. It's got class and it ages really well."

Meanwhile, "Poor Jenny," one of the songs Boudleaux Bryant had taught them, was doing poorly. Cut almost two years to the day after "Bye, Bye Love," it barely dented the Top Twenty. The message was clear: the Everlys had issued one too many cute novelty songs punctuated by rhythm guitar riffs. Don felt this more acutely than the others. Always insecure, he never thought that they had it made and saw their career as a constant "next." At the same time, he was getting more confident in his writing and was itching to cut something a little more mature. On the long hike back from Australia in January 1958, he wrote "('Til) I Kissed You." "I wrote it about a girl I met on that trip," he said. "Her name was Lillian, and she was very, very inspirational. I was married, but . . . you know." For the flip side, they used another of Don's songs, "Oh, What a Feeling." Both were head and shoulders above anything the Bryants had submitted lately.

The bickering between Rose and Bleyer came to a head when the Everlys insisted on cutting "Let It Be Me." Originally a French song called "Je t'appartiens," it had been a minor hit in 1957 for Jill Corey. Don heard the song on a Chet Atkins album. "It was one of the great songs of my lifetime," he says. "We still close the show with it. I heard it on *Chet Atkins in Hollywood* as an instrumental. I said to Chet, 'I love that melody. Is there a lyric?' He said, 'Yes, and it's a great one.' I went to Archie and told him I wanted to do it with strings. Wesley just sat there pouting through the whole session like a kid." It was cut in New York—the first non-Nashville session for the brothers.

Aloha—and goodbye Sue. Don and Sue flanked by Phil and Robin Luke, Hawaii, 1959
Photo courtesy of C. Escott

The Cadence contract expired on or around the first of March 1960. Bley-er made no serious attempt to keep the Everlys, refusing to offer a guarantee against future earnings. Rose had begun scouting out a new record deal early in 1959, knowing he had a strong hand. Artists with a track record in rock 'n' roll were few and far between, and the Everlys were the third or fourth most bankable act on the market, after Elvis, Pat Boone, and Ricky Nelson. As early as July 1959 Rose let it be known that he was looking for a ten-year contract with a guarantee of one hundred thousand dollars a year.

The company that showed the most interest was Warner Bros. Records. Launched in September 1958, it had released almost one hundred singles during its first year; fourteen of them had reached the Hot 100, but only Edd Byrnes's grimly memorable "Kookie, Kookie (Lend Me Your Comb)" had made a serious dent. President Jim Conklin needed name acts with clout in the marketplace, and he had Warners' deep pockets to dip into. The Everlys seemed heaven-sent. The deal, as it was announced in January 1960, didn't quite give the Everlys the one-million-dollar guarantee that Rose wanted, but it offered fifty thousand dollars a year over a ten-year term—supposedly the

A playboy's nightmare: The Everlys enlist
Photo courtesy of Showtime Archive, Toronto

richest record deal in history to that point. "Unbeknownst to me," says Don, "Wesley had written himself into the contract. He wanted us to cut Acuff-Rose songs only, and you can't have a recording career that way."

Peace was assured for a while because the brothers hit a grand slam on their first at bat for Warners; "Cathy's Clown" was their biggest record ever. They were still recording in Nashville, using the same crew of pickers and engineers. "We'd find the song, do the arrangement, go in, tell the musicians what we wanted, tell the engineer," says Don. "We'd produce it in the studio. There was nothing for Wesley to do but time it. His part and Archie's part has been overplayed. Basically, they did not like or care about the music in the way that Phil and I did. I loved it. They looked at it as money. Their idea of what was going to hit was sometimes absurd."

The well-publicized and acrimonious split from Wesley came after the brothers wanted to revive the old Bing Crosby hit "Temptation." "I woke up one morning and I'd dreamed [the arrangement]," said Don. "That's when the shit hit the fan with Wesley. He hated 'Temptation'; I loved it. If he'd owned the publishing, he'd have loved it too." The brothers' five-year management deal with Rose was due to expire in May 1962, but they terminated it early, leading to a lawsuit and mutual recrimination. "Wesley took 'Love Hurts' that we'd recorded and had in the can," says Don, "and he covered us with Roy Orbison. The arrangement was ours, and it was written for us. We couldn't release it as a single because we didn't know if Acuff-Rose would license it or not because we were in a lawsuit with them. It got that bitter."

In the wake of the lawsuit, the brothers moved to California, and they didn't return to Nashville for two years. They came back then to recut all of their Cadence hits in stereo for Warners. By this point, Bleyer had folded Cadence and sold the masters to Andy Williams. "He bought it so that his old stuff couldn't be repackaged—like he's done to us the last twenty-five years," says Don, extracting what little humor he can from the situation. Using much the same session men on the recuts, the sound was predictably close; only the indefinable edge that separates a hungry artist from a sated one was missing— along with the sparkle that comes from singing something for the first time as opposed to the thousandth time. Wesley Rose was at the sessions, and a queasy peace prevailed. It made sense to come to terms with him, says Don, because he controlled their publishing until the end of the decade.

After two years on Warner Bros. when anything they touched, no matter how tangentially, turned to gold, things suddenly went sour. The Everlys finagled a joint six-month enlistment in the marines in 1962 to beat the problem of Don joining the army for a two-year hitch, then emerging to see Phil going in. Then, in October 1962, the brothers left for England to tour with Frank Ifield and Ketty Lester. It was in London that Don's problems with prescription drugs in nonprescription quantities surfaced. He was flown back to the United States. Wire service reports said that he had suffered food poisoning or a nervous breakdown, but the truth was that he had overdosed. Phil finished the tour alone. The whole period is a blur for Don. "We went into the marines. I had some personal problems around about '62, then I woke up and the Beatles were here."

Don and Phil had a sneak preview of the change that was going to come. They'd returned to England on a make-good tour in the fall of 1963, starring with Bo Diddley, Little Richard, and—at the bottom of the bill—the Rolling Stones. "We arrived, and there was a group of photographers and reporters waiting, and they wanted to know what we thought of the Beatles," said Don. Like everyone else, the Everlys wanted to know what a "Beatle" was.

When the Everlys' career faltered, it wasn't because of squabbles over management and publishing or even drug problems but because their day had passed. When that happens, it doesn't matter how good the records are. Oddly, Europe in general and England in particular kept faith with the Everly

Brothers when they couldn't buy airplay back home. Don, by now remarried to the British actress Venetia Stevenson, remembers the sixties English tours as among his happiest days. "I began to have a really wonderful time of my life in England, working. I felt pertinent to the situation. I didn't feel discarded," he says. He and Phil took it in their stride when people told them that they sounded like the Beatles.

In some ways, the Everlys' mid-sixties recordings were their best, but radio wouldn't touch them. "Being the Everlys in the sixties was a handicap," says Don. "We didn't fit between the Holding Company and whoever." Don desperately wanted to be a part of what was happening. He saw a place for the Everlys in the age of Aquarius, but it's doubtful that Phil did, and the bookers certainly didn't; they saw an act that should be feeding the already growing nostalgia for the pimply innocence of fifties music.

Later, the Everlys were present at the birth of the California country-rock scene, and there the pattern repeated itself. Rather than pick up with country music where they'd left off in 1955, the Everlys jumped at a suggestion from Andy Wickham at Warner Bros. in England that they do a concept album in which their current take on country music would be intercut with excerpts from old Everly Family radio shows from the early fifties. That album, *Roots*, which deserves to be talked about in the same breath as the Byrds' *Sweetheart of the Rodeo*, flopped and became some of the best music ninety-nine cents ever bought.

After the Warner Bros. deal ended, the Everlys signed with RCA, which held out the promise of returning to Nashville to work with their old mentor, Chet Atkins. Their two RCA albums, *Pass the Chicken and Listen* and *Stories We Could Tell*, were as consistent and innovative as anything they had ever cut, but the only publicity they got during their RCA contract was when they split up. Just as they'd lived most of their lives in public, so they split up in public. The rift came in July 1973 onstage at Knott's Berry Farm in the Disney complex.

They worked apart for a decade, cutting solo albums. Don quickly returned to his roots in Nashville. "In '74 I passed back through. I saw Wesley and my mother and father, and looked around. L.A. was chewing me up, and I said, 'I'm moving back.' Best thing I ever did. I came back in '75." He made peace with Wesley to the point of cutting some albums for Acuff-Rose's Hickory label. Soon after Don returned, his father died. Ike had played with his sons on and off since they first broke through, but had never tried to use their success as a springboard to relaunch his own career. His only album was cut for Cadence, and it remains unissued, the tapes apparently sequestered away by Margaret Everly.

After their reunion in 1983, Don and Phil began recording for Mercury in Nashville and charted a few country hits, but they're currently without a contract. They still work together, Don based in Nashville and Phil in Los Angeles. More than anything, Don wants to cut a state-of-the-art country record. "I'm going to finish my life out with my roots in music, " he declares. His problem is that the country market is now much like the pop market he once knew so well. Youth is everything. Don feels that his songs are better than ever, his band is hot, and his voice has mellowed well with age, but it's tough being an Everly Brother in the 1990s if you have an ambition to do more than play for folks who want to Remember When.

Even so, life holds no other serious option for Don Everly. He isn't starving—and isn't likely to be any time soon—but it seems like a raw deal when you've put your major vices behind you, the creativity's flowing, but you're denied because you were—and are—an Everly Brother.

"Old men," says Don, "need applause, too." ◉

FOR YOUR LISTENING PLEASURE

Don Everly's solo recordings for A&M and Hickory have yet to be caught up in the reissue sweeps. Everly Brothers compilations abound. The most complete edition of the Columbia and Cadence recordings is on *Classic Everly Brothers* (Bear Family BCD 15618; three CDs). Rhino has issued the entire Cadence catalog over several CDs; *Songs Our Daddy Taught Us* (R2-70212) is unreservedly recommended. *Walk Right Back* (Warner Bros. 9-45164; two CDs) trawls through the Warner years, and Rhino's four-CD set *Heartaches and Harmonies* (R2-71779) is an overview of the brothers' entire career.

IV

Guitar Stars and True Believers

James Burton

. . . .

PLAY IT, JAMES!

James Burton cradles a dark red 1953 Telecaster. The finish is cracked in a few places and the fretboard is worn, but it's got the look. You know that history just has to be bound up in that instrument. If you were driving by a pawnshop window and saw it, you'd pull across three lanes of traffic and back up just to look at it. Burton plays a few trademark runs, then says, "Man, I wish I had a cent for every copy of every record this guitar was on." It would probably clear the national debt.

Burton isn't doing so badly, though. He and his wife, Louise, recently elected to return to Shreveport, Louisiana, a city Burton left when he was seventeen. They're hedging their bets by keeping their houses in Beverly Hills, Burbank, and Las Vegas, but for the present, Shreveport is home again. The Burtons have bought perhaps the most spectacular property in Shreveport, a Southern gothic mansion and five acres on Cross Lake once owned by a B-movie producer. Apparently *The Creature from the Black Lagoon* was shot on the lakeshore frontage.

Burton is still on the road much of the year, and when he's home he occasionally seems lost in the house's labyrinth. "They say there's a mile of pathway," he says during the guided tour of the grounds.

James Burton has witnessed history, but it's hard to know how and to what extent it registered. James picked and ran. Ran because there was always another job waiting. He worked with at least two of the great tragic, doomed figures of our time: Elvis Presley and Gram Parsons. Add to that almost a decade with Ricky Nelson, several years with Emmylou Harris, Bob Luman, Dale Hawkins, and more recently John Denver, and more sessions than even Burton remembers, and you have some sense of his prolificacy. Perhaps part of his reticence is due to unwillingness to poop on his old employers, but it's more likely that James simply didn't see what he didn't want to see.

One unremarked, but remarkable, thing about James Burton is that he retained the name "James," avoiding the nickname "Jim" or "Jimmy." The reason has some peculiarly Southern logic behind it; he has a younger brother named Jimmy. The family lived in Dubberly, Louisiana, out near Minden, when James was born on August 21, 1939, but he grew up in Shreveport, which he has always called home.

The way that some people have a natural facility for an instrument leads you to think there might be something to reincarnation. It seems to come to them so effortlessly it's as if they were doing it in another life and just picked up where they left off. That's the way it was with James Burton. He claims to have taken no lessons; just picked it all up from listening and sitting in. His first guitar was a Rex, then a Stella that he rigged up with a high action to use as a Dobro, and then, when he was thirteen years old, he walked into the J&S Music Store in Shreveport and experienced love at first sight. It was the '53 Telecaster.

Burton's style, combining finger-picking and flat-picking (he holds a flat pick between his thumb and first finger and has a finger pick on his second finger) evolved quickly and naturally. "To finger-pick, you don't really need a thumb pick," he says, "so I used a flat pick to get the speed, then I could still use finger picks. When I started playing slide guitar I used the same style; I never liked using a thumb pick because I liked the up and down strokes you could get with a straight pick."

Burton's style combines country music's emphasis on melody with the drama of the blues. It's commonplace now—it's called rock 'n' roll guitar—but it was a new idea in Shreveport circa 1954. James tuned in the R&B radio stations in town and further afield. "We started searching for those far-out channels on the radio," he says. "There was one station in Del Rio, Texas, that we used to listen to a lot, and Gatemouth Page had a show on the radio that we could pick up." His favorite guitarist was Les Paul, although he never had any plans to copy him. He says he took his cue from vocalists, whom he credits for giving his work its natural fluidity and emphasis on melody. He also loved the steel guitar, and he remembers playing on- and offstage duets with the steel player on "The Louisiana Hayride," Sonny Trammell. The sweet, sustained notes of the steel became part of his concept of how the electric guitar should sound.

Although he went on to work many sessions with charts and written music, James never became more than marginally proficient at sight-reading. "People wanted my sound and my style," he explains, "so they would integrate that into their writing. If they wanted someone to play a written-out guitar solo, why hire me?"

In 1955 James Burton became part of the staff band on "The Louisiana Hayride." All the show's early stars, such as Hank Williams, Webb Pierce, Kitty Wells, Elvis Presley, Johnny Cash, Jim Reeves, and Faron Young, had left

James and Jim Kirkland
Photo courtesy of R. Bennett/C. Escott

165

town by the time Burton signed on; only Johnny Horton and Slim Whitman remained. Even so, the experience of playing behind guests and regulars gave Burton adaptability, which was ultimately what paid for all the houses.

Between Hayride dates, the underage Burton was sitting in at honky-tonks like the It'll Do Club with the Dale Hawkins band. They made a demo tape of "See You Soon, Baboon" at the KWKH studio. The tape was played over the air and impressed Stan Lewis, the owner of Stan's Record Shop and later Jewel/Paula Records. Lewis signed Hawkins to a management deal, then pitched the act to Chess Records.

Every magazine article about Burton always repeats his claim that the first record he played on was Dale Hawkins's "Suzie Q." Cut in February 1957, the record's influence exceeds its rather lowly peak of Number Twenty-seven on the Hot 100. It has become a staple, thanks largely to Creedence Clearwater Revival, who later took it into the Top Twenty. On every version, someone tries to copy James Burton's lick, a lick perfect in its utter simplicity and devilish execution. Burton was seventeen years old then, not fifteen as he usually says, but the log sheet filed with the American Federation of Musicians noted that he was still too young to have a Social Security card.

Dale Hawkins, from Goldmine, Louisiana, took the writing credit on "Suzie Q" together with Stan Lewis. Chess surreptitiously assigned a third share to a deejay in care of his wife. One of Lewis's relatives played drums, and Lewis produced the session (in the sense that turning the tape machine on can be called "producing") at the KWKH studio after it went off the air. The entire deal rankles Burton. He maintains that "Suzie Q" was an instrumental that he wrote to which Hawkins put words. Hawkins essentially agrees, but seems disinclined to hand over a share of the copyright.

"Suzie Q" was the sort of first record that a picker of Burton's caliber should have made, but it wasn't his first. That was "Just for a While"/"You Never Mention My Name" by Carol Williams (Ram 45MS-101, for the discographically minded). Ram was a Shreveport label named after a local record store. Burton's presence on Carol Williams's record is unmistakable. It would have been a pedestrian mid-fifties country record if not for him. Both sides are two-and-a-half-minute guitar workouts with vocals on top. Burton plays the intros, plays under the vocals, plays the fills, and then takes his solos as well. Music is literally bursting out of him; Carol Williams didn't stand a chance—neither did the record. Burton would never be that busy on a record again.

Burton played the hillbilly nightspots around town until he got a call from Horace Logan, the general manager of the Hayride, who doubled as the manager of a Hayride regular, Bob Luman. Logan believed that Luman had what it took to make it in rock 'n' roll, and he thought that Burton had the licks. Luman, Burton, and the bass player James Kirkland tested the waters on a couple of Hayride shows, then started working together. A few weeks later, they headed to California.

Bob Luman's first entry in the statistic books is for "Let's Think about Living," and for that he had to wait until 1960. In 1957 he had eyes to challenge Elvis. Logan got him on Imperial Records, and James can be heard to particularly good advantage on Luman's early Imperial sides. "Red Cadillac and a Black Mustache " is the one that critics like to cite because it's a song of Berryish wit, but James's solos on less well known songs like "Make Up Your Mind" better showcase his clear articulation of ideas at any tempo.

Exactly how Burton and Kirkland came to leave Luman stranded in Los Angeles is still unclear. When Horace Logan quit the Hayride it was to go to California to work with Fabor Robison at Fabor Records. Logan took Luman with him, and Burton, not yet eighteen, tagged along. To help meet the rent, Burton played on Fabor sessions. Then Logan secured a semi-regular spot for Luman on the country music radio show "Town Hall Party" in Compton, California, and landed him a part in a sub-B movie called *Carnival Rock*.

One day Ricky Nelson was in the Imperial offices when he heard Luman rehearsing "Red Hot" with Jimmie Haskell. He knew at once that Burton and Kirkland were playing exactly what he had been hearing in his dreams. "The guitar player was unbelievable," Nelson said later, "and the bass player was playing this slap style I really liked. That *was* rock 'n' roll as far as I was concerned." Burton, Luman, and Kirkland had rented a house in Canoga Park, and the next morning there was a telegram on the door inviting Burton and Kirkland down to the studio where "Ozzie and Harriet" was shot. The invitation pointedly didn't extend to Luman.

Nelson made Kirkland and Burton fairly regular fixtures on "Ozzie and Harriet" and used them as a backing duo when they weren't working with Luman. Then, in December 1957, Luman, Burton, and Kirkland returned to Shreveport for Christmas and played a short tour with Buddy Knox. In January 1958 Ozzie Nelson called Burton and Kirkland offering them a regular spot on Ricky's shows. "He sent me a telegram, and I signed the telegram and sent it back to him," said Burton. "I didn't know it was gonna happen that fast. The wheels were really turning, and I didn't hardly have time to think about being so young and away from home."

The Nelsons invited Burton to stay in their home, and he spent a year or two there before finding his own place. Kirkland toured with Nelson for almost a year before opting to return to country music with Jim Reeves. Burton

James and Emmylou Harris
Photo courtesy of Sylvia Corley

then called up another Shreveporter, Joe Osborn, to join the group. There should be a story or two from the time spent with the Nelsons, but James just remembers it as a good time.

The first Nelson session that Burton worked was the one that produced "Waitin' in School" and "Stood Up," but it's not him taking the solos—it's Joe Maphis. On every Ricky Nelson record after that for the next seven or eight years, though, it's James Burton. Nelson's sessions were supervised by Jimmie Haskell, and Haskell had the sense to allow Burton a lot of freedom. On "Believe What You Say," for instance, James is using banjo strings for that extra twangy sound. His work is astonishingly consistent. He never wastes a note, and his solos are so melodic you could set words to them. "Milestones [in] their self-assured precision and tonal development," is how the *Guitar Player* writer Steve Fishell described Burton's solos, adding "[Burton's] full round bass notes, and crystalline, hard-driving highs wrote the book for state-of-the-art Fender tone."

Burton remembers Nelson as intensely shy and understandably a little insecure at first about his musical skills. "He loved the screaming and everything," says Burton, "but he'd always sing with his eyes closed. I guess it was partly shyness, but that was like his trademark." On television, Burton was usually more animated than his boss, mugging into the camera during his solos. He illuminates the records, and there's a case to be made for saying that it is his work that elevates Ricky Nelson records to greatness.

Burton continued with Nelson until 1965. Just before he quit the lineup, he played on a couple of albums, *Country Fever* and *Bright Lights and Country*

Music, that hinted at his future direction with Mike Nesmith, Gram Parsons, and Emmylou Harris. Those sessions were also one of the first occasions that his Dobro got an extended workout on disc, although diehard fans know that "Jimmy Dobro," who saw a solitary release on Philips in 1963, was in fact James Burton.

By 1965 James was bored. It had reached the point where Nelson was only on the road one month a year. He had been blown out of the water by geeky British groups and didn't know where to go. "The records weren't selling that great," says Burton, "and Ricky slacked back on appearances. He was trying to get another record deal and didn't know what kind of music he wanted to record. It was getting boring to just go down and pick up the weekly paycheck and not play music. Then I got a call from Johnny Cash to do a TV pilot, and Ricky didn't want me to do it because I was under contract to him, but eventually we worked it out."

The television show turned out to be the pilot for "Shindig," and Burton was drafted into the backing crew. "[Producer] Jack Good said, 'I want you to be a regular on the show every week,' " remembers Burton, "and I said, 'Fine.' He said he wanted me to put a group together, so I got Glen Hardin on keyboards, Delaney Bramlett, and so on. We needed a name, and Jack came up with 'The Shindogs.' He said, 'You'll be bigger than the Beatles!' " The statistic books tell us that one Shindogs record got up to Number Ninety-one on the Hot 100.

After a year on "Shindig," Burton disappeared into the studios for several years. "I didn't know there was that much work in the world," he says. "I'd sleep maybe three or four hours a night. I was doing five or six sessions a day, sometimes seven days a week. I'd do an Everly Brothers session, then a Merle Haggard session, then maybe a Johnny Mathis session, then a Fifth Dimension date, then Phil Spector, and so on. We'd book 'em so tight. The nine o'clock session would end just as the next was scheduled to begin at noon. We had a cartage company, and at one minute to noon they'd arrive and pick up our instruments and take them to the next studio. I'd just run to my car. Finally, we had to allow for an hour's overtime, and maybe forty minutes into overtime we'd ask to go."

Burton maintains that playing so many different styles kept him fresh and kept the music exciting. Often, after playing all day, he'd head to the Palomino and sit in at night. Unlike the Nashville session ace Grady Martin, Burton never kept a log of the sessions he worked, and as album jackets rarely gave credit to session men then, much of what he did is undocumented. Every so often, you'll hear a late-sixties Los Angeles record and swear it's James Bur-

James plays his Paisley Tele for the King
Photo courtesy of Sylvia Corley

ton on guitar. It probably is. His Dobro work on Merle Haggard's Jimmie Rodgers tribute album is well worth checking out, as is his interplay with Stephen Stills and Richie Furay on Buffalo Springfield's "A Child's Claim to Fame."

It was Burton's work for Haggard and Buck Owens that gave the Capitol A&R man Ken Nelson the notion to record him in a series of duets with the steel guitarist Ralph Mooney. "He said, 'I've got a lot of requests for an album of you guys. Would you be interested in doing a record together?' Ralph and I both said we would. It was a fast thing. Ralph was living in Vegas and he drove over to my house and we wrote a couple of quick things. We cut the album in three sessions." Unfortunately, it shows.

Unlike most pickers of legendary status, James Burton has never really entertained the notion of being a front man. There are two albums and a few pseudonymous records that were cut to ease the boredom of being a Ricky Nelson sideman, and that was about the extent of it. He still talks about leading his own group, but not with much conviction.

Then, in 1969, came the call from Memphis. "I was in the shower 'cause I had three or four sessions that day, and my wife answered the phone. She said, 'You got a long distance call from Memphis, some guy named Joe Esposito.' It didn't ring a bell with me, so I said, 'Take his number.' She said I should take the call, so I did, and Joe said, 'Hi, James, I got someone here wants to talk to you,' and Elvis got on the phone, and we talked maybe two and a half hours. One of his opening lines was that he watched 'The Ozzie and Harriet Show' every week to see me play with Ricky. He wanted me to be his lead guitarist and manage his band.

"It was a tough decision because I was so busy I was almost a walking zombie. I thought about it, and I thought it would be interesting to go out and do some live gigs."

Surprisingly, James and Elvis had never met. Elvis had got his first big break in Shreveport, and Burton remembered seeing some of the shows. Later he had played on the backing tracks for some of Elvis's anonymous sixties soundtrack albums, and he'd had a call to do the 1968 comeback special, which he'd had to refuse because he was committed to working sessions with Frank Sinatra. With their shared history, they felt like old pals, which left Burton confident about accepting the gig. Elvis gave him two or three months to work off his studio commitments and assemble the band.

From the beginning it was obvious that Elvis's base of operations was to be Las Vegas, so Burton decided to buy a house there as a home away from home. "I made the mistake of staying in a hotel the first two times," he says. "It was like a circus every night, wall-to-wall people. The last show was over at one-thirty, and I was wound up so tight, and there'd be twenty or thirty people from out of town, and we'd visit. Then I came to need to the privacy of my own house." Burton's session work followed him out to Vegas; occasionally people would fly in to work sessions with him before or after the Presley shows.

In 1969 Elvis was thirty-four and at the top of his game. The best young songwriters were submitting to him again, and he looked set to resume his reign. Eight years later, he'd completely lost it. The voice became a wobbly vibrato over which its owner seemed to have only marginal control, and the hits were tailing off. Elvis had lapsed painfully into self-parody. James is guarded about the decline, reiterating endlessly that he never saw Elvis take illicit drugs, although he admits that the prescription drugs Elvis took and the weight fluctuations *might* have contributed to his physical decline. And that, says James, *might* have affected his music. Might, might, might. Even James Burton, raised in the hamburger culture, knew that the Presley breakfast of champions, comprising a dozen eggs and a pound of bacon, fell somewhere short of ideal. Then, when the weight came off, it came off fast. There was something weird about that, James thinks.

James also worked many of Presley's recording sessions, including those held at Graceland toward the end of the singer's life. "He could call his own shots there," says James, "but it was no good for the musicians. He'd call a session at six o'clock, and he'd show at two in the morning, and we were tired. The worst thing you can do to tire yourself out is nothing. Someone would say, 'Let's go eat,' then someone else would say, 'No, Elvis might come down early tonight.' And when Elvis showed up he didn't want to see nobody sitting over in the corner yawning. We'd been up since eight o'clock in the morning, and he's just beginning."

Presley liked recording "live" with the rhythm section, but, as Burton says, "it was rare for Elvis to do more than four or five takes—usually if he didn't have it in two takes he'd forget it. He had an amazing photographic memory for lyrics. Very rarely would anyone have to write out lyrics for him. He'd learn them off the demo in one or two tries."

In 1971 Burton cut his last released solo album to date. Elvis's producer, Felton Jarvis, had booked studio time, but Elvis fell sick and couldn't make the date. Jarvis told Burton that he had contacted A&M Records about doing an album with him, and with the studio booked, the project fell into place very quickly. Too quickly. Burton went with established favorites like "Fire and Rain" and "Mystery Train," and the record fell flat.

Then came the morning of August 16, 1977. "We left Burbank that morning to meet Elvis in Portland," remembers Burton. "We went to Vegas to pick up the horn players and the vocalists, and then, when we were heading to Portland, the pilot made an announcement that he'd had a call telling us to land as soon as possible, but he didn't say why. He put us down in Pueblo, Colorado, and told us to call Vegas. We were thinking that Elvis had canceled because his father was sick. When we got to Pueblo, Marty, the trombone player, called Vegas and I went to call my wife. I'd got halfway to the phone when I saw Marty coming toward me. He had a strange look on his face, and his eyes were red with tears. He put his arm around me and said, 'Elvis passed away.' A cold chill went over me."

Through the last four years with Elvis, Burton had been working with Gram Parsons and then Emmylou Harris. He had met Parsons on the Byrds'

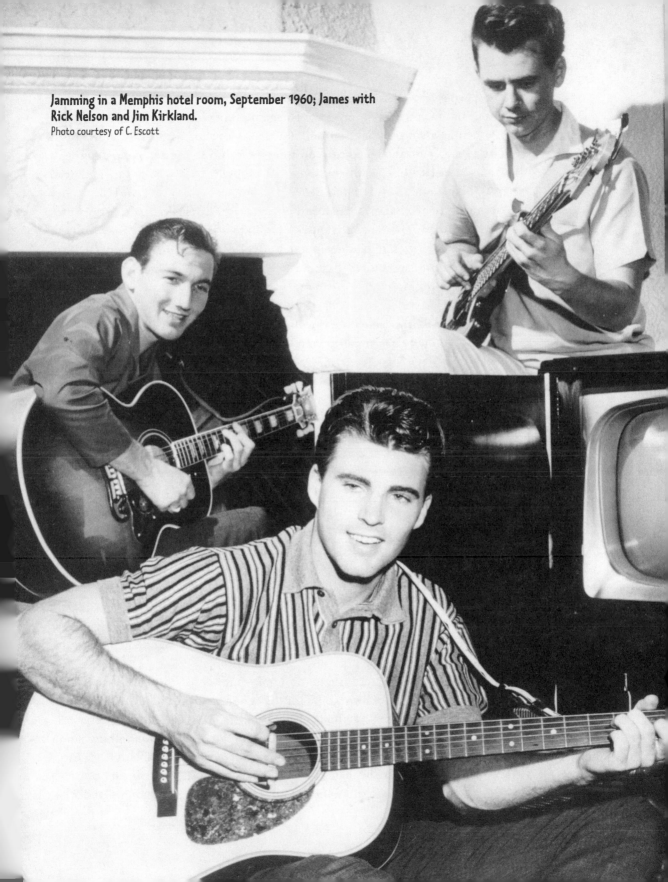

Jamming in a Memphis hotel room, September 1960; James with Rick Nelson and Jim Kirkland.
Photo courtesy of C. Escott

Sweetheart of the Rodeo sessions, and they'd sat in together at the Palomino Club. Then Burton got a call from Merle Haggard asking if he'd be interested in co-producing Parsons's album. "I said, 'Sure, I'd love to,'" he said, "so we left it with Gram, who was going to send some tapes up to Merle. Then about two weeks later I hadn't heard anything so I thought it was off, then I got a call from Gram saying, 'Well, I don't guess I'm gonna do this thing with Merle, but Warner Bros. offered me a deal, and my manager, Ed Tickner, is putting it together.' He wanted me and Glen D. Hardin to work on it."

Tickner negotiated tour support, but Parsons didn't make it very far down the road before he died. If there was weirdness at the sessions or on the road, Burton either didn't see it or didn't want to see it. Tickner picked up with Emmylou Harris after Parsons's death, and Burton became part of Harris's Hot Band. Their touring schedule dovetailed around Presley's shows for a while, but Burton finally had to quit when Harris wanted to spend more time on the road.

Since then, Burton has worked on the road with John Denver. They met on a television special just before Elvis's death, and Denver tried to recruit him then. James still works plenty of sessions as well. He's an equal opportunity picker; if he's available, and if the budget stretches to double scale, James Burton will pick. "This is my career," he says. "The more things I do, the better it is for my career. You need to pace yourself and not overdo it, but I try to make myself available." One of the results has been that, in a business characterized by sniping and backbiting, it's hard to find anyone with a bad word to say about James Burton. He comes, he picks, he's great, and if there's a few minutes left at the end of the session he'll demonstrate his solo on "Hello, Mary Lou" for the other pickers.

If James Burton is to record again as a solo act, he allows that he'll have to sing. "Clapton sings, " he says, "so does Chet [Atkins]. I *know* I'm that good. Now might be the right time to start on something like that. Studios aren't that busy, and I have some offers. I need to put my project together. I still think I'm nineteen playing 'Hello, Mary Lou,' but time's passing."

Guitars are the safest ground for James Burton; he's often uneasy talking about the people he has worked with. Experiences—good and bad—are usually called "interesting" without elaboration. If he has backstage stories, he keeps them to himself. He becomes truly animated only when talking about his guitars and his vintage car collection. The man who played with Elvis Presley *and* Elvis Costello, the man who has plugged in his guitar in north Louisiana beer joints and Vegas supper clubs, still wants to play. He knows that's what he was put on this earth to do. Perhaps a definitive solo album is the last career hurdle he has to jump. The suggestion sits in the air for a moment, then James says, "I'd pay to hear that myself." ☺

FOR YOUR LISTENING PLEASURE

Records with James Burton's name on the front are few and far between. The one with Ralph Mooney, *Corn Pickin' and Slick Slidin'* (Capitol ST 2872), has been reissued in Europe (See For Miles SEECD 377), but there's too much corn and slick ("My Elusive Dreams," "Spanish Eyes") and not enough pickin' and slidin'. The A&M album, *The Guitar Sounds of James Burton* (SP 4393), has never been reissued. Then there's a very rare album that was never officially released, *The TCB Band* (Inergi ILP 1003), on which James leads Elvis's road band.

Merle Haggard's tribute record to Jimmie Rodgers, *Same Train—Different Time,* has been reissued by Bear Family in Germany with additional tracks (BCD 15740) and by Koch International in the United States (KOC-3-4051-2). Burton is all over two volumes of Ricky Nelson's Imperial recordings, *The Best of Rick Nelson* (EMI E2-95219) and *Legendary Masters Series* (EMI E2-92771).

James's work with Gram Parsons and Emmylou Harris has been reissued on *GP/Grievous Angel* (Warner Bros. 26108), a twofer that holds more good music than should be legally allowed on one CD. A planned boxed set of Elvis in the seventies should contain a good sampling of James with the King.

Roy Buchanan

. . . .

THE MESSIAH WILL COME AGAIN

Roy Buchanan broke the mold. Usually the record comes out, then the articles follow, then the concerts start selling out, and then there's a television special. With Buchanan, it was the other way around. First there were the laudatory articles, then the sellout concerts and the first television show, and then the first album. Only gradually did it become clear that Roy Buchanan had been around the block more than once, and that what was hailed as his first album was indeed his first album, but far from his first recording.

Roy Buchanan was the product of a peculiarly Southern weirdness, probably made all the weirder by its transplantation to southern California. He was born in Ozark, Arkansas, on September 23, 1939, but grew up in Pixley, California, about fifty miles north of Bakersfield in the San Joaquin Valley, where his father preached to exiled Southerners at the Pentecostal Church of God. Roy always said his mother sang better than Billie Holiday. "Once a month," he told Bill Millar, "they'd get together with the black church for a revival meeting, and that's how I got into black music. I've always been partial to black guitar players, Blind Boy Fuller, Jimmy Nolen, Pete Lewis. The old black cats won't ever be beat." Buchanan learned the steel guitar when he was nine and left home when he was fifteen, heading first for Los Angeles and then San Francisco.

Just after he left home, Roy heard Elvis—the first white music he loved ("He sounded like he'd been to the same church as me, " Roy once said). Then, a couple of years later, he joined the band of Dale Hawkins, the go-for-broke rockabilly singer from Louisiana. Roy used to say that he had crafted the anthemic lick that introduces and punctuates Hawkins's only major hit, "Suzie Q." In fact, the lick was originated by James Burton, but after Buchanan took Burton's place in Dale Hawkins's band, it was Roy's job to replicate it twice a night. Roy can be heard on one or two of Dale Hawkins's records, though.

And then there was a stint in Canada with Dale Hawkins's cousin, Ronnie Hawkins. As Ronnie's original band, with the exception of Levon Helm, drifted back to Arkansas, he drafted new recruits, tantalizing them with his now-famous promise of low pay but more pussy than Frank Sinatra. Roy worked with the Hawks for a month or so, imparting some of his technique to Robbie Robertson, who was to be the group's permanent guitarist. Talking to *Musician* magazine, Robertson remembered Buchanan as "*really* very, very good, the most remarkable guitarist I had seen. I can remember asking him how he developed his style, and he said with a straight face he was half wolf. He was always saying he wanted to settle down, but he needed to find a nun to marry."

As far as we know, Roy's first solo recordings were made for the tiny Bomarc label in 1959. One side was "After Hours," one of Roy's favorite vehicles for slow blues exploration. Originally written and recorded by the pianist Avery Parrish with the Erskine Hawkins Orchestra in 1940, it was dubbed the national anthem of black America. Roy would return to it endlessly. The first version shows that many elements of his style were in place early on. He was already experimenting with feedback, fuzz tone, and distortion, and had apparently sliced his speaker cones for an even dirtier sound.

By 1963 Roy was based in the Washington, D.C., area. His wife, Judy, was from there. He played the local clubs and, when gigs were scarce, worked as a barber in Bethesda, Maryland. Hardy souls have tried to piece together his early recordings both as session man and featured player, but when he spoke to Bill Millar, Roy was typically dismissive of both. "Play 'em now, I feel like a good puke," he said, a judgment he later broadened to include most of his records. One of Roy's early records, issued as "The Jam" by Bobby Gregg and Friends, actually cracked the Top Thirty in 1962. Roy was quick to point out that "Friends" was not entirely accurate.

The late sixties found Roy teaching guitar and playing regularly at the Crossroads, a club in Bladensburg, Maryland. Word about him gradually began filtering out, partly as a result of underground tapes. Then, quite suddenly, Roy started attracting a lot of attention. His arrival is usually dated to February 1971; it was during that month that *Rolling Stone* published an article by Tom Zito (reprinted from the *Washington Post* two months earlier) extolling Roy's virtues in the exaggerated terms that were the norm then for rock journalism. The contract with Polydor Records is always thought to have been a consequence of that article, but Roy was already recording for the company. His first album had been cut—and scrapped.

Polydor had been in business in the United States less than a year when Roy Buchanan was signed. The deal appears to have been negotiated by Bob Johnston, who, as Columbia Records' Nashville boss, had been responsible for Bob Dylan's Nashville sessions and Leonard Cohen's *Songs from a Room*. Late in 1969 Johnston, now operating on his own, appears to have placed Buchanan with Polydor and assigned him to the producer/musician Charlie Daniels.

Daniels's career had bisected Buchanan's at various points. Originally from North Carolina, he had covered all the bases from bluegrass to psychedelia by the time he showed up in Nashville. Johnston had encouraged him to move there, giving him session work on albums by Dylan, Cohen, and others. "I'd met Roy when he was Dale Hawkins's guitar player," says Charlie. "There had always been an underground buzz thing with him. All the guitar players knew who he was—the inside people. Nobody had done anything with him, though." It appears that Roy's stature among fellow pickers was such that even Les Paul had come to Maryland to hear him play.

In some ways it was typical of Buchanan's career that his first album wasn't released. He and Daniels worked at it on and off for several months, begining with the song "Baltimore" in October 1969. That track featured Daniels playing a Claptonesque lead with Buchanan as his foil. The other abandoned songs included Daniels's "Black Autumn," which contained the orgasmic instrumental passage that later became the centerpiece of Buchanan's "The Messiah Will Come Again."

There was general dissatisfaction with the album (tentatively titled *The Prophet*), but it probably reached the test-pressing stage before it was canned. The way that Daniels remembers it is that "some critic from Baltimore heard the tapes and said it was shit, and that scared everyone at Polydor to death. I just stopped working on it, and then it got so I couldn't get in touch with Roy, so I thought, piss on this." Between the time *The Prophet* was recorded and the time it was scheduled for release, Roy sold out Carnegie Hall (probably the only act to do so without a record on the market). By now, he had a new manager, Jay Reich, who added his voice to those who were saying that *The Prophet* should stay in the can.

Tom Zito produced another set of tapes around March 1971, but a second projected album, featuring part of a concert Roy had given at Gaston Hall, was also canned. Roy's first public television special, "The Best Unknown Guitarist in the World," aired in November 1971. The first album to actually appear, modestly titled *Roy Buchanan*, was recorded (Roy said in five hours) in July 1972 and released that September. It was basically his live set committed to tape. A year later, it had sold a respectable two hundred thousand copies. The cut that gave some indication of Roy's disturbing talent was "The Messiah Will Come Again," a spoken parable delivered in a hushed affectless monotone. The very ordinariness with which he delivered it underscored its strangeness. The song closed with a solo based on Daniels's instrumental passage from "Black Autumn." The notes spun up out of the darkness. Nothing like this had been heard before.

As he would with most of his albums, Roy professed himself disappointed with this one. For anyone who didn't know what else he was capable of, it was astonishing—or at least astonishing in parts. Pickers now had a new act to beat. Someone had just moved the goalposts. Roy knew the value of playing a few notes with frightening precision, but he could spit them out like bullets from a machine gun at double or even quadruple time, never sacrificing a sense of order. He had refined his touch so that he could isolate overtones by playing one string with a pick, simultaneously brushing another string with his fingernail. His trademark, though, was the note that soared crazily out of the silence as he hit a string, bent the note, and simultaneously cranked up the volume.

The *Second Album* (if there could have been a less imaginative title than *Roy Buchanan*, this was it) was cut in November and December 1972 and released the following February. Most of the originals had been composed on the way to New York by Roy and his pianist, Dick Heintze. Production was handled by Polydor's A&R director, Peter Siegel, who paired Roy and Heintze with some session men. The focus was on the blues, and the result was Buchanan's most consistent album. Even he had fewer bad words for it than for most of his records. It became his most successful album too, eventually selling over half a million copies.

By this point, the invitations were tempting Roy far from Maryland. Back in 1969 the Rolling Stones had offered him the job of replacing Brian Jones, and John Lennon had asked him to sit in on a Plastic Ono Band session. Roy blew the chance of working with Lennon by OD'ing on downers and passing out on the console. Success seemed to simultaneously attract and repel him. "This star business," he said, "scares the hell out of me." As a matter of preference, he would play small bars close to home, but if he had to go out on the road, he would play big venues for the maximum return so that he could head back to Maryland as quickly as possible.

One problem Roy never convincingly licked was that of finding a singer to front his band. Someone had told him that instrumental albums didn't sell, so for his third album, *That's What I Am Here For*, he used Billy Price, who sometimes gave the impression that he and Roy were in different bands. Price and the rest of the band (with the exception of Heintze) were from Jay Reich's hometown, Pittsburgh. Reich also produced the album, which was, as he says, "a blatant attempt to sell some 45s." The purists in the press corps were appalled, and the singles didn't sell.

The producer Ed Freeman, who had worked on Gregg Allman's first successful solo album, brought in another singer, Bill Sheffield, for Roy's final

Polydor studio album, bizarrely titled *In the Beginning* (or *Rescue Me* in Europe). It had its moments, but it was essentially untruthful about Roy Buchanan. His swan song on American Polydor was *Live Stock*, mostly cut in New York in November 1974. Roy wanted to be free from Polydor so he could take up Ahmet Ertegun's offer to join Atlantic. Polydor agreed to release him provided they could get a live album and retain worldwide rights to his Atlantic records outside North America.

Roy signed with Atlantic in March 1976. Ahmet Ertegun assigned him to Arif Mardin, who had produced the mega-selling Average White Band albums. It was the AWB feel that laid heavy over Roy's first Atlantic album, titled with grim irony *A Street Called Straight*. The breakthrough didn't happen, and Ertegun persuaded Roy to let Stanley Clarke produce the next one. Clarke was a jazz-fusion bassist who had starred in Return to Forever and who seemed to have no understanding of the traditions on which Roy was drawing. Some cuts were made at Clover Studios in Los Angeles, owned by Steve Cropper. Clarke didn't even know who Cropper was, but Roy and his management insisted that the Stax veteran come out of the office to play a duet on an overly long version of "Green Onions."

Buchanan's final Atlantic album, *You're Not Alone*, appeared the following year. It was followed by a two-year layoff from recording, which was in turn followed by a solitary and awful record for Waterhouse Records in Minneapolis. That was followed by five years out of the studio. Then, in 1985, Roy signed with the Chicago-based blues label Alligator Records.

In interviews toward the end of his life, Roy seemed at pains to emphasize that he was free of the drug and alcohol abuse that had plagued him for years. Those assertions made his death in August 1988 inexplicable to those who weren't privy to the truth: Roy Buchanan's street called Straight never ran for more than a few blocks. The official verdict was that he had been thrown into the drunk tank after being arrested close to his Reston, Virginia, home and had hanged himself there. Judy Buchanan challenged that conclusion, but others indicated that the nature of his death, while tragic, was consistent with another suicide attempt and a history of self-destructive behavior. For years, Judy kept Roy's body in cold storage hoping to gather the funds necessary to prove police brutality.

Roy Buchanan fitted the picture of a genius, unconstrained as he was by societal and musical norms. He never made a truly great record that you could give to your grandchildren and say, "This is the defining work of Roy Buchanan," but in Buchanan's case, a solo here and a solo there together add up to genius.ⓖ

FOR YOUR LISTENING PLEASURE

Polydor compiled the best of their albums and abandoned tapes onto a two-CD set, *Sweet Dreams: The Anthology* (Polydor Chronicles 314-517-086). Rhino did the same for the Atlantic recordings (*Guitar on Fire,* R2-71235). Flyright Records in England has issued a primer on early Buchanan (*The Early Years,* Krazy Kat KKCD 02).

Danny Gatton

. . . .

UNFINISHED BUSINESS

But for a quirk of fate, Danny Gatton would have been what he looked like: a sheet metal worker. He was short and pudgy, and he nursed his beer and cigarette like he was sitting in a bar on the Jersey shoreline after work. He got an F in charisma, lacking every star trapping imaginable, and stared down at his boots when he had to talk about himself. Yet in some ways, Gatton was one of the great guitarists. Certainly in terms of sheer technique he was stunning, and he had the rare ability to make all those notes take on form and substance.

Gatton knew his history, which so often is a creative dead end. Guitarist-historians end up parroting their favorites and becoming a compendium of stuff they've figured out how to play. Gatton was different. He knew Sol Hoopii, Les Paul, and Scotty Moore, and he could throw in little quotations from their work, just like Charlie Parker used to interject a blast of "White Christmas" into his solos. Gatton's genius, if that's what it was, lay in his ability to synthesize an almost impossibly broad range of styles, and in his mastery of guitar mechanics.

Danny Gatton was born in Washington, D.C., at 88 Elmira Street—as noted in the title of his first Elektra album. Before World War II, his father, Daniel W. Gatton Sr., was a rhythm guitarist in a band called the Royalists. Gatton says that his father played in the percussive rhythm style of Freddie Green with the Basie orchestra. Danny was born on September 4, 1945. By then, his father had given up the guitar as a living, but there was still music to be heard in the house. It was his uncle who introduced the six-year-old Danny Gatton to the music of perhaps his greatest influence, Les Paul.

Paul, along with Charlie Christian and the first generation of rockabilly pickers, formed the core of Danny Gatton's listening. Les Paul was the principal influence because of his technological innovation as much as his music. Gatton was always as much intrigued by the technology of the guitar as the music itself. He slowed down Paul's 45 rpm records to 33 rpm to get a better understanding of how the overdubs were layered. When asked, he cited the astonishing "Little Rock Getaway" as his favorite cut.

Danny Gatton
Photo courtesy of Elektra/Nonesuch

Gatton tried to emulate Les Paul by rigging up primitive overdubbing equipment at home with two tape decks. "I would play a track on the left machine," he said, "run it into the right one with a Y cord, and play along with it. I created echo by doubling a part and playing a little bit behind myself, which is real hard to do when you're about twelve."

The D.C. area has been home to some great guitarists, such as Link Wray, the godfather of the power chord. Gatton denied that Wray was any kind of influence at all. "I never was much of a fan," he said. "I'm not trying to brag, but by the time I heard 'Rumble' I could play better than that. My heroes were always at the other end of the spectrum. Now I like to hear that kind of stuff, but back then it was no challenge."

Around 1959, when he was in junior high school, Gatton joined a band called the Offbeats. They played the Top Forty hits of the day, and that gig led to other bar-band jobs that eventually led to Nashville. Gatton moved there for a few months late in 1967. He was working with a band that played at a club in Printer's Alley. After they packed it in, Gatton toyed with the idea of trying to break into the studio scene, but found himself without contacts in what was then a closed shop. "A couple of years later," he said, "I found I lived three doors down from Scotty Moore."

Gatton met Lenny Breau in Nashville. The son of the Canadian country singers Hal Lone Pine and Betty Cody, Breau was perhaps the most technically brilliant guitarist of our time. He could, for instance, play lead and rhythm at the same time. Given a small private income and a limitless supply of drugs, Breau would have played jazz. As it was, his day jobs were mostly in country music (he was in Anne Murray's backing group for a while). For over twenty years, he was in the process of "getting it together." Then he was murdered in 1984. Gatton thought Breau was the best ever.

"Lenny was living in this apartment in Nashville," Gatton told *Guitar World*, "with no heat, no lights, nothin' but running water and a candle. And still he was playing the most beautiful music you ever heard. It was really sad. It was a crime." Breau and Gatton made an odd study in physical contrast. Gatton was chubby; Breau was gauntly thin. Breau, like Robert Johnson, had elongated, talonlike fingers. Gatton had short, stubby fingers that often got mashed in the course of doing body work on his cars.

By June 1968 Gatton was back in the D.C. area and had gotten married. His wife worked for the government; he did body work and other sheet metal work, and he went back to playing the bars around D.C. a few nights a week. By 1974 he was part of a country band with an uncountry name: Liz Meyer and Friends. Then he formed his own trio, Danny and the Fat Boys. It was around this point that the rare albums and underground tapes started making the rounds. In 1975 Gatton and the Fat Boys recorded a hard-to-find album for Billy Hancock's Aladdin label. Hancock claims to have bought the label name off the original owners, although there are probably a few lawyers who would like to argue that point.

The Fat Boys broke up, and Gatton's career took one of its hiatuses. He returned to music with a group called Redneck Jazz Explosion. Buddy Emmons played pedal steel guitar. They hit the local spots around D.C. and made a few ventures beyond; the one that everyone remembers was to New York to play the Lone Star. The band was documented on a 1978 release, *Redneck Jazz*, funded by Gatton's parents. It's something of an all-star session for its day and budget. Along with Gatton and Emmons, there's Chuck Tilley (who had worked with Roy Buchanan) and Evan Johns on vocals. Typically, the front cover photo was of Gatton's guitar—not Gatton himself. Other pickers began to conjecture about his "Dingus Box," a contraption that controlled tone and special effects that he clipped onto the guitar behind the bridge.

The group dissolved when Gatton cut his hand badly, severing some tendons. After a year away from the guitar, he let one of his buddies persuade him to go to Santa Cruz, California, to do some work outside music. His return to playing came with an invitation to play on a Commander Cody album. That led to an invitation to audition for Roger Miller in 1980. For years, Miller's regular guitarist had been "Thumbs " Carllile, who positioned his guitar on his lap like a lap steel. Carllile quit Miller's lineup after Gatton's audition but later returned. They played together for about a year and a half, a period that Gatton remembered as one of the high watermarks of his life.

Although he played Vegas and other spots with Miller, Gatton was still based in D.C., holding down an irregular gig at a club in Georgetown in a band fronted by Billy Hancock. Hancock was friendly with Robert Gordon, who was then spearheading one of those rockabilly revivals that never seem to quite happen. Gordon invited Gatton to play on one of his albums, then asked him to go out on the road. For a while, Gatton played with both Miller and Gordon, but eventually settled for a year or so of steady work with Gordon. He was dismissive of that period. "I had to play like I was twelve years old again," he said, "but then if you play with other people, you have to play what they want you to play."

Many of those who saw Gatton with Gordon have far fonder memories of the music they made together. It sounded like magic from one of the ringside tables. For years a bootleg tape of one of the gigs made the rounds among pickers, leading Amos Garrett to dub Gatton "the humbler." After the gig with Gordon ended, Gatton quit the business again for a while. "It was John Previti, who's my bass player now, who got me back into it," he said. "He called me up to do a little four-piece jazz gig, and it was really a lot of fun. I got addicted to it all over again, and it kinda evolved into another band, called the Drapes, with Billy Windsor singing. I brought the nucleus of my jazz band into his band with the horns and all, and we started doing soul music. We got the idea to cut some tunes, and that was when people started approaching me about management. I figured it was really time to make a move. I couldn't just sit out on the farm forever; I mean, this *is* the thing I do best.

"In my mind, I'm still sixteen and I've got forever, but the realization is coming that I don't. I gotta make a move. I like playing, writing, producing, and the only thing I can't handle is the travel—but that goes with the territory."

In 1987 Gatton released another record on the NRG label (the initials of his mother, Norma Rae Gatton, who distributed the record from her home in Georgia). Titled *Unfinished Business*, it's a bewildering mosaic. Side one of the vinyl version opens with "Cherokee," which is Gatton's salute to Les Paul; side two opens with Charlie Byrd's "Homage to Charlie Christian." Throw in an original blues, the old Santo and Johnny hit "Sleepwalk," and a goosed-up version of Arthur "Guitar Boogie" Smith's "Fingers on Fire," and you get some idea of the bases Gatton could cover. The problem was knowing where to file him. The album's cause wasn't helped by the cover art (courtesy of Shorty's Art & Sign, White Plain, Maryland), which featured a pencil drawing of four vintage automobiles with three guys playing in the rear of the garage. It was obviously full of deep personal significance for Gatton, but it wasn't a jacket likely to reel in the unsuspecting listener.

Then Elektra Records came calling with checkbook in hand. Major label deals can be a curse as much as a blessing. Budgets are bigger, distribution nightmares end, but the company wants to insure its investment by assigning a producer with the brief to come up with something for radio. Gatton said that Elektra gave him a fairly free hand when he was signed, only insisting that he produce a solely instrumental album for his debut. Their only suggestion was that he cut the theme from "The Simpsons" (the Hand-D-Gas fart at the end is probably Gatton's comment on the idea). When he went out on tour in support of the album, he worked with a vocalist and mixed instrumental and vocal numbers on a roughly fifty-fifty basis. "The vocal numbers are set up so I can play in them," he said, "but too many hot licks gets old. Something's got to keep this thing normal." Elektra's insistence upon a solely instrumental album at least made possible a clear, perhaps definitive, statement of what Danny Gatton could do.

At most of his gigs there was a little cluster of pickers sitting close enough to study his right hand. His explanation of his right-hand technique was typically self-deprecating: "It came about out of basic laziness," he said. "I taught myself bluegrass banjo when I was twelve or fourteen, and then I discovered I could play steel guitar with a flat pick and fingers, and I took those techniques and applied them to the guitar. Then I met Lenny Breau, and he had a real long fingernail on his little finger, and he used it for his high notes and little chords to get this whole different sparkling little sound. I use that little finger for chord voicings, and it gives me a whole different texture." This explanation was delivered deadpan as if he were talking about how he dropped in at the bar on the way home from work, and met someone he hadn't seen since last week.

The title cut of the first Elektra album, *88 Elmira Street*, was a direct homage to all the rockabilly pickers who influenced him. The listener can pick up quotations from the work of Scotty Moore, Al Casey, James Burton, and others. "I was playing Scotty Moore's original guitar on that track," said Gatton. "It's a Gibson ES-295, and I bought it trashed out twelve years ago. It sounded incredibly good; it had some magic in it, but I didn't know it was Scotty's. Then Billy Hancock kept offering me all kinds of money for it, way more than it should have been worth, so I said, 'What's the deal?' He said, 'I think you've got Scotty Moore's guitar there.' He got out all these old photos, and this one had a different bridge and tailpiece and had a chip out of it exactly like Scotty's, so we called him and he confirmed it."

"Blues Newburg," from *88 Elmira Street*, sounds like a tribute to another D.C. guitar legend, Roy Buchanan, but Gatton said not. The two men had an uneasy relationship. Buchanan felt an often intense jealousy toward Gatton, and for his part, Gatton is somewhat loath to admit Buchanan's influence at all, although it seems all over "Blues Newburg." "I live in a town called Newburg," said Gatton, by way of explanation, "and we bought a house out in the country that was a wreck. Everything that lives, walks, or flies gets into the house—like I had a snake in my bedroom one time. So I had the blues in Newburg. It's a well-known area around D.C. for seafood—you can get Lobster Newburg and so on—and I had Blues Newburg."

Perhaps Gatton's strength lay in refashioning familiar pieces so that you heard them in a different way. He would state, restate, and paraphrase the theme, then dig into the changes. It was all a little more cerebral than Buchanan. Gatton was preoccupied with tone and texture—every note and every voicing seemed to be the product of endless experimentation.

Gatton must have been one of the first, perhaps *the* first act in what can loosely be called rock music to make his major-label debut at age forty-six, but he wasn't the product of major-label culture and didn't belong there. He explored a musical backwater of his own invention, but the public wasn't buying into it and Elektra dropped him. To Gatton, it was a relief as much as anything. He later recorded a jazz album for Blue Note and another record for a local label.

Then in October 1994 came the news that he had committed suicide. Those close to him say that Gatton, curiously like Roy Buchanan, was prone to bouts of depression. He had had a domestic argument, then stormed out of the house and over to his garage to work on his car. Later there was a gunshot. ⑥

FOR YOUR LISTENING PLEASURE

The two Elektra records and the Blue Note record are still available. A sampling of Gatton's work with Robert Gordon has been reissued by Bear Family as *Black Slacks* (BCD 15489) and *Red Hot* (BCD 15446). *Unfinished Business* and *Redneck Jazz* are available from Norma Gatton, NRG Records, P.O. Box 100, Alpharetta, GA 30201. The cassette-only issue titled *Vintage Masters, 1971–1976* is available from Joe's Record Paradise, 2253 Bel Pre Road, Silver Spring, MD 20901, a store that occasionally turns up copies of the Aladdin album.

Marty Stuart

· ·

ET'S BUS AND HANK'S GUITAR

Marty Stuart's self-appointed role has been that of making new country music true to old country music. In Marty's scheme of things, that means stretching and testing the boundaries without losing sight of what's country in country music. Given the current climate in Nashville, it's a challenge that gets harder every day. More than anything, Marty wants to be a success. He's been grooming himself for this since he was twelve. Along the way, he hopes somehow, some way, to introduce the kids to Roy Acuff. It might be too much for one man to take on.

Nearly every singer in Nashville pays lip service to country music's early stars—even if their teenage years were spent listening to Kiss and the Eagles. They're all George Jones fans now. Marty Stuart does more than pay lip service. It is, when all is said and done, one thing to toss an allusion to Ernest Tubb into your song, it's quite another to have Tubb's tour bus in your driveway, as Marty does. And in a music that cherishes the verbal tradition, he's a walking reliquary of anecdotes. He tells a story that's too long to repeat about Lester Flatt after his first heart attack. Even those who've already heard it spill Coke over themselves when he reaches the punch line.

Marty Stuart is passionate about many things; chief among them is what he perceives to be the dilution of real country music. "There's a comedy tape that Tommy Collins did called 'The Pissed-Off Preacher,' " he says with a characteristic nod toward something that almost no one has heard. "The preacher gets up, and he says, 'Good morning. I'll get right to the sermon. Your flowers are so lovely, but I'm tired of so much shit going on around here.' When I started on my new album, I listened to the radio, and people were going to Number One with bubblegum music. I've pictured myself in the middle of Sixteenth Avenue with my guitar saying, 'This belonged to Hank, this bus belonged to Ernest, and these songs belong to me.'"

Stuart's hillbilly pedigree was come by honestly. He was born in Philadelphia, Mississippi, in 1958. His early musical education was courtesy of the Columbia Record Club. "My grandad was an old-time Mississippi fiddle player," he says. "My uncle had a bit of James Dean about him and he loved Johnny

191

Photo: Raeanne Rubenstein
Photo courtesy of MCA Nashville

Marty's long-term future may yet be as a host;
Here, he and Mel Tillis are guests of Lorianne Crook at TNN
Photo courtesy of Larry Delaney/Country Music News

Cash, and my dad loved Flatt and Scruggs and string music. We got Lester and
Earl and Johnny Cash from the Columbia Record Club on the same day, and
about a week later a cousin gave me *Meet the Beatles*. I said, 'Nah!'"

Stuart got his first guitar when he was nine and, as he says, got the feeling that "this shovel fits my hand real good." He would go to country music
shows and ask to carry the stars' guitars. He worked tent shows and revivals
with the country gospel duo of Jerry and Tammy Sullivan, witnessing the talking in tongues; all this while most kids his age were still watching Saturday
morning cartoons. When he was twelve he went to Bill Monroe's Bean Blossom Festival, and he remembers, "Lester Flatt was such a hero, I stood by his
bus all afternoon waiting for him to come out. It was a walk of an eighth or a
quarter of a mile from his bus to the stage, and I walked behind him, studying
him. I knew I belonged in that world."

It's part of Marty Stuart lore that he invited one of Flatt's band, Roland
White, to his house for supper when the Flatt show was playing near Philadelphia. White returned the favor by inviting him to Nashville and taking him out

to a gig in Delaware with the band. On the bus, Flatt heard Stuart play and set about bringing him into the band. He joined as a mandolin player when he was thirteen, remaining with Flatt until the veteran performer's death in 1979.

"Lester's last year was a great education to me," says Marty. "He was a wealthy man. He didn't need to perform, but he and his wife had split up after forty-three years, and he'd had open heart surgery. Life just fell apart on him, and the only thing he had left was the applause. He didn't want to play festivals and auditorium shows, he wanted to play little schoolhouses where he and Scruggs started. We played shows some nights in places where there was a wood stove in the middle of the floor to keep it warm. I *loved* that. It was like going back to the source."

From 1980 until 1986 Marty worked with Johnny Cash. They met when Stuart saw Cash's phone number in a producer's phone book and called to ask him to participate in a tribute to Flatt. "Cash was my man," he says. "He could sing a song about a train, and I could jump on that train and believe." Marty was alternately and sometimes concurrently Cash's supporting act, backup guitarist, son-in-law, photographer, and producer.

At a precociously early age, Marty Stuart had made the transition from fan to fellow performer. He didn't find it in the least upsetting that some of his idols had not only had feet but torsos of clay. "Nah, we all have feet of clay," he says dismissively. "What made it all right about someone like Johnny Cash was that he was the first to admit it. When he screwed up, he'd raise his hand and say so. Guys like Cash, they were in the cotton field one day, and a star the next. No one was handing out instruction books on how to do that."

The down side of being an industry wunderkind is that Marty Stuart has evolved in public, and unlike many of his heroes, who seemed to emerge with a fully formed style, his artistic dead ends are on display like a presidential nominee's old girlfriends. "It's like I started in the mail room and worked up," he says, "and I do regret I've had to work it all out in front of the public, because there's some embarrassing tapes that'll get released sooner or later."

The earliest sampling of Marty Stuart currently available is a 1982 album for Sugar Hill that is far from embarrassing. Marty, with his Clarence White beard, is only barely recognizable. It is, as he says, a back-porch record. "I'd been working with Cash, and I missed playing acoustic music. The most fun I'd ever had onstage in my life was with Doc and Merle Watson, so I brought in Doc and Merle, and Earl Scruggs and Johnny Cash. I knew they all loved each other." The album, *Busy Bee Cafe*, has an almost complete absence of commercial gloss; in fact, the bass is the only electric instrument. There's no spikiness, but it's no youthful folly.

After Marty left Cash, he set about hustling a record deal. The first stop was Cash's label, Columbia Records, where he was signed by Rick Blackburn. It should have been a spiritual homecoming because not only Cash but so many of Stuart's heroes, including Flatt and Scruggs, had recorded for the label. Instead, Marty was confronted with the world as it is. "I thought it was the natural place for me to be, but Don Law [Columbia's head of country A&R from 1951 to 1967] wasn't there. There weren't any creative geniuses, and there wasn't any loyalty. If you're selling, you're selling—if you ain't, you're out. They gave me a quarter million dollars to learn the record industry, so I don't have any real regrets, though I wish they'd stood beside me through at least one more record. It was a good cold shower."

The Columbia deal yielded one quick hit, "Arlene," in 1986. Marty was touted for next-big-thingdom, and when it didn't happen, Columbia canned his second album and cut him free. The hard feelings aren't buried too deep, and he points out that there were five songs on the album that went on to become hits for other people.

He stayed in Nashville, but went back to Mississippi every now and then to work again with the Sullivans. He later repaid some of his debt to them when he produced their album, *A Joyful Noise*. The spiritual odyssey that led Marty back to the Sullivans and their music is movingly recounted in his liner notes.

Searching for direction, he says he had a moment of epiphany in the Country Music Hall of Fame. "I looked at Hank Snow's suits, Merle Travis's guitar, and Roy Rogers's boots, and I thought: This is where I'm comfortable. I understand this end of it. It's the bubblegum music people have been trying to get me to make that I have no passion for. I got into country music because Buck Owens made me smile, and because Bill Monroe made me holler."

Moments of insight usually founder on the nuts and bolts of following up, but this one didn't. Marty bought *Billboard*, checked the records he liked, and found that MCA's Tony Brown had produced most of them. "I knew Tony. He had been with Elvis when I was with Lester, so I called him and said I wanted to make a tape. Tony wanted to put me with Richard Bennett, which was OK with me because Richard had put the twang back into Nashville on Steve Earle's *Guitar Town*. The other reason I liked MCA was that they were sticking with Patty Loveless even though she hadn't had much success up to then. Artist development was real important to me because I had so much knowledge, and I needed to refine it."

Since then, Marty's self-appointed challenge has been to make music that's different, but not different enough to alienate the faceless programmers

Marty visits his mother, Hilda
Photo courtesy of Larry Delaney, Country Music News

who ultimately determine who makes it and who packs their bags and goes home. All of his heroes, he says, had explored something different but had somehow stayed radio-friendly. "You must have radio, and I love radio, and it's OK to innovate. Jimmie Rodgers, Bill Monroe, Waylon Jennings, these people didn't break the rules so much as just kept going with them. Nobody was doing that, so somebody had to do it—and I was bored!"

Marty's also trying to make records as "live " as possible in the age of the endless overdub and the deep six-figure studio budget. "We sure do spend a lot of time spittin' on them and buffin' them up—to make 'em sound rough!" he says. He wants to do what the stars of yore did: hone material on the road, then bring the road band into the studio and capture the feel they've worked up on the road. Billy Ray Cyrus made a big issue of doing that, but most singers only pay lip service to it, because no one wants pickers screwing up at today's studio rates.

The theme that Marty returns to endlessly is Old Made New Again. "It's been told to me that I spend too much time in the past," he says, "and when my future kicks in I'll take that into consideration. In the meantime, it's been

Yukkin' it up with Little Jimmie Dickens
Photo courtesy of Delaney/Country Music News

a great place to wait around, but I ain't trying to stand at the edge of town, beating a drum and trying to summon Hank Williams back to the county line." Country music's current resurgence doesn't surprise him. "Everyone's amazed that country's doing such good numbers right now," he says, "but I've been waiting on this since I was a kid. But if we don't watch it, it'll slip away from us again. When I was in the sixth grade, Johnny Cash came to Jackson, Mississippi, and my mom took me to see Cash. It was like going to see the Lord. The next day I got laughed at, but now I notice at our shows with Travis Tritt, there are a lot of people under thirty years old, and a lot of 'em say, 'I hated country music till I heard you or Travis or Garth Brooks.' I'm really proud to be one of those who can bring this new crop of people in, but when I've got their attention, I'm gonna play 'em 'Swinging Doors' and move them on down the trail. I'm like Tom Petty and Wynton Marsalis, carrying something forward."

The first two MCA albums, *Hillbilly Rock* and *Tempted*, did pretty well and spawned several decent-sized hits. Then he went out on the No Hat tour with Travis Tritt. Their duets on "The Whiskey Ain't Workin'" and "This One's Gonna Hurt You" brought his music before more people than ever before. "When I looked at Travis's crowd I thought they were gonna look at me like I was Roy Acuff," he says. "And even if I was five years older, I don't think I could pull it off, but right now I can balance both worlds."

The attachment to country music's past is represented in a well-stocked private collection of hillbilly memorabilia. "Here's what I'm holding out for," he says only half-jokingly. "We'll buy the Barbara Mandrell Museum across from the Country Music Hall of Fame, we'll build a walkway across, and we'll call it the Marty Stuart Wing. What I have no interest in is building a podunk tourist trap. I couldn't put Hank Williams's guitar or Johnny Horton's fishing lure into a place like that. I don't *own* those things; I'm in charge of them for now. I'm holding great pieces of Americana, and they need to be given back."

Historians generally make lousy musicians. They tend to genuflect toward the past. Marty is a self-appointed keeper of the keys, but at the same time, he's on MCA Records trying to hold his own against Trisha Yearwood, Vince Gill, and Reba McEntire and fighting for airtime on radio. In the studio, he can talk all he likes about Grady Martin licks on Johnny Horton records, and if he's lucky, someone will know what the hell he's talking about, but when the "Record" button is pushed he has to be very much in the here and now.

"The star thing," as Marty calls it, is something he's wanted since he was twelve. He works at it twenty-four hours a day but, as he says, "treats it with all the irreverence it deserves. There's a difference between singers and stars. Star is a role. That happens to be what I am. I'm not a brain surgeon—I am a country star. I take it seriously, and I don't. Everywhere the bus stops, someone knows Marty, but it's real important to me that Marty stands for something."

Never before has country music been more dominated by artists and industry people who have no sense of its history. Marty Stuart is almost alone in his appreciation and unaffected respect for country's roots. Now, or sometime soon, country music will need him more than he needs it.

POSTSCRIPT

Since this interview with Marty, conducted in December 1992, the Country Music Foundation has made plans to move, and Marty's dream of a Marty Stuart Wing is a distinct possibility, if not quite yet a reality. ◉

FOR YOUR LISTENING PLEASURE

The Sugar Hill album, *Busy Bee Cafe,* featuring Marty with his Clarence White beard and a host of guests, is available on SHCD 3726. The *Tempted* album contains several of Paul Kennerley's immaculately constructed songs and is a good romp, but perhaps Marty Stuart's best album to date has been *This One's Gonna Hurt You.* It contains the duet with Travis Tritt from which the title is taken, as well as several genuinely innovative attempts to move the goalposts.

Delbert McClinton

Years ago, someone said that all the great rhythm 'n' blues singers have voices like tenor saxophones, an observation never truer than in Delbert McClinton's case. The voice is no put-on; it's simply one of the great instruments in popular music. What it lacks in subtle shades it makes up for in raw power. Listening to thirty years of Delbert, you realize that the core values of his music have changed remarkably little, even during his flirtation with mainstream Nashville. Cowboy hat or no cowboy hat, there will always be a little too much roadhouse in Delbert McClinton for him to be comfortable in prime time. By way of consolation, and it might not be much consolation to a singer trying to pay off IRS bills and alimony, his records from twenty years ago still sound fresh and untainted by fads.

198

Delbert, the son of a beautician and a railroad switchman, was born in Lubbock, Texas, on November 4, 1940. In 1951, when he was eleven, the family moved to Fort Worth. He'd already absorbed Lefty Frizzell, Hank Williams, Bob Wills, and the other hillbilly kings by then, but it was hearing rhythm 'n' blues in Fort Worth that gave him a sense of where he was headed. Delbert— curiously like Doug Sahm—was influenced by Ray Sharpe, a blues singer with a hillbilly streak a mile wide, remembered by those who remember him at all for a solitary hit, "Linda Lu."

By his midteens, Delbert was playing the joints on the Jacksboro Highway leading out of Fort Worth, places so tough that, as Ronnie Hawkins used to say, you had to show your razor and puke twice just to get in. Delbert's band, the Straitjackets, backed up most of the visiting stars: Big Joe Turner, Junior Parker, Sonny Boy Williamson, and—in Delbert's eyes—the greatest of them all, Jimmy Reed. Strip Jimmy Reed down to his component parts, and there's almost nothing there. He was barely proficient on guitar or harmonica, and his lyrics—although often wry and darkly humorous—were delivered under the heavy burden of alcohol. Somehow, the whole magically outstripped the sum of the parts. One night in 1958 Delbert and the Straitjackets were to back him. "Our microphone was terrible," he says. "It had come with a little tape recorder, and I knew Jimmy Reed was gonna be working with us, so I went out

Photo courtesy of C. Escott

Photo courtesy of Showtime Archive/Toronto

and bought a new Shure microphone. That very night, he threw up on it. I still got it. Now *that's* history!" Delbert once said that he was working a joint that burned, but he dashed back inside to get that microphone. Good people have an innate sense of what's important.

His name suavely reconstructed as "Mac Clinton," Delbert started recording in 1960 for a Fort Worth wheeler-dealer, Major Bill Smith, who became famous before his death in September 1994 for his emphatic insistence that Elvis was alive and anxious to talk. In 1961 Delbert played harmonica on Bruce Channel's recording of "Hey! Baby," which Smith leased to Mercury, and which went on to become one of the biggest hits of 1962.

Delbert was sent out on tour with Channel, and in June 1962 they touched down in England. One night in Liverpool a girl took them to hear the Beatles, then staking out much the same territory as Delbert. They traded licks for a few nights, and Delbert almost certainly gave John Lennon the impetus to put a harmonica solo on their first Parlophone record, "Love Me Do," although he didn't play on it, as has often been reported. A grainy photo is all that remains of this brush with the soon-to-be-famous. While he was in London, Delbert cut a four-song session for Decca Records that resulted in one single.

Back in Texas, Delbert formed the Ron-Dels with Ronnie Kelly. They grazed the Hot 100 in 1965 with "If You Really Want Me To, I'll Go," a song that has been revived periodically by Doug Sahm, Waylon Jennings, and others, not least Delbert himself. It was one of many promising starts that fizzled out. By 1970 he was getting the feeling that Fort Worth was a dead end, so he hitched up with a young divorcee and went to Los Angeles. Shortly afterward, she left him, an experience etched unforgettably in "Two More Bottles of Wine."

Still on the West Coast, Delbert reestablished contact with a hometown buddy, Glen Clark, and together they got a contract with Earl McGrath's newly formed Clean Records. Clean was distributed by Atlantic but was doomed to fail. Their first single, the original version of "I Received a Letter," made the smallest possible dent in the Hot 100, and Clean folded just weeks after the second album was released. It was a pattern that would dog Delbert's career to the point where he came to regard himself as a jinx.

In 1974 Delbert returned to Fort Worth, got married, and signed with ABC Records, a contract that yielded three stellar albums before ABC in turn folded. One album in particular, *Genuine Cowhide*, is perhaps the best evocation of the spirit of fifties roadhouse blues recorded after the fact. It's not just good for a white boy, or good as an exercise in nostalgia, but *good*. Real good. Delbert's versions of songs like "Before You Accuse Me" or "Let the Good Times Roll" don't beg comparison with the originals, they simply exist as little paeans to doing it right. Critics loved *Genuine Cowhide;* the public ignored it. "Critics' favorite." How record company people like to spit out that phrase.

Shortly after the third ABC album, *Love Rustler*, ABC duly folded its record division and sold off the assets to MCA. Delbert's contract was one asset that MCA figured it could do without, and he was terminated. He played some artist showcases in Nashville and was picked up by the Macon-based Capricorn label, which brought him to Georgia and placed him with the staff producer Johnny Sandlin. The first Capricorn album, *Second Wind*, cut with the Muscle Shoals rhythm and horn section, is perhaps his finest work.

Throughout his career, Delbert has assiduously recycled his old songs. The lead cut on *Second Wind*, "B-Movie Boxcar Blues," had first seen the light of day on Clean Records. It was a Pilgrim's Progress through the underbelly of America, as revealed in a sequence of two- and four-line cameos: "Made a truckstop for toothpick and water/Got a ride with a fruit picker's daughter"; or "The way she did what she did when she did what she did made me think of you." Apparently Delbert had written the song, and Glen had titled it. "I was working at a veterinarian supply warehouse," says Delbert. "I played it for Glen, and he laughed and laughed. He said, 'Boy they won't ever play that, it's too nasty,' and then he asked me what I was gonna call it. I said, 'Man, I don't know.' He suggested 'B-Movie Boxcar Blues'—and it stuck." The Blues Brothers heard it on *Second Wind*, covered it, and it went double platinum.

Perhaps the high spot on Delbert's first Capricorn album was the gorgeous, slow-burning "Take It Easy. " Like all the great soul records, it married laziness with tightrope tension in a way that just about defies easy explanation. It was pulled as a single, but with radio playing nothing but disco, it fizzled and died.

Capricorn kept the faith and brought Delbert out to the Record Plant in Los Angeles in January 1979 for a second kick at the can. Emmylou Harris had just scored a Number One country hit with his "Two More Bottles of Wine," so Delbert rerecorded it. Then he dipped back into the Delbert and Glen songbook for "I Received a Letter" and "I Don't Want to Hear It Any More," figuring that no one had heard the originals anyway. Delbert says that he had written "I Received a Letter " before he left Fort Worth, but a final verse came to him recently while he was driving. "I don't think I'll ever record it again," he says unconvincingly, "but I may try and get someone else to do it."

Just as the second Capricorn album, *Keeper of the Flame*, was being shipped, the company's phones were being disconnected. The Curse of Delbert had struck again. Very quickly, he signed with Muscle Shoals Sound, which had struck a deal with Capitol. His first Capitol/MSS single, "Giving It Up for Your Love," gave him his only Top 10 hit to date. The first MSS album was tagged after the Bobby Charles masterpiece "Jealous Kind." The song had kicked around since the fifties, when Clarence "Frogman" Henry cut it, but Delbert's version is definitive. It could have been the start of something, but the follow-ups sputtered and died, and—true to form—Muscle Shoals Sound dissolved shortly after Delbert's second album for them. "By the time that happened I was pretty disenchanted with making records," he says, "and I didn't record again for a little over eight years." It was 1989 before a live album appeared on Alligator, followed by a deal with Curb Records in Nashville.

"My music," says Delbert, "is equal parts country, country swing, rhythm 'n' blues, and roots rock 'n' roll. I've always been very comfortable mixing those together. Radio and record companies want to categorize me, though. Record stores don't know where to put me. I don't fit in any category that's available." Inevitably, he has thought about buying a hat and doing straight country, but he knows it would be unnatural. "The satisfaction I get is from people coming up and saying, 'Don't change it,' and I won't change it. I'm like a painter who paints what he wants to paint. If people don't discover him for two hundred years, that's their loss. If you put your heart into something and do it real, there's got to be a point when it rises to the top."

In the studio, Delbert still tries to cut live with the band, something almost unheard of since the advent of multitrack. "I am hell-bent on getting live vocals," he insists, "because I have such a difficult time doing overdubs. You lose the spontaneity, which is the truth in music. A mistake doesn't matter. Some southwest Indian tribe purposely puts a flaw in every blanket they make to show the imperfection of mankind. I feel the same way about music. You can polish something till it don't shine."

Delbert and his girlfriend, Wendy Goldstein, moved to Nashville in February 1989. They had a child—Delbert says he has one every fourteen years—and he set about rediscovering his muse. He has been seen on TNN, and on specials. Since Curb Records signed him, he made some inroads into the country market, more than could be hoped for a performer past fifty. With any luck, he'll get his 'n' hers Mercedes for his garage, if that's what he wants. If it doesn't happen, posterity will probably judge him as one of the finest interpreters of roadhouse music and the writer of a few exceedingly fine songs.◉

FOR YOUR LISTENING PLEASURE

Mercury Nashville has reissued the Capricorn albums, *Second Wind* (314-518-008) and *Keeper of the Flame* (314-518-009). The first two Curb albums, *I'm with You* (D2-77252) and *Never Been Rocked Enough* (D2-77251), are both worth having.

Dwight Yoakam

· ·

HILLBILLY DELUXE

When Dwight Yoakam arrived in 1986, he was immediately bracketed with Randy Travis and Steve Earle. In an industry with an obsessive need to categorize everything, they were the New Traditionalists. The comparison looks pretty lame now—the categorization more so. All the three ever really had in common was that they all had their first hits in the spring of 1986, which means that New Traditionalism, whatever it was, ain't so new anymore.

Dwight Yoakam resisted whatever temptation he had to pick up where Buck Owens left off; instead, he went on to produce a small but quite remarkable oeuvre. The boundaries have stretched, but the core values have remained the same. The common threads have been the spiky, brooding quality of his writing, an implicit or explicit debt to Bakersfield (i.e., Buck 'n' Merle), and Pete Anderson's nuevo-rockabilly productions.

When he burst on the scene, Yoakam seemed in need of a copy of *How to Win Friends and Influence People.* Never short of opinions, he reveled in having a soapbox at last and mouthed off about Nashville's betrayal of country music, about Columbia Records' dismissal of Johnny Cash, about western hats. If you had a subject, Dwight Yoakam had an opinion. These days he's less abrasive, but still verbal; his slings and arrows are couched in generalities rather than aimed at specific targets. Ronald Reagan's famous self-exculpatory "I don't recall . . ." will never be part of the Yoakam vocabulary. He recalls it all. By his own admission, he is anally retentive of detail. As a songwriter, he could wish for worse.

Dwight Yoakam came by his affinity for hillbilly music honestly. He was born in Pikeville, Kentucky, in October 1956, and the first music he heard came from his father's and his uncle's record collections. "There was just enough stuff there to educate me musically in an offbeat fashion," he says. "It was a non–radio programmed education. And even though we moved out of rural Kentucky when I was a kid, we'd go back to my grandparents' house and I'd hear the Louvin Brothers, Bill Monroe, and so on. In the late sixties you could still hear unadulterated country music on the radio in the South—even

live radio in Kentucky. That drive from Columbus, Ohio, back to Kentucky was part of the fabric of my upbringing. The generation before us were still regional in their outlook. There were no nightly national TV newscasts. Our upbringings have become more homogenized, and—tragically—regional cultural ethnic expressions have been lost."

Bluegrass music figured large in Yoakam's scheme of things. It's no secret that the bluegrass patriarch Bill Monroe influenced Elvis Presley, Carl Perkins, and most of the rockabillies. Yoakam feels he's the heir to that tradition: "There's a degree of confrontational persistence needed just to survive in those [mining] areas," he says. "Those people stand flat-footed, square-jawed, and stare down some of the most horrific conditions. Their music was an articulation of that; it was an almost paradoxical expression of joy in confronting adversity. That's what you hear in bluegrass music, like the Stanley Brothers and Bill Monroe, and I owe the majority of my writing instincts to that music. The term 'bluegrass' itself has become festivalized. I prefer the term 'mountain music'—hillbilly music in its true form."

Yoakam also underscores the point about Monroe being one of the forgotten father figures of rock 'n' roll. "If you'd put an electric guitar and a set of drums behind Bill Monroe in 1938, you'd have had rockabilly music fifteen years earlier," he says. "Put on Bill Monroe singing 'Rocky Road Blues' and I'll show you where rock 'n' roll got fifty percent of its cool."

Yoakam is proud of his Southern blue-collar background, almost to the point of inverted snobbery. The economic precariousness of those years has colored his approach to life. "There was always a question about whether we would be able to maintain our level of existence. It's given me an uneasiness about security—and the world. You hear that in country music. The cultural ethnicity of country music is the *Grapes of Wrath* culture."

After graduation from high school, he attended a few semesters at Ohio State, then went to Nashville for a year or so. He even auditioned at "The Grand Ole Opry." "I had a more jagged and emotional approach to country music than what was going on at the time in Nashville," he says. In the early seventies Nashville was trying to find the lowest common denominator between country music and easy listening. Yoakam returned home, and then, in 1976, he and a friend headed for Los Angeles. His buddy came back; Yoakam didn't.

"I was drawn to Los Angeles by my earlobes," he says. "The country-rock sound, and the Bakersfield sound of Buck Owens and Merle Haggard. If you want to define it, I'm a country-rock artist without the hyphen. The Eagles, the Byrds, and Creedence came from rock toward country. I came from country toward rock." Yoakam had also dabbled in theater back in Ohio, and California held the vague promise of movie work.

Yoakam started playing the hillbilly nightspots around Los Angeles. In 1980, at a club in the San Fernando Valley, he met Pete Anderson through a mutual friend. "This guy, a steel player, said there was a guitar player I should meet," he said. "So I went and listened, and Pete was incredible. I got up on-stage, sang a couple of Merle Haggard songs, and we hit it off." Anderson's style, heavily influenced by James Burton and what Grady Martin played with Johnny Horton, dovetailed with Yoakam's unreconstructed vision of country music.

Yoakam's first six-song EP, produced by Pete Anderson, was issued on AK Records and then reissued on the Oak label. It introduced Yoakam to the record business at its nuts-and-bolts level. He even codesigned the jacket and carried the artwork to the typesetter. "I wanted it to look like those early albums I saw when I was a kid," he says.

One of the extra players Yoakam conscripted for the sessions was Gene Taylor, a pianist then working around Los Angeles with the Blasters and other local bands. Taylor remembers Yoakam as desperately committed to his music: "He was living in a little duplex and driving a beat-up El Camino. The tires were bald, the brakes were shot, and it was raining when we went to record. I never thought we'd make it. The piano went out of tune after every take, but Dwight was *really* into his music. You knew he was gonna make it or crash and burn out trying. He believed in himself totally, and his attitude was, 'This is my music. This is what I do. If you don't like it, get the fuck out of my way.'"

The deal that brought Yoakam's self-financed EP to Oak Records and then to Warner Bros. went something like this: Oak was owned by a producer-promoter, Ray Ruff, whose sister worked for Tab Rex, who pressed and distributed Yoakam's EP. "Ray Ruff loaned me the use of the label," says Yoakam, "because there was an awareness of Oak in country radio, but we P&D'd [pressed and distributed] the record through Tab Rex, who also did Tupelo Chain Sex and a lot of alternative bands. After it was reissued on Oak, it sold maybe five thousand copies. In an accounting sense, I never saw a dime from it, but in the larger sense, it launched my recording career."

The EP got Yoakam and his group, the Babylonian Cowboys, on the road with the Blasters, which led to a little press coverage and a deal with the Halsey agency, and it was Halsey who started courting the record companies. Paige Levy, then Paige Rowden, from Warner Bros., came to Austin and saw Yoakam play with the Blasters. "Paige went back to Jim Ed Norman, head of Warners

207

Dwight with Buck Owens (left) and Bill Ivey of the Country Music Foundation
Photo courtesy of Larry Delaney/Country Music News

in Nashville, and more or less demanded that he sign us," is the way Yoakam tells it. At the same time Yoakam was signed, Norman reportedly had to have his arm twisted into signing Randy Travis. Yoakam was placed on the newly reactivated Reprise label in November 1985, and the company bankrolled some additional sessions to flesh out the EP. The additional sessions, and virtually all of Yoakam's subsequent sessions, were held at Capitol studios, a decision based, he says, on romance. "That's where Buck cut, where Merle cut. It was our connection to our predecessors in West Coast country music. The acoustics and dynamics are also incredible."

To introduce Yoakam to radio, Warners issued a promo single on the Warner Bros. label shortly before Reprise was officially relaunched. It coupled live versions of "This Drinkin' Will Kill Me" and "Miner's Prayer." The first single culled from *Guitars, Cadillacs, Etc., Etc.*, a revival of Johnny Horton's "Honky Tonk Man," climbed to Number Three, and the album quickly went platinum.

Yoakam's retrofit style was at odds with the numbingly strict formatting of country radio, and he didn't help his own cause by mouthing off about radio.

His spikiness and immodesty were the precise antithesis of the Shake 'n' Howdy tradition that country singers were supposed to uphold, and the antithesis of the unassuming modesty that country stars were supposed to wear like a crown of thorns. You could fault Yoakam's social skills, but beneath the punk veneer lay a real concern about country music—a well-justified concern when you consider that Marie Osmond was Number One on the week Yoakam broke through.

The following year, 1987, saw Yoakam's first album with a production budget deeper than four figures. It was appositely titled *Hillbilly Deluxe* because it was essentially a glossier version of *Guitars, Cadillacs, Etc., Etc.* Once again, Reprise pulled an oldie for radio, a heavy-handed revival of Elvis's "Little Sister." The album's true delights were hidden away. Songs like "1,000 Miles" showed how Yoakam had mastered the use of detail to bring a song to life. "I'm preoccupied with details because they're the catalysts for life's journey," he says obscurely. He draws a parallel to Chuck Berry, still the master of the perfectly placed detail. "Chuck Berry is *the* genius of everyday life-detail chronicling. He's the poet of the hamburger stand. 'The coolerator was crammed with TV dinners and ginger ale.' How cool! That's brilliant writing! The eloquent articulation of commonplace details."

Yoakam's words of appreciation for Chuck Berry brings to mind Elvis Presley and Carl Perkins standing in the old Sun studio thirty-five years earlier singing snatches of "Brown-Eyed Handsome Man" and enthusing about Berry's gift for throwaway detail. "You'd be hard pressed to find a novel with such a poetically concise description of an airplane landing as you'll find in 'The Promised Land,'" says Yoakam. "Chuck Berry should be the admonishment for every aspiring songwriter. Don't become lazy. The other thing he never did was repeat pronouns or definite articles like 'the,' 'it,' and so on, and I don't even think that lack of repetition was conscious."

Hillbilly Deluxe spawned four Top Ten singles, showing that Dwight and country radio were slowly cozying up to each other. His reputation got another boost when he coaxed Buck Owens out of retirement to form something akin to a father-and-son act. Owens had been dropped by Warner Bros. in the early eighties, worked off his commitment to "Hee-Haw," and then retired into self-imposed exile in Bakersfield to nurse his investment portfolio. He says that Yoakam persuaded him that there was still a place for him in country music, and their relationship was cemented with a joint Number One hit, "The Streets of Bakersfield." It was Yoakam's first Number one—and Owens's first since 1972. Even so, it's hard to know exactly how Owens perceived Yoakam. Yoakam saw his music as an art form; Buck just saw it as something he did.

"The Streets of Bakersfield" hinted at the eclecticism that Yoakam was beginning to introduce to his basic mix, an eclecticism he needed to introduce if he was to survive. The song was delivered as a two-step with an accordion break from Flaco Jiminez, who was, after all, the real sound of Bakersfield, with its large transient Hispanic population. The album that followed, *Buenas Noches from a Lonely Room*, reaffirmed that Yoakam had already made two statements, one stripped down and one deluxe, about his roots, and now he was ready to move on.

"Buenas Noches from a Lonely Room" is the quintessential California country song title. It evokes the desolation of a hillbilly wracked by an uncontrollable obsession and cast adrift in a vast melting pot of twenty million souls. The phrase doesn't even appear in the lyrics of the song but is, in Yoakam's words, "an abstraction from the lyrics. It was a summary, a thesis of what that song was about."

All this talk, rife with literary allusions and detailed syntactical references, raises the inevitable question of whether Yoakam is too smart for a hillbilly singer. It's a subject on which he has pronounced views. "Look," he says, "I've got a long way to go before I'm literate enough to hurt myself. I've got many miles before I run out of Illiterate Highway. I was educated by the public school system of this country, and I suffer from its shortcomings, from the fact that it's a herding pen for young bodies and minds. I've come to realize how little I know, specifically vocabulary and semantics. [In songwriting] I engage in the articulation of thought and ideas through the use of words. That's about syntax, semantics, and vocabulary."

A diminished vocabulary obviously didn't hurt Hank Williams. He is popularly supposed to have read nothing more erudite than *Billboard* and comic books. Yoakam again: "I don't want to take anything away from Hank Williams, but he would have been just as brilliant—maybe more brilliant—had he perhaps read Ernest Hemingway. That stereotype of Hank Williams reading nothing but comic books is typical of the way people who market ethnic music in this country—who've carpetbagged it—perpetuate the myth that you can't be a really great country or blues artist unless you're illiterate and self-destructive. *They're* the ones who burn those artists up, use them, abuse them, then put them in coffins and collect the royalties on their estate."

He's right, of course. Hank and Lefty died broke. Their ignorance hurt them there. It led Williams to mistrust anyone who appeared to have a shard more education than he had, and it led Lefty to sign 2 percent, 1 percent, or no-percent contracts because they were shoved in front of his face. "My education was poor," says Yoakam, "but I'm not going to carry that around in my pocket as a badge of low self-esteem that I'm going to put on every time I'm in the company of someone who happens to run a record label. I know his game. I know what he's really trying to do is rape me."

Shortly after *Buenas Noches,* Yoakam took a sabbatical. It went against the grain of the record, tour, record, tour cycle that keeps you on the road two hundred-plus days a year, every year. Yoakam, a homebody at the best of times, decided to take a break to avoid burnout. Perhaps he realized as well that traditional fan loyalty in country music was a thing of the past. At one time, three or four hits guaranteed a twenty-year career. Now the market is much more akin to the pop market; it chews you up and spits you out. Yoakam knows that the key to longevity is not burning out. He didn't want road weariness to cloud his work, so he went into a holding pattern and released a slightly premature greatest-hits anthology.

The fourth album (or fifth, if you count the hits package), was *If There Was a Way.* The songs were still consistently good, and that alone flew in the face of conventional wisdom which says that an artist who writes the majority of his own material will spend twenty years writing his first album, and then fall flat on his face trying to produce a comparable body of work every year.

Yoakam's market is hard to penetrate. At first he was embraced by the college crowd, which, as usual, quickly moved on to something else. Now his following seems to be mostly mainstream country, with some of the rock audience along for the ride. Whatever he does, he swears it will always be rooted in country. "When I started," he says, "people thought I had some Hollywood take on country music; they didn't realize my background. Now maybe they're gettin' it."

The kinder, gentler Dwight Yoakam who gives interviews these days is closer to acceptance by the country music establishment, but shows no signs of moving to Nashville to be embraced by it. As Nick Hunter, one of his first boosters at Warner Bros. in Nashville, points out, Yoakam will need their support, because if someone is trying to extend the boundaries of country music, it's much easier to do so from within.

No one can dispute that Dwight Yoakam cares desperately about country music: its past, its present, and its future. The years in Los Angeles have helped him bring his roots into even sharper focus. While most singers wait for their A&R man to make the rounds of the music publishers in Nashville to find songs for them, Yoakam is resolute about sitting in his canyon in Los Angeles and writing his own. In them, he captures much of the haunted, spiritual quality of true hillbilly music.

Tim Hardin

. . . .

NO REASON NOT TO BELIEVE

Navel-gazing singer-songwriters are simply boring; politicized singer-songwriters even more so. The earnestness. The so-called progressive agenda. The dreary self-absorption of an immature mind. It all usually resolves itself to whining over minor chords. So what made Tim Hardin so special? He was mercifully apolitical, but was self-absorbed to a fault. He went on record in *Time* as saying that he was too involved in his personal life to write about what was going on in the world. Perhaps it was the blues that let Tim Hardin endure. Perhaps it was the poetry of half a dozen uncommonly good songs. Perhaps it was the almost brutal honesty.

The problem started when Tim Hardin's records were filed under "Folk." He wasn't a folknik. His work was a twisted road map of spiritual highs and lows. He seemed to feel everything more acutely than everyone else, to the point that his mind must have been a burdensome thing. His singing was one of the few really convincing white takes on the blues. He called himself a jazz singer when he was pressed. "To know jazz is to know God," he once said, and the jazz feel was there in the way he phrased, hung onto notes, and bent them and played with them.

With the ambiguity that was so typical of him, he once said that Ray Charles had called him the "third light of the blues" (Lightnin' Hopkins was first apparently, Ray himself was second, and Hardin was third), but it's as likely that Hardin *wished* Ray Charles had said that about him. "I'm a better singer than Ray Charles, and Ray Charles told me so," he told another interviewer on another day, but in Hardin's scheme of things interviewers only existed to be put on. In the same vein, he often said that he was Beethoven reincarnate. You could say that was another put-on or, worse yet, uncontained vanity, but look at the back cover photo on the *Bird on a Wire* album. Damn, it could be Ludwig van at age thirty.

If Tim Hardin's life had one recurrent theme, it was excess. He took everything to the limits—then stretched them. He ate in binges, drank to excess, smoked constantly, doped himself up excessively, loved suffocatingly. He once found some hyacinth oil he liked and sprayed, not just one room, but

Tim Hardin
Photo © David Gahr

every room of his house with it. Everything was always done to excess. He loved
the idea of being in love and being part of a little family, but he couldn't do it.
He loved the vision of the simple, centered life that he found in pop-spiritu-
al books like *The Prophet*, but he was never able to find it for himself. He did-
n't know how to make himself fit into the world, so he tried shutting himself
off from it. That didn't work either, because he was wretched company for
himself. At one time he lived with a wolf and a malamute and bayed at the
moon with them. When he was bad he'd blame it on the moon.

Separating the self-created myths from the person is almost impossible,
because Tim Hardin truly lived those myths. It wasn't as simple as saying that
multiple personalities lived in him; it was an extension of his creativity. He
was constantly reinventing himself. Finding someone who could make him
feel rooted as the same person was one of the great challenges he faced, and
one he almost never met.

The first myth, which cropped up in the earliest pieces about Tim Hardin and was then repeated in the way misinformation tends to be, was that he was related to the outlaw John Wesley Hardin. As far as we know, he only wanted to be. He was born in Eugene, Oregon, on December 23, 1941. Contradictorily, Hardin always poked fun at those who asked "What sign are you?" but he later lied about his birth date because he preferred the readings for another sign. He had one brother and one sister. His mother, Molly, once had a career in classical music; his father, Hal, had once played bass, but he worked at his in-laws's mill when Tim first remembered. Later, when asked about his father, he would say, "A fool . . . just a fool."

Hardin knew he wasn't like the rest of the boys in a lumber town. He was small and wanted to act. He played Billy Bigelow, Gordon MacRae's part, in a high school production of *Carousel*. When he left Eugene, though, it was in an almost absurd test of manhood. He joined the marines. It was, he said later, "a legal loophole that allows the prisoner to sign himself into another prison—from parental care to the military." He hated it once he was in. He was stationed at Okinawa, San Diego, and Twentynine Palms, California. He later said that his platoon corporal became the first American casualty in what became the Vietnam War. What is certain is that it was in the marines that Hardin became addicted to heroin. He was one of the many good men who disembarked from the east with a habit.

Hardin left the marines in 1961 and headed back to Eugene for a short spell, then went to Greenwich Village. He enrolled at the American Academy of Dramatic Art, but it reminded him too much of high school. He skipped classes and was dismissed. In the Village he started hanging out with Karen Dalton and Richard Tucker, and it was almost certainly their influence that made him think seriously for the first time about playing music. That's what he was doing when he moved to Boston around 1963. He later said he taught one semester of musicology at Harvard, although that might have been more myth. High school diplomas are usually reckoned to fall somewhere short of the requirement to teach there.

While Hardin was in Boston he got a call from Erik Jacobsen. A onetime banjo player, folkie, and lately producer of Chris Isaak, Jacobsen was just starting out in management and production when a group called Two Guys from Boston told him about Tim Hardin. When they got back to Boston, they told Hardin to phone Jacobsen. Hardin's opening remark was one that Jacobsen would hear often in the years to come: "You got money?"

Jacobsen did, in fact, have a little money, as well as an idea for a dance craze song, and he invited Hardin down to New York to work on it. Jacobsen was living on Prince Street in the Village then, and Hardin arrived with a flask of whiskey in his pocket that he'd been nipping from all the way down. He asked for marijuana and asked if Jacobsen knew where he could score some heroin. Then he started to sing, and the doubts that had been coursing through Jacobsen's mind to that point were erased, along with the idea of getting Tim Hardin to work on a hully-gully song.

Hardin moved back to Greenwich Village in 1964, and Jacobsen set up an audition for him at Columbia Records. Cass Elliott and the Mugwumps were there. "It was," says Jacobsen, "the counterculture meets Columbia Records. Tim was smoking pot, then he went to the bathroom, came back and passed out. It was a nightmare." The demos didn't give Columbia much incentive to sign him. His early songs were mostly rejuggled clichés.

Jacobsen kept the faith after Columbia took a pass, fronting Hardin fifty dollars for every song that had at least two verses and a chorus. Some of the demos later emerged on *Tim Hardin 1* and *Tim Hardin 4;* others later surfaced on an Atlantic album called *This Is Tim Hardin.*

The blues lick that Tim called the "Hi-Heel Sneakers" riff is all over the early demos. It underpinned half of everything he wrote for around a year, but the way he phrased was unlike any blues record. His singing was influenced in part by Ray Charles, in part by jazz singers like Mose Allison, and in part by Lefty Frizzell. It was the way that Lefty worked his inflections into country songs that intrigued Tim. "Lefty was a stylist," Hardin said later, at a time when Lefty's name was on almost no one's lips.

One of the demo sessions that Jacobsen remembers well was with the veteran R&B drummer Sticks Evans. It was held at a small studio in New York, and Hardin brought along a fellow dope addict, who sat out in reception. When they emerged from the session, the reception area had been cleaned out. The lamps, tables, typewriters, Rolodexes, even the "Men" and "Women" signs from the washroom doors were gone. Jacobsen had to pay for the lot. Later, Hardin wondered why there were deductions against his royalty checks.

Jacobsen and a partner signed Hardin to their Sweet Reliable Productions (an unfortunate choice of name for a company that tried to book Tim Hardin), and they placed him with the partnership of Charles Koppelman and Don Rubin. Jacobsen and Koppelman-Rubin were working jointly on the Lovin' Spoonful, and Hardin came into the fold about six months after the Spoonful got together. The Spoonful's John Sebastian had worked with Hardin since the Columbia demo session. Later Hardin uncharitably claimed to have taught Sebastian everything he knew. "What he's doing is something I already did, but he's making it and I'm happy for him," he said unconvincingly.

Koppelman and Rubin found a home for Hardin at the newly formed Verve-Forecast label. In 1965 Jerry Schoenbaum had launched the Folkways and Forecast divisions of Verve, itself a division of MGM. Hardin's first single, "Hang On to a Dream," was issued in February 1966; *Tim Hardin 1* followed in July. It was made up of newly recorded songs sitting uncomfortably between some demos. Placing old and new side by side made it clear what a change had come over Tim Hardin's music. Much of the blues swagger was gone, to be replaced by confessionalism and an almost painful self-obsession. "When I heard 'Ain't Gonna Do Without,' it made me cry," said Hardin, who claimed to be unaware that one of the old blues demos was going to be on the album. "It was a studio joke, a joke on 'Hi-Heel Sneakers.'" Hardin also claimed to be unaware that strings were going to be overdubbed onto some songs. "They said John Lennon said that would be a really good idea, to try and placate me," he recalled later in England.

Hardin's life had taken some twists and turns between the time he started working with Jacobsen and the release of *Tim Hardin 1*, and those changes were charted in his music. All the songs he is best remembered for come from an eight-month period in 1965 and 1966. He went to Los Angeles for a while in 1965, and there he met the Lady from Baltimore. He called her Susan Moore in the songs, but her name was Susan Morss, and she was an actress then, working as Susan Yardley. She didn't come from Baltimore; her family was from Vermont and New Jersey, but "Baltimore" rhymed with "Moore," and "Jersey" didn't. The old-money ambience that Hardin evoked in "Lady Came from Baltimore" was true enough, though, and so was the contempt with which he was greeted by Susan's father. He had been a major general in the army and was then a prosecutor in New Jersey. He loved the trappings of authority—the uniforms and the titles—the very things that Hardin was trying his damnedest to avoid. Tim Hardin *wanted* to be John Wesley's great-grandson.

The nature of many of Hardin's previous relationships can be inferred from "Lady Came from Baltimore." He was a user on every level. "He learned a lot of bad tricks from low elements," said Jacobsen. "He had a total disregard for others' feelings. He was selfish and self-absorbed. He was a user without a nice bone in his body." It's old news that for an addict, everything takes second place to the addiction. Hardin would tell women he loved them, that he was writing songs for them, then he'd get their credit card and skip. Susan, as the song says, touched him in another way.

"She was the star of a show called 'The Young Marrieds,'" said Hardin. "Two rooms, big rooms, full of bags of mail every week." Typically, he latched onto one small, compelling detail. "Some of the letters were terrible. A girl who was five foot three, weighed two hundred and twenty pounds, terrible complexion, greasy hair, and she'd ask, 'How can I look like you?' That's a caricature of sadness. But Susan was a beauty, man." They didn't get tight until they moved to New York in 1966. Susan more or less supported him for a while and didn't see much of a future for him in music. *Tim Hardin 1* changed that.

Tim and Susan moved back to Los Angeles just before *Tim Hardin 1* was released. They found an old Spanish house on Miller Drive. The photo for the front cover of *Tim Hardin 2* was taken from the back courtyard early in 1967. Hardin had a studio set up in the house and mailed tapes back to New York. In the months before the birth of his son, Damion, he was making a concerted effort to free himself of his addiction to heroin, but he started using again during a trip back to Eugene. He wrote "Black Sheep Boy" on that trip, back in his old bed at his grandmother, Manner Small's, house. Damion was born shortly afterward, on February 28, 1967. Tim published a poem on impending fatherhood as the liner notes for *Tim Hardin 2*. He hadn't liked Jacobsen's liner notes for *1*, so he had decided to write his own meditation on the irreversibility of what he and Susan had undertaken. It was almost a prayer for the strength he knew he would lack.

None of Hardin's albums sold well. He had a cult following that, according to Don Rubin, probably accounted for sales of between ten thousand and fifty thousand per album. Sales aside, you can make a case for *Tim Hardin 2* being one of the ten best albums from the sixties. The backings—finally— were sympathetic. The strings didn't sound as though they had been gratuitously pasted on at the last moment, and Hardin had finally got over the "Hi-Heel Sneakers" lick. The irony was that the most money Hardin saw from *Tim Hardin 2* was when Bobby Darin covered "If I Were a Carpenter." Once again, he was outraged. He later claimed that Darin had his version playing in the headphones so that he could ape Tim's phrasing. "Tim and I were out driving," said Susan, "when 'If I Were a Carpenter' came on the radio. I thought it was him, it was so close. The brakes screeched. The door slammed. He was stomping on the side of the road, screaming and swearing."

In the months after *Tim Hardin 2* was released, Tim, Susan, and Damion were on the move. They went to Hawaii for a while, then San Francisco, where they lived for four months on a houseboat, and then back to Los Angeles. During that time Hardin should have put a group together and toured to stoke album sales, but he had a combination of stage fright as well as a tendency to burn promoters by not showing or trying to play when he was out of commission. Erik Jacobsen remembered one incident shortly before he gave up on Tim Hardin. He had booked him into a club in Chicago, and Hardin had cajoled a credit card from the club owner to go buy a suit. When the bill came in, there were five suits on the tab; he had sold the others to raise money for dope. Jacobsen's departure from Hardin's camp was enforced in a particularly ugly way, and Jacobsen's admiration for Hardin's talent still can't overcome his personal disgust.

A beleaguered appearance with Laura Nyro at the Academy of Music in Philadelphia was caught by Michael Cuscuna, lately the owner of Mosaic Records, then a journalist. "He stumbled onstage," wrote Cuscuna, "and proceeded to sing pathetically, make incoherent remarks, tell stupid jokes about his friend Bacardi, and ruin some of his best tunes. The encore was a pathetic tribute to, parody of, imitation of, or interpretation of Ray Charles. I couldn't tell what it was, and probably Hardin didn't know either." A reputation like that spread quickly. Even clean and sober, Hardin would sometimes dismay audiences that had come to hear the greatest hits. He simply didn't appreciate commercial exigencies.

The closest Hardin had to a steady band was the group that worked on *Tim Hardin 3*, the live album from Town Hall in New York recorded in April 1968. A new manager, Steve Paul, gave him the money to assemble the band, composed for the greater part of jazz musicians. Tim had heard Donald McDonald play drums and hired him on the spot. The flautist Jeremy Steig introduced Tim to pianist Warren Bernhardt, who would work with him on and off for several years. The vibraphonist Mike Manieri and the bassist Eddie Gomez were well known around the New York jazz scene. Tim later explained the rhythmic concept they tried for: "The essential was the pulse, counting by ones, instead of groups of four, so that each bar was a [single] beat, which gives you freedom." But as good as they sounded together, there wasn't enough work to keep them together after Town Hall.

Hardin's ability to perform was undermined still further by chronic respiratory problems. He was living in Colorado (for the air quality, he said) when he played Town Hall. After the Town Hall gig, he went back to Colorado, talked briefly and unconvincingly of raising horses, then decided that he needed the pace of the city. He and Susan moved to Woodstock, New York, and took a brownstone in New York City too.

In August it was announced that Hardin had pleurisy, and pleurisy was also given as the reason that he had performed poorly on a tour of England the previous month. Certainly, he had problems with his lungs. The liner notes to *Tim Hardin 3* catch him in the throes of a coughing spasm: "The way I smoke it doesn't make any difference what brand it is. With my problem which is an immediate . . . you know . . . just a regular . . . phlegm . . . WAAGH!" But the problem in England was more familiar. Koppelman and Rubin had booked him into the Royal Albert Hall, and he had a sold-out tour with Family lined up. A few songs into his set, he nodded out onstage after dismissing the backing group in front of the audience. The tour was canceled.

Hardin returned to England in 1969 to take what was known as the sleep cure for heroin addiction. The theory was simple but flawed. Most addicts can't get over the withdrawal phase, the theory went, so they should be tranked up on barbiturates to get them through withdrawal. The problem was that they still emerged with a psychological addiction to heroin and, in Hardin's case, a new addiction to barbiturates.

The Verve deal ended shortly after Tim and Susan moved to Woodstock. Columbia Records, now with Clive Davis at the helm, took another chance on him and moved recording equipment and an engineer up to Woodstock. If Hardin felt like recording at three in the morning, the engineer was woken up. The result was *Suite For Susan Moore and Damion*, an inchoate piece of often painful confessionalism. It was as personalized a record as has ever been made. There were no songs on the album for Bobby Darin to cover, but in a strange twist of fate, Hardin covered Darin's "Simple Song of Freedom" for his first Columbia single, and it gave him his only Hot 100 hit as a singer. It was the sort of feebleminded political statement that Hardin had spent his life not making.

Susan left soon after the move to Woodstock. The liner notes to the second Columbia album, *Bird on a Wire*, contain a twisted little poem castigating her for taking Damion and going to Los Angeles with another man. Susan says she left with Julie, one of Tim's old groupies who was their babysitter then, and that the poem was Tim's way of not facing up to the fact that she had left him because of his return to hard drugs.

Shortly before she left, Susan found a house for Tim in Woodstock. It was the old Hellman estate, built with mayonnaise money, a gorgeous, rambling house, wood paneled and with a thirty-foot vaulted ceiling. It was set in fifty acres on the side of Bear Cat Mountain, bordering on a federal wildlife preserve, but idyllic as it was, it was unsuited for someone who had trouble with his own company. Oddly, though, Hardin rarely sought out the company of the other musicians who lived in Woodstock then: Dylan, the Band, Paul Butterfield, or Van Morrison. He made an appearance at the Woodstock Festival, though. At home, he walked around at all hours, writing fragments of songs on bits of paper.

Hardin was trapped in Woodstock. His driving license had been revoked, and even though he had given up heroin again, he was drinking so heavily that he was still unable to play anything other than the occasional date. He didn't sleep a lot. He had a girlfriend from Sweden for a while, then brought Jane Harbury, an expatriate Englishwoman he had met in Toronto, to live with him for a year or so. A Dutch couple kept house. He tried to pretend to visiting interviewers that he was reveling in the life of a country squire, inviting them to sample the water and displaying a northwesterner's knowledge of the types of lumber used in the construction of the house. The truth, as always with Hardin, was sadder. He had run dry, and it frustrated him, angered him every day. His life had been creation, and it was as if the faucet had been turned off.

Once, when Susan had come downstairs in the morning, entire songs would be littered around the house; now there were only couplets. Here he was in a perfect setting for creativity, yet nothing came. Susan says that he came to regard her as the muse that unlocked his songs, but the problem, she believes, was probably more prosaic. Like most alcoholics and substance abusers, Tim Hardin had lost touch with his feelings, and with them went his songs. The last Columbia album, *Painted Head*, was a fine, undervalued record, but it did not contain one original song. Later Hardin explained his barrenness by saying that he was not a writer; he was primarily a singer who happened to have written a few songs along the way. "Nobody should care who wrote the song," he said. "It's ruined the presentation of a lot of people, like yours truly."

Hardin eventually left Woodstock and, in February 1972, went back to England, where, as a registered addict, he could acquire drugs on the National Health Service. He was still drinking heavily, too: a bottle of brandy a day; more if he could get it. Columbia Records rented a flat for him. Interviewers were wheeled in. Hardin would pace restlessly; he looks like a cornered animal in photographs from that time. "I'm very healthy, very alive," he said unconvincingly to Michael Watts at *Melody Maker*. "I'm completely back on an even better course." He told Watts that he wrote constantly, "but I only come up with tunes after months and years," he said. "The words make the line of the melody because I sing improvisationally."

"It was like living a horror movie," wrote Justin de Villeneuve, Hardin's manager of the day. De Villeneuve, who had previously managed Twiggy, had been bowled over by Hardin's talent before he came to realize that Hardin was unmanageable. "Like most addicts, he could never tell the truth," said de Villeneuve, "and was the most cunning liar. His lies were so imaginative, they held me in grudging admiration. He could stop anybody on the street, tell them the most amazing tale, and take a fiver [five pounds] off them." When Hardin started to nod out onstage, de Villeneuve remembers firing a peashooter at him to wake him up. The easier access to drugs did nothing to improve Hardin's unreliability. The story was the same as before. Gigs were missed, promoters burned, and there were psychotic incidents in airports and on board planes.

The last fully realized album, *Tim Hardin 9*, was released in England on GM Records (and on the Antilles subsidiary of Island Records in North America) in 1973. There were a couple of fairly new songs; one of them, "Shiloh Town," stood with the best stuff. The free-floating melancholia was focused. It was an antiwar song, presumably rooted in the Civil War but sufficiently vague to invite any level of meaning.

The story of the years in England is really a book in itself. Tim and Susan reconciled briefly in London. He hoped that she could help him find the place where the songs had been, but she couldn't. He even lost the songs he had, signing away his copyrights. Gaff Management bought Hardin some Carnaby Street suits and platform shoes and sent him out on tour with a four-piece band to support *9*. A fellow GM artist, Lesley Duncan, backed him. After that tour, he barely played at all in England.

He came back to the United States in 1976 and went to live in Seattle for a while. An old school friend, Phil Freeman, taped a concert at the Community Center for the Performing Arts in Eugene that was issued as *Homecoming Concert*. Shortly after, Hardin moved to Los Angeles. He took a house close to Damion's school, enabling them to reestablish contact. He tried to work his way back into the music business. Erik Jacobsen saw him in a studio in Los Angeles. "I asked, 'Who's that?'" he remembered, "and someone said, 'That's Tim Hardin.' He had bloated up to two hundred pounds and he'd lost all his hair. I never would have recognized him."

Hardin had been clean in Seattle, but back in Los Angeles, he quickly fell into the old trap. He called Susan insistently, emotionally blackmailing her with threats of suicide. She took Damion and left in September 1980. During those last troubled months, Hardin worked with Don Rubin again. They had two tracks ready for an album; one of them was "Unforgiven," a song that Rubin later placed with Joe Cocker. He pitched it to Eric Clapton as well, but Clapton's track was never finished.

Tim Hardin died in Los Angeles on December 29, 1980. When the Los Angeles County Coroner's Office handed down its verdict on January 26, 1981, it was of death from acute heroin-morphine intoxication due to an overdose. There were obituaries—short "Famous Long Ago" obituaries. His death came three weeks after John Lennon's and got very short shrift in comparison.

For all his protestations that he didn't want to be thought of as a songwriter, his songs are far better known than his records today. Here's a brief sampling of who has recorded what. Comparisons emphasize that no one has yet eclipsed the painful intimacy of Tim Hardin singing his own little signed confessions:

"Don't Make Promises": Marianne Faithfull, Helen Reddy, Three Dog Night

"Hang On to a Dream": the Nice, Cliff Richard, Françoise Hardy

"If I Were a Carpenter": Joan Baez; Johnny Cash; King Curtis; Bobby Darin; Dave, Dee, Dozy, Beaky, Mick, and Tich; Waldo De Los Rios; Lee Dorsey; the Everly Brothers; the Four Tops; Burl Ives; Waylon Jennings; Al Martino; Matt Monro; Robert Plant; Leon Russell; Bob Seger

"Lady Came from Baltimore": Joan Baez, Johnny Cash, Bobby Darin, Cliff Richard

"Misty Roses": Fifth Dimension, Johnny Mathis, the Youngbloods, P. J. Proby, Astrud Gilberto

"Reason to Believe": the Beat Farmers, Glen Campbell, the Carpenters, Cher, Marianne Faithfull, Rick Nelson, Rod Stewart, Andy Williams ◎

222

FOR YOUR LISTENING PLEASURE

Polydor in the United States has issued all of *Tim Hardin 1, 2,* and *4,* as well as several unreleased demos from the pre-Verve period on *Hang On to a Dream* (Polydor 314 521 583). The live album *(Tim Hardin 3)* is scheduled for rerelease with additional titles.

V

Lost at a Fairground

Playing Favorites

. . . .

In addition to all the musically correct stuff, some genuinely oddball items come my way. Here, in no particular order—and for no particular reason—are some that appealed.

PORTER WAGONER, "The Rubber Room," on *What Ain't to Be, Just Might Happen* **(RCA LSP 4661)** Part of country music has always been played out in the theater of the absurd. No one made the connection more obvious than Porter Wagoner, and the classic of Porter's absurd period is the *What Ain't to Be* album, released in 1972. For the front cover, Porter has dyed his hair unnaturally blond, and he has the unsettling smile of someone who doesn't have his plug all the way into the socket. He's wearing a psychedelic shirt and a high-buttoned pukey green jacket with a light green pinstripe, offset by a black cravat and a brooch.

In common with the best absurd country classics, like "Please Don't Go Topless, Mother," "The Rubber Room" is desperately serious. Over the backdrop of a poor man's Jimmy Webb string arrangement, Porter sings lines like "When a man sees things and hears sounds that ain't there, he's headed for [pause] the rubber room." The engineer throws gallons of cheap echo on words like "psycho" and "doom" and, of course, "rubber room," which becomes "*rub-ub-ub-ubber room-oom-oom-oom.*"

The next track is "If I Lose My Mind," in which a man sees someone else making love to his wife in the driveway and, in the best oedipal Southern tradition, goes home to Momma to lose his marbles. "If I lose my mind, Momma, I wanna be here [another pregnant pause] with you/Have them lock me up but see I have good care." If Gladys had still been alive, where would Elvis have gone after Priscilla ran off with that judo instructor? The same theme is picked up on "Comes and Goes." Porter's mind is spinning like "tor-nay-der winds" as it "comes and goes."

Someone called Rex Teal wrote the one-paragraph liner notes. "I only wish it were possible for every person to spend a day on the lake with Porter Wagoner," he wrote in conclusion.

Take a life jacket, for God's sake.

THE BLUE SKY BOYS, "Down on the Banks of the Ohio" (Bluebird 78, reissued on RCA Camden CAL 797 and Bluetone BSRCD 1001/2) The very name "Blue Sky Boys" is something of a paradox because their music has much of the darkness you find in Celtic ballads of death and walking spirits. They were a singing brother act, Bill and Earl Bolick, and they called themselves "Blue Sky Boys" to avoid being lost among all the other brother acts that were recording back in the thirties, such as the Dixon Brothers, the Monroe Brothers, and the Delmore Brothers.

"Down on the Banks of the Ohio" comes from the Bolicks' first recording session, in Charlotte on June 16, 1936. The song is fairly well known; Olivia Newton-John got a white-bread version onto the charts in 1971. It's a murder ballad, kin to songs like "The Knoxville Girl," itself derived from an English ballad, "The Wexford Girl." In the Bolicks' hands much of the eeriness and creepiness comes to the surface. When they sing "Come my love let's take a walk/Just a little ways away," it carries a dreadful premonition of what is about to happen. The Bolicks' unerring sibling harmony was never used to better effect. A lifetime of singing together gave one brother the telepathic knowledge of where the other was heading. They come together on a note, then one goes high and one low, and in between there's a haunting overtone, which seems like a third voice coming out of the ether.

At last sighting, the Blue Sky Boys were both still alive. They fell out occasionally but performed together on and off into the seventies. The lack of daily practice makes some of their later recordings rustier, but by way of compensation their voices deepened and coarsened a little. "On the Banks of the Ohio" is available now only on a bootleg CD, but with no likelihood of RCA releasing the Blue Sky Boys legally, we'll not complain.

BILLY WALLACE AND THE BAMA DRIFTERS, "That's My Reward" (Mercury 70876) Here's a record that wasn't merely out of style when it was cut, but was never in style. Billy Wallace probably thought he was cutting rockabilly, but even rockabilly was never this spare. The backing is just an acoustic guitar and a string bass beating it out at a good clip. During the solo Billy shouts, "Play it, Mister Gibson," but it's never clear if "Mister Gibson" is the picker or the guitar itself.

Billy Wallace had written a few exceptionally fine songs before this. One of them was "Back Street Affair," perhaps the first country hit to address the issue of cheating without the escape hatch of moralizing. "That's My Reward" is the story of a man who has not merely been dumped but dumped upon. At least one of the couplets is as wonderful as anything in country music:

> You rule my nights, you rule my days
> Who started the rumor that they freed all the slaves

225

Wallace has a creaky oldtimer's voice, which makes his pretension at rockabilly that much more absurd, but it's the very unusualness of every aspect of this record that accounts for its charm.

FAIRGROUND ATTRACTION, "Ay Fond Kiss," on Ay Fond Kiss (RCA PD 74596) British rock always left me pretty much cold. It usually tried too hard and lost the sway, the loose-jointed swing of the best stuff. It was like the sadly true caricature of white people's dancing that Steve Martin did so well. British blues was even more absurd—a contradiction in terms, really. Guys hovering in front of electric fires in their bedsits, practicing and practicing until they could cram three or four times as many notes as necessary into every bar. What did they accomplish in the end? The notes were just notes; they had no form and told no story. On some level, it all seemed to be learned, like the way Abba learned English phonetically and sung without understanding the lyrics.

The British folk-rock brigade, like Fairport Convention and John Martyn, were closer to the mark. At least their music was rooted in something that was theirs, rather than something borrowed. Then came Fairground Attraction. They had a big hit in England with "Perfect" in 1988, a song that mixed British streetcorner busking with James Burton licks and a melody that stayed with you after one hearing. A song about perfection had to be perfect, and this was indeed a perfect record.

The group issued two albums, then broke up. It was a musical marriage, apparently an incompatible one, between Mark Nevin, Eddi Reader, and two backup men. Nevin had learned American music, but it never sounded as though it came from a manual, and he had a feel for combining textures in a way that actually worked. Eddi Reader has a deeply sensuous voice, a gorgeous Scottish accent, and a dynamic range that goes from a whisper to a scream. She knows the value of holding something back.

On "Ay Fond Kiss," Eddi whispered. It was a Robbie Burns poem about the pain of parting set to a very spare musical backdrop. It was probably a demo, and wouldn't have been released at all if the group hadn't broken up, leaving RCA with half an album. Like all the best country and folk songs, this one ached with unfulfillment and longing. Eddi's tenderness and restraint only heightened its impact. She never once sank to bathos.

After the rift, Mark Nevin went to Nashville for a while, and Eddi Reader stayed in Scotland. She made a solo album for RCA in England with her new band, the Patron Saints of Imperfection, but without Nevin's songs and musicality it came up short. Good, but not great. Certainly not perfect. A second solo album, this one with some of Nevin's songs, was a Top Five album in England, but it too was uneven. Meanwhile, "Perfect" was picked up by Kathy Mattea at Mercury in Nashville, who missed the point by a mile.

WANDA JACKSON, "Silver Threads and Golden Needles" (Capitol F-3575), reissued on *Right or Wrong* (Bear Family BCD 15629) Like almost everyone outside Wanda Jackson's immediate family, I first heard "Silver Threads and Golden Needles" sung by the Springfields. Linda Ronstadt did it later, and the song went on to become something of a standard without ever quite being a major hit. Wanda cut it first, though. It was sandwiched between two rock 'n' roll songs on an afternoon session at the Capitol Tower in September 1956, with Buck Owens earning forty-one much-needed dollars on rhythm guitar.

Dusty Springfield first heard "Silver Threads" on Skeeter Davis's *End of the World* album, and the first thing she did when she sang it with the Springfields was to change "Silver threads and golden needles cain't patch up this heart of mine" to "Silver threads and golden needles cannot mend this heart of mine." That gave some indication of what had happened to the song as it made its way from country to pop, but it wasn't until I finally heard Wanda's version, with a complete verse I'd never heard before, that the song really hit home:

227

> I grew up in faded gingham where love is a sacred thing
> You grew up in silk and satin where love is a passing game
> I know now you never loved me, and I know I was a fool
> To think your pride would let you live by the golden rule

There's the anguish that comes from loving one above your station in life. The song addressed an immemorial theme in folk music: the young woman who is slighted for loving one she cannot have after she has been seduced by him. It finds its echo in old British ballads like "Lord Greggory" and "Lord Thomas and Fair Eleanor." In "Lord Greggory" the maiden and his Lordship exchange pocket handkerchiefs after their dalliance:

> For yours was pure linen, love, and mine was coarse cloth
> Yours cost a guinea, love, and mine but one groat.

Wanda's youth and innocence were never put to better use than on "Silver Threads and Golden Needles." She catches all the hurt of one who has seen her young dreams dashed. It's the hurt of someone for whom things are never going to go right. The studio logs reveal that it took fourteen takes to nail the song, but on that fourteenth take, with tempers probably starting to fray and the studio clock ticking remorselessly away, she caught the artless simplicity of the country song.

JERRY AND TAMMY SULLIVAN, *A Joyful Noise* **(CMF Records CMF-016)** This is an act of devotion in more ways than one. It was produced in 1991 by Marty Stuart and his producer at the time, Richard Bennett. The Sullivans are traveling evangelists, a father-and-daughter team. Stuart had worked with them in leaner years and had gone back on occasion for spiritual rejuvenation. In these times, when we're used to preachers being caught with their hands in the till or with their pants around their ankles, the Sullivans have a genuinely affecting humility. Their music comes from brush arbor meetings—all-day outdoor singings and prayings under a makeshift shelter. No theme parks. No glycerine tears sparkling in the television lights. No financial targets.

Tammy takes most of the lead vocals. She sings in a full-throated style that wavers off key sometimes to great effect. So many female country singers overemote and drench their work in soap opera bathos, but there's none of that here. Tammy closes off her mind and sings from the heart. She could make Megadeth walk on their knees to Lourdes.

Bennett and Stuart keep the production sparse and to the point. There are no drums. The pulse is carried by the bass and rhythm guitars. It's so simple, such a perfect formula, one that everyone knows is there but nobody except the Sullivans seems to use anymore. Starday Records used to issue albums like this thirty years ago. Most of them were poorly cut in one afternoon. Today, Country Music Foundation Records is probably the only label in Nashville that would take a chance on this. It's an executive version of a Starday record. Time was spent; money was spent. Well spent.

BROTHER CLAUDE ELY, "Send Down That Rain" (King recording), first issued on *Satan Get Back* **(Ace CDCHD 456)** For years there was a tape circulating of Brother Claude Ely singing "There's a Leak in This Old Building." As soon as it became clear that it dated to around 1953, it also became clear that Elvis Presley's "We're Gonna Move" wasn't so original. "We're Gonna Move" had in fact been cloned note for note from "There's a Leak." "We're Gonna Move" is credited to Vera Matson, although it was actually written by her husband, Ken Darby, who doubled as music director of *Love Me Tender*, the movie in which the song appeared. Elvis was cut in as co-writer, and it had always been thought that his presence in the composer credits was engineered by Colonel Tom Parker.

Could Elvis have had a hand in cloning "We're Gonna Move" from "There's a Leak"? Perhaps. Ken Darby, whose other credits included the music direction of the film versions of *The King and I*, *Porgy and Bess*, and *Camelot*, as well as "'Twas the Night before Christmas," would have thought Brother Claude Ely was from another planet. Elvis, though, had either heard

Brother Claude or singers much like him when he was growing up.

The holiness shouts were probably among his earliest musical memories. Brother Claude's link to Elvis is stronger than that one song, too. Brother Claude played guitar, more accurately *thrashed* the guitar, in a murderous frenzy and sang as uninhibitedly as any white man had ever sung. That he, or someone very like him, did not extend Elvis's sense of the possible is inconceivable. Here was abandon, total abandon.

"There's a Leak" was recorded at a church in Whitesburg, Kentucky, in October 1953. It is a wonderful recording, worthy of its underground reputation, but when Ace Records in England summoned up the courage it must have taken to issue a Claude Ely compact disc, they included the rest of the program from Whitesburg. "Send Down That Rain," unissued to that point, is the stellar cut. It draws a parallel between rain needed to nourish the barren fields and the Holy Ghost rain that will be visited upon the wicked. "There's fire in that rain, boy, there's fire in that rain," yells Ely. You can almost see the snakes passing from hand to hand, the eyes rolled upward, and the uncontrollable twitching. If you never bought into the Neil Young nonsense about music saving your soul, you need to hear Brother Claude Ely.

The final surprise comes with the photo. Brother Claude is a venal-looking preacher with a lecherous smile and a sparkling gold tooth. His features are coarse and slightly bloated, and he's wearing a cowboy hat. If I'd had a row of potential Brother Claude Elys in a police lineup, I'd never have picked this one.

DOUG AND ANN HOOKER PRESENT: Blossom, *Playing for Your Pleasure* (self-produced cassette; no catalog number) It was colder than you would have ever imagined if you'd heard that the temperature in southern England that day was around thirty-eight degrees. A damp, chill wind blew off the North Sea straight into an outdoor shopping plaza in Canterbury, Kent. During the Second World War, Canterbury was almost razed, with the providential exception of the cathedral. Eastern parts of the cathedral were completed in 1174, four years after Archbishop Thomas à Becket was murdered there by the emissaries of Henry II. Eight hundred and twenty years and five hundred yards away, there is now a dismal shopping center built on the ruins of craprously built stores that had themselves been built on the postwar rubble of the old city.

Almost nobody was shopping that day. It was January, at the height of the post-Thatcher recession, and Canterbury was like New Orleans after Mardi Gras, but without the feeling that there had ever been a party. Such shoppers as there were looked pinched and gray and hurried about their business.

In the middle of the central promenade was Blossom, an 1830s fairground organ playing jarringly happy music from the organ equivalent of piano rolls: "Daisy, Daisy," "The Beer Barrel Polka," "The Happy Wanderer," and so on. Unmanned and without an audience, it seemed all the more surreal. The colors were gaudily Victorian, their richness and opulence contrasting with the cheap glitter of the goods in the window displays all around. There were scenes of hay wains and villages nestling in the Downs. A wooden courtier stood under an arch in the center of the organ, bewigged and ready for presentation at court. When the percussion was triggered, the courtier raised and lowered his arm in time, holding a Union Jack. To one side of him was a minstrel's guitar. The top of the hollow body rose and fell with a wooden clap for percussion. On the other side was a cymbal synchronized with the guitar. The combined effect was that of the mathematical precision of a Bach fugue.

It's almost impossible to fully explain the feelings that this lonely musical automaton generated. It was a requiem for a glorious England that wasn't so glorious but whose last vestiges still survived at my first rememberings. It conjured up the memory of being lost at a fairground with an organ playing eerily in the background, and of retired colonels, now as long dead as the empire they served, tending their herbaceous borders and officiating at country fêtes.

I stood before Blossom until the cold got under my coat and then under my skin. Around the back, Doug and Ann Hooker sat in a trailer that the British exotically call a caravan, squatting over an electric fire. They advertised four cassettes but had only one in stock.◉

Fairground Attraction. Busking in Blighty
Photo courtesy of C. Escott

231

Index

232